BY LOVE
TRANSFORMED

BY LOVE
TRANSFORMED

R. T. KENDALL

JOY STRANG, GENERAL EDITOR

Charisma
HOUSE
A STRANG COMPANY

Most Strang Communications/Charisma House/Siloam/FrontLine/Realms products are available at special quantity discounts for bulk purchase for sales promotions, premiums, fund-raising, and educational needs. For details, write Strang Communications/Charisma House/Siloam/FrontLine/Realms, 600 Rinehart Road, Lake Mary, Florida 32746, or telephone (407) 333-0600.

By Love Transformed by R. T. Kendall
Joy Strang, general editor
Published by Charisma House
A Strang Company
600 Rinehart Road
Lake Mary, Florida 32746
www.charismahouse.com

Unless otherwise noted, all Scripture quotations are from Holy Bible, New International Version. Copyright © 1973, 1978, 1984, International Bible Society. Used by permission.

Scripture quotations marked KJV are from the King James Version of the Bible.

Scripture quotations marked NAS are from the New American Standard Bible. Copyright © 1960, 1962, 1963, 1968, 1971, 1972, 1973, 1975, 1977 by the Lockman Foundation. Used by permission. (www.Lockman.org)

Scripture quotations marked THE MESSAGE are from *The Message: The Bible in Contemporary English,* copyright © 1993, 1994, 1995, 1996, 2000, 2001, 2002. Used by permission of NavPress Publishing Group.

Cover design by John Hamilton Design
www.johnhamiltondesign.com
Interior design by Terry Clifton

Library of Congress Cataloging-in-Publication Data

Kendall, R. T.
By love transformed / R.T. Kendall. -- 1st ed.
    p. cm.
ISBN 1-59185-981-6 (casebound)
1. Christian life--Meditations. 2. Bible--Meditations. I. Title.
BV4501.3.K455 2006
242--dc22

                              2006019336
                            First Edition
                  06 07 08 09 10 — 987654321
                Printed in the United States of America

To Steve and Cindy Vetter

Contents

Foreword

Although I was raised in a Christian home and born again at a young age, it wasn't until I started reading the legendary writings of godly men and women from times past such as Maria Woodworth-Etter, Andrew Murray, Watchman Nee, and C. S. Lewis that I began to grow spiritually. I learned from these writers that transformation is not instantaneous. Becoming spiritually mature takes time—and requires us to pay a price.

It's the same in the natural world. Weeds grow quickly, but mature trees that bear fruit and can weather storms take time to grow. If we as believers are to withstand the storms of life and become like mature trees that bear fruit in due season, then we must pursue the things that will help us grow.

Some believers are satisfied to remain at their current level of Christian maturity, but God is calling us to grow up in Him. In the process, we will come to know Christ and become conformed to His image.

R. T. Kendall is a modern-day spiritual giant who has helped me in my own walk with God. Known as a theologian, pastor, and expository teacher of the Word, Dr. Kendall served as minister of Westminster Chapel, a leading evangelical church in London, England, for twenty-five years. Though he received his doctorate at the prestigious Oxford University in London, England, he is able to take the most complex truths and make them understandable for every believer.

Dr. Kendall emphasizes the need to live our lives based upon the Word of God *and* the Holy Spirit. Without the Word there is no spiritual foundation, but without the Holy Spirit to guide us into truth and be our Teacher, we can't fully comprehend the Word. He brings the Word to life in us.

Dr. Kendall isn't afraid to tackle the tough issues of life, such as what to do when God is silent or when you have been betrayed. He teaches that the path to spiritual maturity includes taking up your cross and facing difficulty. As you become sensitive to the Holy Spirit and walk in obedience to Him, you will have the grace and pure joy of coming to know Christ and will one day receive a great reward.

As I read through more than thirty of Dr. Kendall's books to make selections for this devotional, some of my old paradigms were challenged, my hunger for God increased, and my mind was renewed. His insights and explanations stayed with me, and I would often quote segments I had read to those with whom I spoke throughout the day.

If you desire to grow in your walk with God, the selections in this devotional were chosen just for you. They will help you in your growth process by encouraging you in everyday life situations and challenging you to go to the next level spiritually.

May you be transformed by His love!

—JOY F. STRANG

Preface

I was surprised when Charisma House asked to do a devotional based on some of my books and to make this fit into a 365-daily plan. My immediate thought was to ask Joy Strang if she would be kind enough to determine what is appropriate for such a book, to make the decision as to what to include and where to put it. My dad used to say to me as I grew up, "If you want to get something done, ask a busy person to do it." I know exactly what he means by that. There is none busier than Joy, but none more qualified for this kind of task. For one thing, she is an avid reader. She particularly loves old books! I suppose this says something about my style! Second, Joy has a good theological mind. She knows what she believes and would be astute in her choice of what to include in a book such as this. Third, she would know the kind of material that the Charisma House audience would love.

I do thank Joy Strang for this hard work. It took her months and months to read from so many of my books, then to decide what to use and where to put the material. As I have looked at what she has done, I have been very touched and gratified. It is so humbling to see the choices she has made and to think that people would use this in their daily devotional time with the Lord.

I would only pray that what I have written would never become a substitute for praying and reading the Bible—but only as a supplement to one's Bible reading.

I thank Lillian McAnally for the editorial work she has done in preparing this volume; I am also grateful for the encouragement from Barbara Dycus. Many thanks to Ann Mulchan, Deborah Moss, and the product development team at Strang Communications Company. I thank Stephen Strang, too, for his trust, friendship, and desire to put my books, mostly written in England, into print in the United States.

When Louise and I are not traveling around the world, we attend Key Largo Baptist Church in Key Largo, Florida. Pastor Steve Vetter has been such a blessing to us. We fondly dedicate this book to Steve and his lovely wife, Cindy.

May God bless you as you read this book.

—R. T. KENDALL
www.rtkendallministries.com

Does God Have Your Attention?

Psalm 120 gives us a number of examples of different ways that God uses to get our attention. Meshech and Kedar symbolize places where we do not like to have to live. Are you living in the "wrong" place? Perhaps you are feeling a little sorry for yourself. But maybe God has put you there so that you will value what really matters. Because of an unhappy situation, where things just aren't the way *you* would like them to be, God gets your attention. He can also use *danger, delay,* or *discord* to get our attention.

> *Woe to me that I dwell in Meshech, that I live among the tents of Kedar! Too long have I lived among those who hate peace. I am a man of peace; but when I speak, they are for war.*
>
> —PSALM 120:5–7

Meshech and Kedar also symbolize places of *danger.* Kedar, for example, refers to the Bedouins who were a perpetual problem to the travelers. Are you one of those people who enjoy living on the edge of danger, but now find yourself in trouble?

Another part of the distress, *delay,* is found in verse 6: "Too long have I lived among those who hate peace." Perhaps your distress is because of a prolonged situation. You have waited and waited for the situation to change. In reality, however, all this time perhaps God has been waiting for you to turn to Him.

God also uses *discord* to get our attention: "I am a man of peace; but when I speak, they are for war" (v. 7). Are you in such a situation of *discord?* Perhaps your marriage is on the rocks; perhaps you are living somewhere where there is nothing but tension. God can use discord to get your attention.

What makes for peace is when we come to terms with the fact that the problem is not merely the situation but *our reaction* to the situation. A man of peace will defuse heated situations, not adding to their misery. Such a man can do this because internally he has discovered and experienced "perfect peace" (Isa. 26:3). It is called the "peace of God, which passeth all understanding" (Phil. 4:7, KJV).

Excerpted from *Higher Ground* (Christian Focus Publications Ltd., 1995).

A Double-Portion Anointing

Y ou may have heard of the "Peter Principle"—an ingenious concept and quite true: everybody is promoted to the level of their incompetence. Either through death, ambition, or lack of good personnel, people are given a job that they can't do. Often, due to pride or selfish ambition, a person is determined to gain promotion; they get it and celebrate. But eighteen months later, they have a nervous breakdown because they can't cope. But, you see, when you operate within the sphere of your own anointing, it's easy.

Once God has given you an anointing, you will always have it because "God's gifts and his call are irrevocable" (Rom. 11:29).

The anointing that will be given to you—whatever it is—will put your faith to the test. The anointing may bring difficulties for you. It may lead you where you don't want to go. You may have to go against personal desire. It may lead you to bless those whom you personally may not have chosen to bless.

If you know you have the anointing, even though you don't have other little things, know that blessing from Him is worth more than all the money in the world. Jesus said, "The kingdom of heaven is like

> When they had crossed, Elijah said to Elisha, "Tell me, what can I do for you before I am taken from you?" "Let me inherit a double portion of your spirit," Elisha replied. "You have asked a difficult thing," Elijah said, "yet if you see me when I am taken from you, it will be yours—otherwise not."
>
> —2 Kings 2:9–10

a merchant looking for fine pearls. When he found one of great value, he went away and sold everything he had and bought it" (Matt. 13:45). What that means is, when you want the anointing more than anything in the world, you'll do anything to get it because you want God's blessing, just like Elisha who would not let Elijah out of his sight.

There's a lesson here for all of us: if we want the blessing more than anything in the world, we can have it because our very desire will be testimony to God's work in our hearts.

Excerpted from *All's Well That Ends Well* (Authentic Media, 2005).

Lift Up My Eyes

Why did the psalmist say these words? Firstly, it is possible that in a moment of *temptation* he was thinking, *Shall I look to the hills like so many others are doing?* Those who were worshiping Baal were increasing in number rapidly. Many were looking to the hills for help, so the psalmist pauses and asks: "Where does my help come from?" But he realizes his help does not come from the hills. Quite the opposite, in fact; his help comes from the Lord.

Secondly, it is possible that the writer was referring to the *tradition* of looking to mountains. There were those who, by looking to the mountains in the direction of Jerusalem, had a good feeling. For "the mountains surround Jerusalem" (Ps. 125:2)

> *I lift up my eyes to the hills—where does my help come from? My help comes from the Lord, the Maker of heaven and earth.*
>
> —Psalm 121:1–2

Have you been wrestling with a problem of temptation from a certain direction, and you know that by looking in that direction, you are looking where temptation will be? Do you know the best way to prevent yourself from falling into sin? It is to keep from falling into temptation. Most of us have a fairly shrewd idea of what will tempt us. What may be my weakness may not be yours, and what may be yours may not be mine.

Perhaps you are looking to tradition for help. I think England is the most traditional country in the world. I sometimes thought Westminster Chapel was the most traditional church in England. Maybe you like tradition. But you can be so tied up in tradition that you never reach the Lord. You can come to church and get a good feeling. But that is just looking to the hills for reasons of tradition. Your good feeling may not be from the Lord at all.

In any case, whether we look because of temptation or tradition, the psalmist says, "[Our] help comes from the Lord," not the mountains.

Excerpted from *Higher Ground* (Christian Focus Publications Ltd., 1995).

Are You Trapped in Bad Company?

Spanish novelist Miguel de Cervantes Saavedra wrote in his masterpiece, *Don Quixote de la Mancha*, "Tell me thy company, and I will tell thee what thou art." There is some truth to that statement. We are known by the company we keep.

We often believe that this concept applies only in our interaction with unbelievers; however, this can be applied to our relationship within the body of Christ, also.

Some years ago I was in a situation where I found myself unwittingly in the grip of someone who I could see was not good for me. The person was a professing Christian, but I found myself in his grip, and I was leaning on him. I realized that this was wrong, and God delivered me from the situation. I was so thankful.

Am I advising you to avoid altogether unbelievers or certain members within the body of Christ? Most certainly not. However, ask the Lord to shine His light on the various relationships in your life.

Could it be that at this moment you are in this snare? You are trapped with bad company, and they are doing you no good. Maybe, however, you have rationalized the situation and made up excuses, concluding that you can be an exception. You wouldn't recommend anybody else to do what you are doing.

> *Do not be misled: "Bad company corrupts good character."*
> —1 CORINTHIANS 15:33

The worst thing that you can do, however, is to begin to think that you are the exception to the rule. For the devil will come alongside and say that you are different, that you can associate with wrong company. Then, before you know it, you are in a trap.

It is a wonderful thing to realize that God delivers us from bad company.

Maybe you are in a situation where you are being wrongly influenced, and as a consequence you have lost the sense of inner peace. Where the Spirit of the Lord is, there is liberty. But bad company causes you to lose the peace that God wants you to have. I ask you, are you in the grip of bad company?

Excerpted from *Higher Ground* (Christian Focus Publications Ltd., 1995).

The Obedience of Gratitude

Although we don't deserve it, there is God's promise to us in our showing gratitude. Gratitude shown, even keeping our vows, contains great promise! God does not have to promise us anything for our showing thankfulness. We ought to be thankful to Him for His goodness. Period. End of story. But I can tell you that He delights in rewarding those who show that they are grateful to Him. God does not have to promise us blessing if we tithe, but He does. (See Malachi 3:10.) God does not have to promise us blessing for forgiveness, for not judging, and for giving to others, but He does. (See Luke 6:37–38.)

> So you also, when you have done every-thing you were told to do, should say, "We are unworthy servants; we have only done our duty."
>
> —LUKE 17:10

In other words, our obedience to show gratitude is required of us. "So you also, when you have done everything you were told to do, should say, 'We are unworthy servants; we have only done our duty'" (Luke 17:10). Obedience is duty. But God is so good, so kind, so merciful! We cannot out-praise the Lord, out-give the Lord, or out-thank the Lord!

He has *chosen* to show His pleasure when we get it right and do it right. For those strong enough in themselves that they need no further affirmation from God or recompense, I say, "Good for you." But I, for one, am not that strong. I need affirmation and all the encouragement I can get. I sometimes come to tears when I read those words of David: "For he knows how we are formed, he remembers that we are dust" (Ps. 103:14). I am so weak that I need all the motivation I can get to press on with any kind of obedience, and that includes the obedience of gratitude.

Excerpted from *Just Say Thanks!* (Charisma House, 2005).

When God Says "Yes"

When God is in something, He grants us success, and it comes easily. This psalm tells us what God does when He says "Yes."

First, He *builds* (v. 1). He supplies the energy and the materials. He supplies the labor and the success that had been so eluding. Things begin to happen—with ease.

Second, God *watches* (v. 1). It is a wonderful thing to know that God is looking after you. If God says "Yes," you don't have to worry.

Third, God *feeds* (v. 2). It is pointless to wear yourself out toiling for food to eat, for if God says "Yes," He just supplies your need.

Fourth, God grants *sleep* (v. 2). I experience times of insomnia; everybody does at times. It is worse if there is a hard day coming up. This happened to me when we went to Hong Kong some time ago. I thought I knew jet lag when I came from America to Britain, but I had never experienced anything like what I felt after flying from Britain to Hong Kong. It was awful. I was scheduled to be on a Hong Kong radio station the next day, but I was awake all night.

> Unless the LORD builds the house, its builders labor in vain. Unless the LORD watches over the city, the watchmen stand guard in vain. In vain you rise early and stay up late, toiling for food to eat—for he grants sleep to those he loves.
> —PSALM 127:1–2

This verse has since helped me to see that sleep comes from God, and if I don't get the sleep I think I need, it will still be OK. The radio interview went fairly well, and I made it through the day.

When He says "Yes," it makes a big difference. But to know this, you may have to fast and pray. If God is hiding His face from you, and you don't know what to do, go and spend a whole day in prayer and fasting.

Within God's will there is no failure; outside of God's will there is no success.

Excerpted from *Higher Ground* (Christian Focus Publications Ltd., 1995).

What Is Your Thorn in the Flesh?

What is *your* thorn in the flesh? Is it a frailty? It may be a physical problem. It may be an emotional problem. It may be a personal weakness.

It may be a fault: a defect, or imperfection—one that feels embarrassing and humbling. You may have prayed about it a thousand times. You may have asked people to lay their hands on you and to pray that this imperfection would disappear. I myself have done this.

It may be a friend. Sometimes a dear friend can be a real thorn in the flesh. Perhaps he is difficult. You want to be with him, but afterward you feel frustrated or all the worse for being in his company. It may be a love-hate relationship. You feel you can't be without this person, but the relationship is always edgy, prickly. You feel that even discussing it would be spontaneous combustion!

> As a father has compassion on his children, so the LORD has compassion on those who fear him; for he knows how we are formed, he remembers that we are dust.
>
> —PSALM 103:13–14

It may be an enemy. This person seems to live to make you look bad! But it may be that your enemy—who keeps you on your toes (not to mention your knees)—is raised up by God to keep you sharp and careful.

Could your thorn in the flesh be that you have known failure? It may have been financial failure, a failed marriage, or a job loss. Or, when facing temptation, you failed, and the whole scenario haunts you daily.

Perhaps someone has lied about you. You cannot defend yourself. People believe the lie. You long with all your being to be vindicated. But God withholds vindication. This could be your thorn in the flesh.

Don't despise your thorn, whatever it is. Don't resent it. It exists by God's sovereign pleasure. It is for your good. It is the best thing that ever happened to you next to your conversion and anointing. It is only a matter of time before you will appreciate it.

Excerpted from *The Thorn in the Flesh* (Charisma House, 2004).

We Are His Field

It is intrinsic to understanding God's sovereignty that we realize what Paul meant when he said that Christians are God's field. He is showing that God owns us. This simply means that God has total rights to our lives. We have no private life; our private life is His. We cannot go on a two-week vacation and say, "God, I want a good time, and You have been breathing down my neck for most of the year. I would like a couple of weeks away from You." No, He'll go *with* us on vacation; we have no time that we can call our own. It is His time. We have no secret thoughts about which we can say, "God, I just don't want You to know about this." We do not own ourselves.

> *For we are God's fellow workers; you are God's field, God's building.*
> —1 Corinthians 3:9

Does this disturb and annoy you? Or does this thrill you to your fingertips to know that you are bought with a price? It is true whether you like it or not! You are His; He owns you. You are God's field; it is not your field. For that reason God can do what He wants with you, and because you are His, you can't get rid of Him even if you tried. You may have said to God, "Leave me alone." But He didn't; He would not.

Because He owns us, God has no obligation to us. God ultimately takes the responsibility not only for saving us but also for our development.

> Every virtue we possess,
> And every conquest won,
> And every thought of holiness,
> Are his alone.
> —Harriet Auber, "Our Blest Redeemer, Ere He Breathed,"
> public domain

It is a mystery that God, who chose me in Christ before the foundation of the world, works for my growth.

Excerpted from *When God Says "Well Done!"* (Christian Focus Publications Ltd., 1993).

Facing Our Greatest Battle

What did David mean when he wrote these words? If he is telling the truth, we are seeing a quality of humility that is very rare. What a contrast to the spirit of today! We are living in an age in which we must catch the eye of other people. The key to success today has mainly to do with pride and self-esteem.

But the key to success in the world is the way of disaster in the things of the Spirit. What is the mother of all battles? Pride. There are many Christians today whose real problem is their pride. They want to be greater than others. This is in contrast to what Jesus said to His disciples: "The greatest among you will be your servant. For whoever exalts himself will be humbled, and whoever humbles himself will be exalted" (Matt. 23:11–12).

> *My heart is not proud, O LORD, my eyes are not haughty; I do not concern myself with great matters or things too wonderful for me.*
>
> —PSALM 131:1

Our pride will cause us to do stupid things. It will delay us coming to terms with the most important thing in the world: our relationship with God Himself. Pride keeps a person from confessing Christ openly, from going out on the streets to witness.

Jesus bore the sin of our pride at Calvary. He knew humiliation. He was naked on the cross. When we see all that the Son of God went through, we must know that there was no other way whereby we could be saved. It is not by our good works or joining a church. It is not by getting rid of a habit, however bad it is.

Something will happen to us when we resign from the rat race and realize that the only thing that matters is for God to have us all to Himself. We will get to know Him, and we will be amazed.

Remember, the key to success in the world is the way of disaster in the things of the Spirit. (See Galatians 5:17.)

Excerpted from *Higher Ground* (Christian Focus Publications Ltd., 1995).

Dignifying the Trial

It is not every day that I can remember where I was when understanding a particular verse in the Bible dawned on me, but I do when it comes to James 1:2. It came to me after losing my temper at a pizzeria in the summer of 1979. I had *so* looked forward to a pizza from this particular place and regarded such as a reward for returning to Disney World a second year in a row. But when the time came, everything went wrong. I became impatient for having to wait forty-five minutes for it, and then it rained so much, my pizza fell out of a wet paper bag into a puddle of water. Now I had to go back and face the same manager—after telling him off the first time. *How could all this happen?* I asked myself.

But James 1:2 had already been on my mind for weeks. As I drove back to the pizzeria that evening, I said to myself, *Either James 1:2 is true or it isn't, and if I plan to preach on it shortly, I had better begin practicing what I preach.*

I have to tell you, this episode was pivotal for me, and I came to my senses for being so upset. Minutes before I returned to the pizzeria to apologize with genuine meekness to the manager, I repented before God for my anger and behavior.

> *Consider it pure joy, my brothers, whenever you face trials of many kinds, because you know that the testing of your faith develops perseverance.*
>
> —JAMES 1:2–3

I decided then and there to *dignify* that situation by accepting the entire matter as something God sent. That is when a new phrase was born to me: "dignifying the trial." It was a divine setup. I not only repented to the Lord, but I also thanked Him for the whole thing. I apologized to the manager, cheerfully waited for another pizza (for some reason, he wouldn't let me pay), and returned to my family at the motel a different person.

Excerpted from *Pure Joy* (Charisma House, 2006).

Greater Suffering Produces Greater Anointing

The main reason for burnout and fatigue is almost certainly because someone has operated beyond their anointing rather than functioning within it. It was because the person could not accept the limits of his or her ability.

None of us can do everything, but to a person who is not content with the anointing or gift that he or she has, there will be trouble ahead. It is humbling to accept our limits, but there is considerable joy and peace in doing so, not to mention an increase of anointing. We can pray for a greater anointing—namely, an ability to do what we previously could not do in our own strength—but until that anointing has come, we must accept the limits of our faith and our ability.

When we are content with the anointing God chose for us, we do what we are called to do without fatigue. "I can do everything through him who gives me strength" (Phil. 4:13). When I become mentally and emotionally fatigued in what I am doing, it is a fairly strong hint that I have chosen to move outside my anointing and what God specifically asked me to do. As long as I do *what* He called me to do and *no more*, I will not be edging toward burnout. God never promotes us to the level of our incompetence. As long as we are content with the calling He has chosen for us, we will live and move at the level He has seen fit to give us.

> *When he has tested me, I will come forth as gold.*
>
> —JOB 23:10

So if it is a great anointing you want, anticipate great suffering at some stage. The anointing is the power of the Holy Spirit to make you do what you do with ease and without fatigue. If you wake up one day with one big enormous trial before you, you should grasp it with both hands and consider it pure joy!

Excerpted from *Pure Joy* (Charisma House, 2006).

God's Plan for You Vindicates Him

God has a plan for you. He has something in mind for you far better than anything that you could come up with. We call it the will of God. You will never do better than His will. Do not ever think you can upstage the will of God. The joy you will experience because you waited on Him is incomparable, because God loves to carry out His plan, as that vindicates Him.

You may say, "Well, He didn't do a very good job with me. I have emotional scars on my life; I had this happen to me when I was a child, and I wasn't treated very nice by my parents," and so on. God says, "I know about that. Do you think that I was looking the other way? I have fashioned you." (See Psalm 139:14.)

God wants to use you just as you are. God wants you to trust Him in all that has happened to you and fashioned you to

> *Before I formed you in the womb I knew you…*
>
> —JEREMIAH 1:5

make you who you are. He has an idea, and if you wait for Him, He will be vindicated, for He wants to show you what you mean to Him!

The Father's idea was that He would send His Son, the Lord of eternity, into the world, long before you and I were born, long before there was ever a church or man in the Garden of Eden. He determined it long before He created the sun, the moon, the stars.

Take note of this: God, who had an idea about His Son and what His Son should do, also has an idea about you and what you should do. It is carefully thought out. The very hairs on your head are numbered. And God loves you as though there were no one else to love. It is the same God who sent His Son into the world to say to us, "As the Father has sent me, I am sending you" (John 20:21).

Excerpted from *Meekness and Majesty* (Christian Focus Publications Ltd., 1992, 2000).

The Difference Between Trials and Temptations

There is a difference between a trial and a temptation, although both come from the same Greek word—*peirasmos*. They are often used interchangeably, though. After all, temptation is a trial (of faith), and every trial is a temptation (to grumble). When the word appears in the New Testament the context helps us to see which interpretation is meant. There are therefore differences and similarities between trials and temptations. Although we must not push the distinctions too far, here are examples of the differences:

> *Let no one say when he is tempted, "I am being tempted by God"; for God cannot be tempted by evil, and He Himself does not tempt anyone. But each one is tempted when he is carried away and enticed by his own lust.*
>
> —James 1:13–14, nas

1. *In their ultimate origin.* Temptations come from the flesh; trials are sent from God. He allowed Satan to test Job (Job 1:6–12). Therefore when we speak of "trial" we see God's fingerprints; when we see temptation, we see our own—or the devil's.

2. *In their immediate origin.* Temptation comes from within; trials usually come from outside us. Job suffered physically, but inwardly—at least at first—there was no apparent struggle.

3. *In their moral relevance.* Temptation, when it is sexual in nature, has considerable moral relevance, but a trial may be what I would want to call morally neutral, such as illness or losing one's keys.

4. *With reference to what is tested.* Temptation will usually attack a weak spot; trials test our strength as well as exposing a weakness we may have been unaware of—as with Job, who turned out to be so self-righteous.

Any trial that God sends—death of a loved one or friend, financial reverse, loss, illness, misunderstanding, losing your keys, failure, disappointment, betrayal, abuse, unemployment, depression, accident, loneliness, missing a train or plane, rejection, not getting that important invitation, or any physical pain—should be seen as having our Lord's handprints all over them.

Excerpted from *Pure Joy* (Charisma House, 2006).

How Do You Get the Most Out of Your Trials?

So how do you dignify a trial? Below are eight steps to getting the most out of your trials.

1. *Welcome it.* Welcome the trial as you would welcome the Holy Spirit, for it is the Holy Spirit who, with the Father and the Son, is behind the whole ordeal. And in this case, He comes with one purpose: for your own good.

2. *Don't panic.* Satan's immediate goal when he is given permission to attack is to get you to panic. This is why he is compared to a roaring lion (1 Pet. 5:8). The reason for the roar is to intimidate and cause fear and panic—to make you think you are defeated even before anything has had a chance to happen.

3. *See the trial as a compliment to you from God Himself.* This is important. The kind of trial He has allowed you to have is very possibly one that could not be granted to others around you. God gave this trial to you for one reason: you are up to it.

> *Out of the most severe trial, their overflowing joy and their extreme poverty welled up in rich generosity.*
> —2 Corinthians 8:2

4. *Never forget that God allowed it.* Satan will want you to focus on yourself, feel self-pity, and blame someone else for it. But realize that this trial has passed through God's filtering process.

5. *Know that there is a purpose in it.* There is an intelligent, meaningful reason God allowed it. It is to refine you, teach you a lesson, equip you better, make you more sensitive, teach you self-control, and help you guard your tongue. In other words, to make you more like Jesus.

6. *Don't try to end it.* Don't try to get out of anything prematurely. God will allow it to last as long as it is supposed to last.

7. *Don't grumble.* It is a sobering thought that God puts grumbling alongside idolatry and sexual sin in the list of evil deeds that brought His wrath down on ancient Israel (1 Cor. 10:1–12).

8. *Know that God wants you to pass the test far more than you do.* There are two reasons for this. First, He loves us so much and rejoices to see us experience pure joy. Second, it brings glory to Him when we dignify the trial by cheerfully enduring it.

Excerpted from *Pure Joy* (Charisma House, 2006).

God Wants Your Worship

I wonder whether we realize that God not only cares about the kind of worship we give, but He also really wants our worship. I find it so moving that God should care about my worship of Him.

Our natural reaction to this idea is to think, *Well, worship of God by little old me isn't going to matter to Him!* We tend to think that God will take more notice of the worship of more important people, like the president of the United States or an eminent man of God such as Billy Graham. It's as if we feel He must say, "Ah, this is more like it!" when He sees these kind of people worship. Maybe we don't say this, but in so many words, isn't it what we so often secretly feel?

> *And said unto him, Hearest thou what these say? And Jesus saith unto them, Yea; have ye never read, Out of the mouth of babes and sucklings thou hast perfected praise?*
>
> —Matthew 21:16, kjv

Yet throughout the Bible is the theme that God cares about each individual as though there were no one else to care for. Whether you are five years old, fifty, or ninety years old, God cares about your worship. He is not interested in your status in life; He looks at *you.*

On Palm Sunday when the children were crying, "Hosanna to the son of David," the chief priests and scribes didn't like it. But Jesus said to them, "Have ye never read, Out of the mouth of babes and sucklings thou hast perfected praise?" (Matt. 21:16, kjv).

You see, not only do so-called unimportant people matter, but God does not care whether or not you are in a strategic position from which to spread His name. You may sometimes think, *I'm not going to be able to do anything for God where I am. Why should He show me anything or give me any insights?*

What matters to God is not how important you are or how useful you are. All that matters to Him is the quality of your worship.

Excerpted from *Worshipping God* (Hodder & Stoughton, 2004).

Why He Hides From Us

All disciplining that comes from our heavenly Father is in reality the hiding of His face. If indeed you are a child of God but haven't experienced the hiding of His face, it is only a matter of time. I say that because we are told, "…he punishes everyone he accepts" as a son or daughter (Heb. 12:6). There is no warning. We find ourselves enjoying His sweet presence when—without any notice—He seems saliently absent.

The funny thing is that what God uses to get our attention may be the very thing that turns us off about Him! You would think He would use a method or technique that makes Him more loveable—or at least more likeable, but often He seems to do the very thing that He must know is making Him look pretty awful in our eyes at that moment. It is when He seems to

> *Verily thou art a God that hidest thyself,*
> *O God of Israel, the Saviour.*
> —ISAIAH 45:15, KJV

turn His back on us. He makes us feel rejected, as though He has dropped us from His good list entirely. It is when He seems disloyal and comes through to us (as best we can tell at the time) as an enemy, not a friend.

To put the purpose of chastening another way, it is given to us that we might *break the betrayal barrier* in our relationship with God. It is what few Christians (in my opinion) manage to do, at least, at first—and some, sadly, never succeed. A breakthrough in the betrayal barrier is one that will put us squarely on the path to joy.

Do you feel as if God has left you? Be assured that He has not left you in the absolute sense; it only seems that way.

When God hides His face it is not because He has completely left you; it only *feels* that way.

Excerpted from *Pure Joy* (Charisma House, 2006).

Hardships That Bring Preparation

Many people today, especially young people, want everything right now. They don't want to be prepared. Or maybe you think you are beyond that stage of being prepared because of your age.

Perhaps you feel unappreciated at work, or the conditions in the office are so oppressive and so difficult that it is all you can think about. You can let your situation throw you and become your downfall, or you can accept it as being part of God's preparation for you and allow it to turn you into one of the strongest human beings that ever lived. That's what happened to David.

> *O Lord, remember David and all the hardships he endured.*
>
> —Psalm 132:1

It may be that at some stage in your life God manifested His power and you knew you had a sure word from Him. There is not a single Christian who, at one time or another, doesn't know the feeling of God speaking to him or her. Then a year goes by, and you begin to think, *Lord, did You really speak to me?*

David had to wait for years before what was promised him was fulfilled. After being anointed as king, he wasn't immediately made king; it was only a word from God. David was still subject to Saul and had to flee from him. His anointing seemed to bring nothing but trouble.

One thing you can do while you are waiting is to submit to everything God allows to happen. All of these hardships David endured were part of his preparation.

We should be encouraged to know that whatever hardship we have gone through, even if the hardship was our own fault, God can take our life, work all over again, and make everything look as though it is the way it was supposed to be.

How do we cope with hardships? We have two choices: either we trust our vow to God, which in the end will give us more bondage and more guilt when we inevitably let God down, or we can trust God's vow to us. We should trust His Word.

Excerpted from *Higher Ground* (Christian Focus Publications Ltd., 1995).

1:10 Break Through the Betrayal Barrier

It is my experience that sooner or later nearly every Christian—virtually ten out of ten—will find some occasion when he or she feels God has betrayed them. But it is also my pastoral experience that roughly only one in ten will breakthrough the betrayal barrier.

Why should I write like this if my statistics are not very encouraging? For this reason: you can be that rare person who *does* break the betrayal barrier.

Most people, when God is smiling on them, can worship with jubilation, give cheerfully to His work, sacrifice time and pleasure for Him, and be expected to volunteer for any help needed at one's church. But let God appear to betray them, and these same people, I am ashamed to say, indicate a rather different story. Such

> *Though he slay me, yet will I trust in him: but I will maintain mine own ways before him.*
>
> —Job 13:15, kjv

people never discover the joy awaiting them on the other side were they to break through the barrier.

Are you wanting more of God? He invites you to break the betrayal barrier. A. W. Tozer used to say that we can have as much of God as we want. I disagreed with that at first. This is because I felt I didn't have as much of God as I wanted! But I have decided that Tozer was right: we *can* have as much of God as we want, but that wanting more of Him gets tested—by the betrayal barrier. It comes unexpectedly and at the "worst" time. It is not my *feeling* of wanting more of God—as when I worship or respond to an inspiring message—that proves I really want more of Him; it is how I respond to things that happen to me later on that proves I really want more of Him.

Excerpted from *Pure Joy* (Charisma House, 2006).

The Path to Joy

Nearly every person God uses a great deal has broken through the betrayal barrier *before* they were mightily used. It is not in the pulpit or on a stage or being seen by thousands when you break the betrayal barrier. It is what happens when you are alone. It happens when you have nobody to comfort you, when you are being misunderstood, when people are pointing the finger at you, when everything seems to go wrong, and yet you say, "Yes, Lord."

> *Teach me to do your will, for you are my God; may your good Spirit lead me on level ground.*
>
> —Psalm 143:10

Here's how you can break through the betrayal barrier:

1. Affirm from your heart that what is happening is God's idea. What is designed to get your attention may be a turnoff, yes, but it is God's idea to do it this way.

2. Realize this is possibly the greatest opportunity you will ever have to know Him intimately.

3. Pray more than ever. Spend every minute you can in secret with Him without the television on or people interrupting you. I don't mean for you to become a recluse or retreat into a monastery, but seek Him with all your heart.

4. Walk in the light God gives you. Confess any sin God brings to your attention. Accept any form of new obedience He puts before you.

A person may be in the spotlight before thousands or behind the scenes as a quiet, self-effacing intercessor. In either case, such a vessel of the Holy Spirit will have had to discover God for himself or herself during the hardest of times. This is so that you will believe in God even if nobody else does. To discover God for yourself means that you believe the Bible and the resurrection of Jesus Christ from the dead even if your hero or mentor denies the faith. And what brings about this kind of maturity is breaking the betrayal barrier. This is the path to pure joy.

Excerpted from *Pure Joy* (Charisma House, 2006).

Grace for the Moment

W hy does God let this happen to me? Why didn't God do this sooner? Why didn't God stop this? All of us have questions like this, and there are no sure answers to questions like these.

Why did God allow Abraham and Sarah to reach the age of one hundred and ninety, respectively, before giving Sarah such "strength to conceive"?

Sarah's foolishness, however, did not remove her from God's purpose for her. Sarah's laughing at God did not make Him change His mind. For God was determined to deal with Sarah herself and make her see His glory. "Is anything too hard for the LORD?" (Gen. 18:14).

Whether we are facing a major decision, sorrow, illness, bereavement, misunderstanding, or perhaps depression—God's grace is never wasted by being given to us before we need it.

> Therefore do not worry about tomorrow,
> for tomorrow will worry about itself.
> Each day has enough trouble of its own.
> —MATTHEW 6:34

Sarah's natural explanation for God's promise and her natural reaction to His own purpose for her have been repeated by all of us many times. We have manipulated providence and prophecy and judged His promises incredible. But God has also been kind to us, as He was to Sarah—even turning our laughter to godly fear. It is a sign that He is dealing with us, that He wants to include us in His great purpose.

Corrie ten Boom once asked her father, "What is it like to die?" He answered her, "When we take the train to Amsterdam, when do I give you the ticket to hand to the guard?" She replied, "Just before we get off." Her father then added, "That is the way God deals with us." God answers our questions when we really need the answers. God supplies the grace when we really need it.

Excerpted from *Believing God* (MorningStar Publications & Ministries, 1997).

God Has a Plan

The path to joy is submitting to God's Plan A or His Plan B. Victor Hugo said, "Like the trampling of a mighty army, so is the force of an idea whose time has come." If I may paraphrase that, I would say that, like the trampling of a mighty army, so is the force of one's anointing whose time has come. But one has to wait on God's time, and if the disciplining continues, God isn't finished with what we need.

> *I know, O Lord, that a man's life is not his own; it is not for man to direct his steps.*
>
> —Jeremiah 10:23

There are, basically, three kinds of chastening, or of God's discipline:

1. *Internal chastening.* This is God's primary way of dealing with us. It is God's way of trying to get our attention via preaching, teaching, hymns, our daily devotions, and through prayer. I call it God's Plan A.

2. *External chastening.* This is Plan B. It is God's strategy utilizing outside factors such as losing your job, financial reverse, putting you flat on your back, being swallowed by a big fish as Jonah was, or whatever it takes to get your attention.

3. *Terminal chastening.* I pray that you or I will never need this. It is the worst scenario for a person who has truly been saved. This manner of discipline, generally speaking, usually takes one of two forms: (1) physical death, as when Ananias and Sapphira lied to the Holy Spirit (Acts 5:1–11), or (2) stone deafness to the Spirit so that one can no longer hear God's voice (Heb. 5:11–6:6).

God does not chasten us idly or without reason; it is exactly what we need for the task He has assigned for us. He has a work for you to do that nobody can do as well as you can. Your own gift, or anointing, is unique. But if your time has not yet come, it is because there is a little bit more work for God to do in you.

Excerpted from *Pure Joy* (Charisma House, 2006).

Faith to Move Into Action

God has a way of bringing our options down to one. He has a way of securing the response to His Word down to one. God did not lead the children of Israel through the land of the Philistines, lest they turn back altogether. He wanted instead to bring them to the place where they would have no choice but to turn utterly to Him. That was "the crunch"—not turning back.

There was nothing to do but to lift up that rod—and watch God do the rest. Moses may have thought, *I've never done this before. I may look like a fool, but here it goes!* Up the rod went. Across the wind came. God did the rest.

They didn't swim across. They walked. They didn't run. They walked. They enjoyed the spectacular sight up close. Some were given the honor of carrying the bones of Joseph. They had pockets full of loot, jewels, valuables. Parents would say to their children, "Take a close look at this. This is our God at work. Don't ever forget it." Pharaoh, in the meantime, made the most unwise calculation to be seen among the Egyptians yet. What was it? The Egyptians thought that they could do what the children of Israel had done.

By faith the people passed through the Red Sea as on dry land; but when the Egyptians tried to do so, they were drowned.

—HEBREWS 11:29

Their most fatal error was trying to continue the pursuit of Israel across the Red Sea, but they realized it too late. For the same pillar of fire and cloud that had been Israel's guidance became Egypt's confusion.

The rod that was used to deliver Israel was used to condemn the Egyptians. The same Word that saves some will condemn others. Faith does what cannot be done by those who do not believe. And yet, faith also does what crying to God cannot do. There comes a time that we must act, do, obey. Lift up your rod. If that is what God has told you to do, nothing else will happen until you do it. Doing it is faith.

Excerpted from *Believing God* (MorningStar Publications & Ministries, 1997).

The Purpose of a Thorn in the Flesh

The purpose of the thorn in the flesh, Paul says, is to keep us from being conceited because of God's unusual blessing. In Paul's case it was because of "surpassing great revelations."

If you say, "I don't have a thorn in the flesh," then I don't suggest you pray, "O, please, Lord, give me one!" I can tell you right now that it is nothing for which you should stand in a line. It is nothing that you pray to get; you will pray to get rid of it. I don't wish it on anybody.

The first qualification for the thorn in the flesh is the fact that the Lord has been extraordinarily good to you. If He has been unusually good to you—you qualify.

> To keep me from becoming conceited because of these surpassingly great revelations, there was given me a thorn in my flesh.
>
> —2 Corinthians 12:7

Is that you? It may not be "visions and revelations from the Lord" (2 Cor. 12:1), but it is nonetheless an equivalent dose of sovereign grace, so wonderful that it is humbling for you to contemplate.

The second prerequisite is that one of your weaknesses happens to be that you tend to take yourself too seriously. If you immediately say, "That's not me," then I doubt that this is true. We are talking here about a thing called "pride." We are talking about a sensitive ego. So if you are *sure* you don't have a problem where pride is concerned, then there is no problem for you! Congratulations! You will not have a thorn in the flesh. You are exempt, so forget it.

Now I don't want to be unfair, but if you think you don't have a problem with pride, then you show you have no conviction of sin. The more you are convicted of sin, and the more you see of God's glory, then the more you will see how proud you are. At first you say, "I'm not that bad," and later you say, "I'm horrible." God peels the layers away—that is why you need a thorn in the flesh.

Excerpted from *The Thorn in the Flesh* (Charisma House, 2004).

The Key to Faith

This verse is a warning and an encouragement to you and me. The warning: if you and I do not make an attempt to receive the praise that comes from God rather than the praise of people, we too will find it impossible to exercise genuine faith. The encouragement: we are not required to have obtained the honor and praise of God, but only to *make an effort* to obtain it. God's commands are not burdensome (1 John 5:3).

He is not demanding that we perfectly repudiate the praise of people and absolutely receive His praise; He is only asking us to make an effort to obtain His praise. Nothing can be more reasonable than that.

What is so scary about this implication is that you and I could continue to miss what God may be up to in His church generally and in our lives in particular. If I choose the praise of people over God's approval, I will be a victim of unbelief. I will render myself incapable of believing God, as He wants me to. I will likewise miss whatever God has chosen to do at the moment. Jonathan Edwards taught us that the task of every generation is to discover in which direction the Sovereign Redeemer is moving, then move in that direction. But if I am found being enamoured with the praise of people during the time God is at work in my day or in my area, I will miss seeing His glory—even if it is right in front of me. That is what happened to the ancient Jews in Israel, and it can happen to us today. I can think of nothing worse than that.

> How can you believe if you accept praise from one another, yet make no effort to obtain the praise that comes from the only God?
>
> —JOHN 5:44

This verse therefore contains an immense encouragement, namely, if I but *seek*—or make an effort to obtain—His honor, I will be able to believe and see what He is up to.

Excerpted from *Pure Joy* (Charisma House, 2006).

Sometimes God Says "Stay"

Sometimes it is God's will for you to just *stay*. You may want to move on—but God may want you to stay. You may say, "It's time to get moving. Let's get the show on the road." But God says, "Stay. In quietness and trust is your strength" (Isa. 30:15).

The ancient people of Israel had to learn this lesson. They had to learn to take their cues from the visible glory of God—the pillar of fire by night and the cloud by day.

Israel was locked into this manner of direct guidance from God. They could only move when the cloud lifted. If the cloud did not lift, they stayed. No matter how tedious and tasteless that particular place in the wilderness might have been, they had to "stay put" until they were released to move on. The cloud did not adjust to the Israelites; they had to adjust to the cloud. It often takes as much courage to stay as it does to move. It may take even more faith sometimes to remain where you are than to explore a new geographical area.

> *Whenever the cloud lifted from above the tabernacle, they would set out; but if the cloud did not lift, they did not set out—until the day it lifted.*
> —Exodus 40:36–37

It may not be mere boredom, however, that tempts you to move on. Sometimes it is opposition. Whatever the case may be, whenever God says, "Stay," it is with a definite purpose. You will never be sorry when you remain where we are, even though you may not know the reasons at the time, if God says you must.

Excerpted from *The Sensitivity of the Spirit* (Charisma House, 2002).

Seek His Esteem

It is a powerful and wonderful thing to have God's esteem. The word *esteem* means to think highly of; it means respect or favorable opinion. Can anything be more fantastic than to have God esteem you—to think highly of you? This is possible not because of your profile, your importance, or performance, but because you want it more than anything else. Profile does not mean that God is pleased with you. There are people who are rich and famous, but they will never experience God's commendation or hear "well done." For these things mean little in heaven. All that is required is to want it—*more than anything*. That's all. This means that *you*—whoever you are—can have God's esteem.

What is required of you is not perfection, but *seeking*—making an effort to obtain—His praise and esteem. You don't have to be the prophet Daniel. Three times the Lord said to Daniel, "You are highly esteemed" (Dan. 9:23; 10:11, 19). Daniel was called highly esteemed not because he was a prophet, but because he loved God

> *This is the one I esteem: he who is humble and contrite in spirit, and trembles at my word.*
>
> —Isaiah 66:2

more than the approval of people (Dan. 6:10). It was his love for God's honor that put him where he was; he could be trusted with a high profile *because* it meant less to him than God's honor.

How much time and energy is required on our part? It all depends. If we *want* His esteem, then we are going to walk in any ray of light He gives to us along the way. We prove we want His esteem by the decisions we make. The honor of God is therefore at our fingertips. It is closer than our hands or our feet, closer than the air we breathe. It is centered in the mind, heart, and will. One could say, therefore, that to have the esteem of God is the easiest thing in the world to achieve because He is eager to show it. And yet to feel and hear His "well done" comes to those who show that it is really what they want by their words and deeds. The reward is pure joy.

Excerpted from *Pure Joy* (Charisma House, 2006).

Who Gets the Credit?

Can you do something good or worthwhile and keep quiet about it? What if you do something heroic, sacrificial, or valiant, and nobody notices? What if someone does know about it, but even he or she says or does nothing to ensure you get sufficient commendation? It may "get your goat" or hurt you deeply. But can you hold your peace and control your tongue?

Can you be content with the knowledge "God knows"? In other words, would His knowledge of what you did be enough for you? Or do you say to yourself, *I know God knows, but surely I deserve to have someone around me to be aware of what I did?* I sympathize with you if that is your thinking. I've been there a thousand times, and it hurts.

> *But Mordecai found out about the plot and told Queen Esther, who in turn reported it to the king, giving credit to Mordecai.*
>
> —ESTHER 2:22

But this is precisely where we show how much God's esteem means. What if God says that you cannot have it both ways, that you have to choose between knowing He knows and having the admiration of people? Sometimes we *can* have it both ways, providing we made the choice for His glory. What if you have to wait until you get to heaven before people have the true picture; is that OK with you? If so, you're *there*; that is the goal you and I must reach: the willingness to wait until we get to heaven to get proper recognition.

Excerpted from *Pure Joy* (Charisma House, 2006).

True Forgiveness

"**H**ow can I know whether I have truly forgiven someone?" Joseph provides a heart-searching frame of reference by showing us how he was able to totally forgive his brothers.

Joseph had much to be bitter about. First, his brothers had treated him with cruelty and disdain. True, he had made them jealous and had not been a very nice guy—he had even been a tattletale. (See Genesis 37:2.) But selling him to the Ishmaelites was a wicked and evil act.

Second, Joseph had been falsely accused. Instead of sleeping with Potiphar's wife, he had resisted the temptation. We all like to think that God will bless us when we are faithful and obedient to His Word, but the thanks Joseph got was imprisonment.

Third, God allowed all of these things to take place.

Joseph had much to be bitter about, then, and many "offenders" to forgive: his

> *You intended to harm me, but God intended it for good to accomplish what is now being done, the saving of many lives.*
> —GENESIS 50:20

brothers who sold him into slavery, Potiphar's wife who lied, and God who let it all happen.

The truth is, Joseph needed to be delivered from bitterness and self-pity. Joseph was full of self-pity. He says so: "I have done nothing to deserve being put in a dungeon" (Gen. 40:15). At that point in time, Joseph had not yet forgiven his brothers, Potiphar's wife, or God.

Joseph had not forgotten his dreams. He knew that one day his brothers would bow down before him. And eventually they did. But when it finally happened, Joseph was a changed man. There was no bitterness. There were no grudges. None. Something had happened to him during those final two years in prison. Instead, when the time came, he lovingly welcomed them and forgave them with tears. It was the moment he dreamed of. But instead of punishing them, which he had the power to do, he wept. Filled with love, he demonstrated total forgiveness.

Excerpted from *Total Forgiveness* (Charisma House, 2002).

Rejoice in the Lord!

Rejoicing is, more often than not, a choice. We all love spontaneous rejoicing. Such comes from answered prayer, the answers to our questions, the manifestation of the miraculous, the success and prosperity we wanted. It takes little faith to rejoice when it is precipitated by happy, external circumstances. But the command to rejoice comes because we don't always feel like rejoicing—and yet Paul said to do it all the time. Not rejoicing *because* of all that has happened but rather "*in all* circumstances" (1 Thess. 5:18, emphasis added). The choice we make to rejoice comes because we simply don't feel like rejoicing. *We just have to do it.*

How do you rejoice when you don't feel like it? The answer is, you find things for which you certainly should be thankful and then discipline yourself to *voice that gratitude.* I go through my journal every morning, item by item of the previous day, and thank the Lord in detail for everything. I have been doing it for over fifteen years. My wife, Louise, and I frequently do this together. Once, when returning to Key Largo in Florida (where we now live) from the airport, Louise said, "Let's thank the Lord for twenty-five things that took place over the weekend." We had a wonderful weekend in Connecticut. We began taking turns and naming particular things. When we finished, Louise said we had mentioned fifty-three things. I think God liked that.

> *Rejoice in the Lord always. I will say it again: Rejoice!…Do not be anxious about anything, but in everything, by prayer and petition, with thanksgiving, present your requests to God.*
> —PHILIPPIANS 4:4, 6

Showing gratitude is the sort of thing you can make yourself do whether you feel like it or not. There are *always* things you can thank God for if you look around. In other words, even if you don't feel like it, do it anyway.

Excerpted from *Pure Joy* (Charisma House, 2006).

How to Obtain Power

In a sense, most of us want spiritual power—to experience signs and wonders. However, we often lack spiritual power because the Word is woefully lacking within our lives. What then is the basis of God's giving spiritual power to His followers?

> *And they were astonished at his doctrine: for his word was with power.*
> —LUKE 4:32, KJV

1. Personal reading of the Scriptures

We have to ask ourselves a question: "Have I read my Bible completely through?" A poll was taken suggesting that the average clergyman spends an average of four minutes a day alone with the Lord. Then we wonder why the church is powerless. Personal reading of the Scriptures is the first step to power.

2. Personal revelation of the Scriptures

When is the last time the Scriptures got hold of you and shook revelation knowledge into your life? Spurgeon said, "If a text gets hold of you, chances are you've got hold of it."

3. Personal rethinking of the Scriptures

Many of us have accepted uncritically a hand-me-down point of view, secondhand Bible revelation, and secondhand doctrine. There is no personal rethinking by which we acquire the real meaning of the verse.

4. Personal release of the Spirit

Release of the Spirit comes from the Spirit Himself. If you want power, then it's going to have to come from the Spirit. The Bible is just about His finest accomplishment. It's His product. He likes it when you like His Word.

The scope for power will be found to the degree that we value His own Word. Power that flows from His name will be in proportion to our love for His Word. When that love is expressed, don't be surprised to see healings and miracles. There may be no need for people to line up to be prayed for. It will happen right where they are.

Excerpted from *The Word and the Spirit* (Charisma House, 1998).

We All Have Reasons to Rejoice

D o you feel that you let God down sometimes? Haven't we all?

He is not asking us to be excited about the bad things that may have happened in our lives or in the world around us, but He is trying to get our minds on something useful and positive because—one day—we will be glad we did.

The rejoicing that Peter experienced after being rebuked and flogged by the ruling council of Jerusalem showed how much he had changed. He was cowardly after Jesus was arrested, but now he was as bold as a lion. God wants to do this for all of us. He lets us have a second chance after we have blown it. This alone is cause for rejoicing.

But there is one further important clarification: we are told to *rejoice in the Lord*. We do not rejoice in ourselves or in things. We rejoice in the Lord Jesus. This we can always do because there is no fault in Him, no disappointment. We rejoice in His person—that He is totally God and totally man. No matter what our circumstances we can always—with integrity—rejoice in the Lord Jesus Christ.

> *And they departed from the presence of the council, rejoicing that they were counted worthy to suffer shame for his name.*
>
> —Acts 5:41, kjv

The same Lord we rejoice in, however, is not only in heaven. He is with us wherever we are. Paul spoke of Jesus being right there with him (2 Tim. 4:17). How could this be if He is in heaven? Is it because He miraculously remains there and yet comes to us where we are? Certainly. But it is also because He lifts us up to where He is! "God raised us up with Christ and seated us with him in the heavenly realms in Christ Jesus" (Eph. 2:6). "Never will I leave you; never will I forsake you" (Heb. 13:5) That is therefore perpetual cause for rejoicing.

God will come again, one way or another, to let us have another chance—and (perhaps) save face! Rejoice in His faithfulness. Rejoice in the way He covers for us and does not expose the skeletons in our closets. God is so kind and gracious. Whatever you are going through, this too will work together for good (Rom. 8:28). So rejoice!

Excerpted from *Pure Joy* (Charisma House, 2006).

Lonely but Never Alone

There are varieties of loneliness. For example, there is the loneliness of solitude—being alone without companions. You live alone. You eat alone. You watch television alone. You spend Christmas alone.

Then there is loneliness of singleness. I think the hardest question I am asked is why does God allow evil—to which I just reply, "I don't know!" The next hardest question I am asked is, "RT, why can't I find a wife?" "Why can't I find a husband?" "Why can't I find a girlfriend or boyfriend?" My heart goes out to such people.

I grant that there are a lot of people who are single and very happy; they don't want it any other way. But many would like to be married—they are so lonely. But there is something worse than being single, and that's being married—but *unhappily.* Part of the loneliness of singleness is sexual frustration. Sex is a God-given desire. Sex was not born in Hollywood but at the

> *And surely I am with you always, to the very end of the age.*
> —MATTHEW 28:20

throne of grace. There is a physical need for sexual fulfillment. Loneliness only adds to this, and my heart goes out to the many who suffer in this way.

Jesus is at the right hand of God. When He was on earth He was tempted at all points, just as we are (Heb. 4:15), but I have to say that He *resisted.* But it is comforting to know that Jesus has never forgotten what it was like then. He therefore sympathizes now. The difference between Jesus and some of us is that once we come out of something, we forget what it was like. Jesus has never forgotten what it was like.

Excerpted from *The Thorn in the Flesh* (Charisma House, 2004).

God Is for You!

I love the psalm in which David says, "God is for me" (Ps. 56:9). To know that God is with us and "for" us is a greater cause for rejoicing. This always make me think of my Grandpa McCurley, who was almost the only relative who stood with me when my theological views changed in 1955. "I'm for him, right or wrong," he said to the rest of the family in those days. That was the kind of support I needed at that time. And yet that is how much God is with us and for us all the time!

This does not mean He approves of all we believe and do. Yes, He is for us—right or wrong, but it does not follow He will uphold my unrighteous cause. He is able to be for me—whether I deserve it or not—in order to demonstrate patience that I might be brought to repentance and get sorted out, if that is what needs to happen. The amazing thing is that He still maintains love and support for me when I am unworthy. He sees the end from the beginning. He does not have to explain Himself for maintaining an everlasting love toward us, even when we are in the wrong. This is why we should not be self-righteous if we feel the presence of the Lord and claim this proves we are in the right.

> *If God is for us, who can be against us?*
> —ROMANS 8:31

God has a way of manifesting His presence to the most unworthy child! That is why He can be real to me. It does not mean I am better than others or that God approves of all He sees in me. He is that way with all His children! He stays with them until they get sorted out. What love! Amazing love! This is why we rejoice always…in the Lord.

Excerpted from *Pure Joy* (Charisma House, 2006).

Show Gratitude—in Everything

The anointing is the power of the Holy Spirit that enables me to do things with ease. It could be greater insight, greater energy, greater joy, or greater blessing of any proportion; and I want a greater anointing. One of the quickest routes to a greater anointing is to show gratitude to God—in everything.

Thanking God *for* everything and thanking Him *in* everything are not exactly the same thing. Not many people thank Him for everything. We may end up doing that—when enough time rolls along that "all things work together for good" (Rom. 8:28, KJV). Then we may thank Him for

> *Give thanks in all circumstances, for this is God's will for you in Christ Jesus.*
> —1 THESSALONIANS 5:18

things that were once evil and caused grief. But I do not counsel that we must thank Him *for* everything at any given moment.

When I sin or fail, I do not say, "Thank You, Lord." I cannot say that I thank God for the events of September 11, 2001. It may well be that all who read these lines live long enough to see God's sovereign hand in it all and find reasons to be thankful. But we are not required to be thankful for everything—for being robbed, raped, lied about, or being betrayed.

We therefore are not asked to be thankful *for* all these ordeals. But it is another thing to give thanks *in* such adversities. And this we are asked to do: "Give thanks in all circumstances, for this is God's will for you in Christ Jesus" (1 Thess. 5:18). Paul and Silas were in jail, but they were praying and singing hymns to God. (See Acts 16:25.) No matter what your present state, give Him thanks—in everything.

Excerpted from *Just Say Thanks!* (Charisma House, 2005).

Do You Want Pure Joy?

Pure joy is promised to all, but it is only received by those who want God and the offense of the cross more than anything in the world. God is a jealous God; He shares His joy with those who honor Him and embrace the stigma.

Do you want pure joy? How much do you want of it? Here is what I recommend to you if this joy is lacking:

1. Be sure that you have totally forgiven anyone who has hurt you or been unjust to you in any way.

2. Embrace any stigma that is associated with the Spirit so that you are utterly willing to look like a fool to those who know you.

3. Dignify any and every trial God puts in your path.

4. Seek the honor that comes from Him rather than getting your ego massaged by the praise of people.

5. Seek His face by praying with all your heart—until this joy is yours.

This joy is nothing else than God Himself. He wants to be real to you. God wants all His children to experience pure joy, but I am not saying that all must have exactly the same manifestations. I have never fallen to the floor in laughter. You may, or may not, speak in tongues (1 Cor. 12:30). The necessary evidence of the baptism, or sealing of the Spirit, is this peace and joy. In my opinion, we delay what God would do in us because of sheer pride or out of fear of what people might think. You may never speak in tongues or fall to the floor, but you must be willing to allow that to happen if you want pure joy.

> *Let us not become weary in doing good, for at the proper time we will reap a harvest if we do not give up.*
> —GALATIANS 6:9

Excerpted from *Pure Joy* (Charisma House, 2006).

The High Price of Complaining

What I want you to consider is whether you have a complaint, and, if so, is it valid? God knows whether it is valid. Do you feel that it has been unfair that you have had to live all these years with that particular man? Or do you think that God has not been fair to you because you never married, and you have complained? Do you have a valid complaint? It may be. God knows whether it is.

But let me ask you this: In your complaining do you roll up your sleeves, or do you let God handle it? The one thing that can be said about the judgment that must never be underestimated is that it will be the day when God is going to clear His name, and the justice will be carried out totally and in an undoubted way.

God knows what people have said. God knows the infidel shakes his fist and says, "If there's a God, why does He let this happen?" God can wait.

But that will be a day when He will be involved. Judgment will be carried out by

> *And do not grumble, as some of them did—and were killed by the destroying angel.*
>
> —1 CORINTHIANS 10:10

an all-wise and all-righteous God who has a perfect memory of everything that ever happened. His Day can be your day, but if you make today your day and do not wait for His Day, then that comes under a different category, what the Bible calls "grumbling."

We will be judged not only on what we have done then, but also on what we have said. Indignation may have led us to complain, but we must always ask ourselves: Do we speak with tongues of gold or tongues of straw?

Excerpted from *When God Says "Well Done!"* (Christian Focus Publications Ltd., 1993).

How to Pray in God's Will

Praying in God's will is carried out at one of two levels (or perhaps both): (1) when you know what God's will is and pray accordingly, or (2) when you don't know what God's will is but pray with groans that words cannot express—that is, words you don't understand.

The first level is, in my opinion, quite rare. It has happened, but not often. It is when I *know* somehow that when I pray for something I also know God heard me and that it will be answered because I prayed in the will of God. I wish I could say that I engage in this kind of praying all the time.

> *In the same way, the Spirit helps us in our weakness. We do not know what we ought to pray for, but the Spirit himself intercedes for us with groans that words cannot express.*
>
> —Romans 8:26

Zechariah and Elizabeth prayed for a son. They did not know that they put this request in God's will and that it was *heard*. But it was—except that they were not notified for a long time. Zechariah had prayed years before in the will of God, but he was not given the grace of the Spirit to *know at the time* he was praying in God's will. Knowing at the time is therefore, in my view, rare.

The second level of praying in the Spirit is when you *do* pray in the will of God, but you do not know what you are praying for. How can this be? Romans 8:26, quoted above, coheres with 1 Corinthians 14:2: "For anyone who speaks in a tongue does not speak to men but to God. Indeed, no one understands him; he utters mysteries with his spirit." When you are praying in tongues you are praying in the will of God, which is why you could pray consciously in the will of God at both levels. This is because when I pray in tongues I abandon my wishes to the Spirit. I do not know what God's will is, true, but I know nonetheless that I am praying in God's will because I am praying in tongues.

Excerpted from *Pure Joy* (Charisma House, 2006).

How to Know the Will of God

I think it might be helpful for some if I were to use a little acrostic, PEACE, on how to know the will of God. None of us want to be deceived when we are open. How may we know we are not being deceived?

First, is it *Providential?* In other words, if you are praying whether to do this or that, does it fall in place? Do you have to nudge the arm of providence, or does it just happen?

Second, *Enemy.* Always put this in the computer when you are wanting to know the will of God: What will the devil think? Would it please or displease him?

Third, *Authority.* What does the Bible say? Is it biblical, in other words. The Holy Spirit will never lead us to embrace what is contrary to Holy Scripture.

Fourth, *Confidence.* What does this do for your own confidence? Your own assurance? Sense of well-being? Because whenever you are in the will of God, it will increase your sense of confidence. It always does that. When you are lacking in confidence, there is something wrong. If what you are about to do diminishes your confidence, there is something wrong.

> *Do not be anxious about anything, but in everything, by prayer and petition, with thanksgiving, present your requests to God. And the peace of God, which transcends all understanding, will guard your hearts and your minds in Christ Jesus.*
> —PHILIPPIANS 4:6-7

Fifth, *Ease.* Does this decision give you a feeling of ease? "To thine own self be true," as Shakespeare put it.

So PEACE. That is how to know the will of God. Now this acrostic can be a kind of guide, and yet, if you develop the godly habit, you will not necessarily need this. I do not say it will not be helpful, but that it will simply confirm what you have found to be true anyway.

Excerpted from *Are You Stone Deaf to the Spirit or Rediscovering God?*
(Christian Focus Publications Ltd., 1994, 1999).

Crowns to Give Him

God wants us to know that He takes notice of everything we do. We are made in such manner as to want recognition and approval. Dale Carnegie, author of the classic best seller *How to Win Friends and Influence People*, states that the strongest urge in the world that people are born with is the desire to feel important. God made us that way. For those who say, "I don't need a reward to do what God tells me to do," I just hope they are not being a bit smug and self-righteous. It is as if they are saying, "I love God so much I would work for Him without any glory whatsoever." Good. And that *is* the way we are to be here below. The problem with the Pharisees was that all they did was to be seen by people (Matt. 23:5), but Jesus put forward the proposition that we should abandon the honor that comes from one another and seek to obtain the honor that comes from God (John 5:44). That is a motivation for how we can be honored—by God Himself, but in His way and in His time. And most certainly at the judgment seat of Christ.

> They lay their crowns before the throne and say: "You are worthy, our Lord and God, to receive glory and honor and power."
>
> —REVELATION 4:10–11

Some will no doubt say, "I don't care whether I receive a reward at the judgment; I will be happy enough just to make it to heaven." I do understand that, but that is certainly *not* the way you will feel when you actually have to stand before Jesus the Righteous Judge. You will wish beyond the ability to imagine with all your heart that you might receive His "Well done." It would be the most awful feeling to be passed by when others were being so blessed.

Not only that, if I understand the meaning of Jesus having many crowns (Rev. 19:12)—plus the theology of some of our greatest hymns—where do you think those crowns come from?

The crowns on Jesus' head are our crowns. They are the crowns given as a reward at the judgment seat of Christ.

We will never—ever—be able to thank God enough for saving us and giving us a home in heaven. But one thing that will be given to us—that will help us show our gratitude—is that we get to take off our crowns and give them to Jesus.

Excerpted from *Pure Joy* (Charisma House, 2006).

Believing God

Faith is *believing God.* The heroes of Hebrews 11 are people who believed God. They are the writer's examples to show that faith itself is not a New Testament innovation. Faith goes way back in time, claims the writer of Hebrews. There is nothing new about it at all. God hides His face in order that we might believe. He withholds the evidence of things visible that we might be persuaded by His Word alone!

Faith, then, is the long parenthesis between the undeniable appearances of God's glory. When God appears, faith is no longer necessary. There are actually times when faith is eclipsed by such a sense of the majesty and glory of God that one is temporarily without the need of faith. These are times of mountaintop experiences, such as when our Lord was transfigured before His disciples (Matt. 17:1–9).

But one is not permitted to live indefinitely on the mountaintops. Like the disciples who "came down from the mountain" (v. 9, KJV), so must we. It is in the valley that we live by the faithfulness of God,

> *Now faith is the substance of things hoped for, the evidence of things not seen.*
> —HEBREWS 11:1, KJV

who periodically reveals Himself so we will not be swallowed up in despair.

These Hebrew Christians were witnessing a long interval. They were discouraged. They had known better days—perhaps some mountaintop experiences. They were perplexed and could not understand the utter absence of the sense of God's presence. The writer comes along and shows them that this is nothing to despise. It is an opportunity to believe.

Although faith is not a New Testament innovation, it is a New Testament norm. The Christian life is a venture of believing God. Seeing is not believing. Believing is not seeing. Faith is an inner persuasion in those who live by the integrity and faithfulness of One whose manifested glory is worth waiting for.

In the meantime, faith accomplishes extraordinary things.

Excerpted from *Believing God* (MorningStar Publications & Ministries, 1997).

What Is Love?

Afresh definition of love can be quite difficult to come by. A two-word defini-tion is "selfless concern," and if I had to narrow it to one word, it would be "unselfishness" or "brokenness." That is what Paul meant by "the most excellent way."

First, Paul describes love as grace renewed. In 2 Corinthians 3:18 he says, "And we…being transformed into his likeness with ever-increasing glory, which comes from the Lord, who is the Spirit." Believers often find themselves going from glory to glory in church or in their quiet time. Often the transition is accompa-nied by suffering, but every experience of being changed carries with it a fresh bap-tism of love, of unselfishness. It is like the calm after the storm. It is this calm that is described in 1 Corinthians 13:4–5. This is a description of grace renewed. It is not only a renewal of faith and trust, but it is a peace that is devoid of bitterness.

> *Love is patient, love is kind. It does not envy, it does not boast, it is not proud. It is not rude, it is not self-seeking, it is not easily angered, it keeps no record of wrongs.*
>
> —1 CORINTHIANS 13:4–5

Second, Paul describes love as guilt removed, and that in two ways: first, we don't feel guilty, and second, we don't make others feel guilty. When grace is renewed, and we are changed from glory to glory, the guilt is removed, and we feel so good. Guilt is the most crippling thing in the world. But when the guilty feeling is gone, the need to make others feel guilty is not there. It is when we feel totally forgiven, totally absolved, that we will find it easy to forgive others.

Third, it is also a description of the Golden Rule: "In everything, do to others what you would have them do to you, for this sums up the Law and the Prophets" (Matt. 7:12). In other words, treat people the way you would like them to treat you. How do you feel when people make you feel guilty? How do you feel when people blame you? It makes you feel like dirt; you feel awful. God keeps no record of wrongs.

Perhaps your marriage is in trouble. If that is the case, start living like this. Don't wait for your wife or husband to do it—you do it. It will heal your marriage. "Do to others what you would have them do to you."

Excerpted from *Just Love* (Christian Focus Publications Ltd., 1997).

To Flow in the Spirit, There Must Be Intimacy

You get to know a person's ways by spending time with them. My wife, Louise, and I have been married for over forty-five years. I know her ways, and she knows mine. When we are asked a question or receive an invitation, we almost always know what the other will say. God wants us to know Him like that.

Flowing in the Spirit means to honor God's "no" as well as His "yes." Paul and his companions were "kept by the Holy Spirit" ("forbidden," KJV) from preaching the word in the province of Asia (Acts 16:6). Really? Are we to believe that the *Holy Spirit*—not the devil—would actually stop people from preaching the gospel?

It seems to me that this would take both supernatural discernment and considerable courage to act on a word from the Spirit like that. This seems to fly in the face of our mandate to preach the gospel to every person (Mark 16:15). How did they know? I only know they listened to the Spirit and obeyed. It must have taken as much courage to obey not to preach as it did to preach.

> *Therefore I was angry with this generation, and said, "They always go astray in their heart; and they did not know My ways."*
>
> —HEBREWS 3:10, NAS

To flow in the Spirit is to have intimacy with Him and to feel what He wants. It is to learn God's ways, His style, His manner of doing things, His way with people, His gentleness, His indignation, His impulses. In other words, do what pleases the Spirit and what He prompts you to do. God wants us to know His ways; it is as though God admits to having a certain kind of personality. God wants intimacy with us, and there is no greater joy than to keep in step with the Spirit.

Excerpted from *Believing God* (MorningStar Publications & Ministries, 1997).

Accepting Our Anointing

Everybody has an anointing. The apostle Paul called anointings "gifts" in 1 Corinthians 12:4–11. They are God's gifts, which He graciously bestows on those who don't deserve them. The difficulty is, ambition gets into the picture, and some don't like it if their own anointing does not result in a high profile. Paul compared these gifts, which I am calling anointings, to the parts of the human body.

Some anointings—such as the eye or the head—have a high profile. Some anointings—such as the hands or the feet—have a lower profile. But whatever the function, they must all work together.

> *Now the body is not made up of one part but of many....But in fact God has arranged the parts in the body, every one of them, just as he wanted them to be.*
> —1 CORINTHIANS 12:14, 18

Some people have an anointing with no apparent profile at all—like the kidneys or intestines, which, despite their hiddenness, are indispensable. (See 1 Corinthians 12:23ff.) God's design is that there should be "no division in the body, but that its parts should have equal concern for each other" (v. 25). Paul draws a conclusion: "Now you are the body of Christ, and each one of you is a part of it" (v. 27).

There are those with a high profile, such as apostles, prophets, and teachers; and there are those in the background who have an anointing (not listed in 1 Corinthians 12:8–10) that the King James Version calls "helps"—a gift to help others (v. 28).

The question is, will we accept our own anointing? Or will we let ambition and personal drive for recognition get in the way?

Excerpted from *The Anointing: Yesterday, Today, Tomorrow* (Charisma House, 2003).

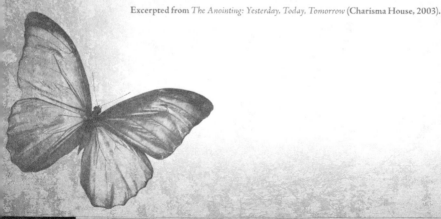

Recognizing His Presence

I think there is a sense in which we can define spirituality as the ability to close the time gap between the moment the Lord appears and our awareness that it is the Lord. Let me put it this way: Perhaps God spoke to you at a particular time or was present on a particular occasion. At the time, it didn't seem as if it was God who was doing the speaking or God who was present at all. What He was doing or what He said you underestimated, if not rejected. Only years later did it become clear to you that you had failed to recognize His presence.

Some of us may take less time to recognize God's presence—weeks or days; others may have it down to only minutes or seconds! So, when our initial feeling is to reject something, we find ourselves thinking instead, *This may be the Lord.*

Perhaps you can think of an experience when something came up that first you

> *He said to me, "Son of man, stand up on your feet and I will speak to you." As he spoke, the Spirit came into me and raised me to my feet, and I heard him speaking to me.*
>
> —Ezekiel 2:1–2

thought God simply wasn't in. Then later, like Jacob, you had to say, "The Lord was in this place. I didn't know it. I wasn't aware of it." (See Genesis 28:16.) Let's not think ourselves so spiritual that we are sure we couldn't possibly miss the Lord's presence. Our very biases may keep us from seeing the Lord when He appears.

Does God tell us what He's going to do? The answer would have to be—sometimes He does, sometimes He doesn't. But when the Lord does appear, we ought to be able to recognize Him. I would hate to think of the Lord appearing and my not knowing Him. I would love to think that the Holy Spirit within me would recognize the Holy Spirit within someone else; then, if I am where God is at work, I could overrule my biases, my prejudices, and my instincts and see that this is God.

Excerpted from *When God Shows Up* (Renew Books, 1998).

The Reward of Obedience

Have you ever wondered what it will be like at the judgment seat of Christ? I don't know where it will be—whether at a place on the earth, in the sky, or in a newly created part of God's universe. But you and I will be there. It is hard to imagine having confidence, or boldness, on that day even though John said that this is possible if "love is made complete among us" (1 John 4:17).

It seems to me that our hearts will be pounding out of our chests. Surely it will be the most sobering, terrifying moment we have ever experienced.

You and I will be judged at the judgment seat of Christ in part by whether or not we accepted our anointing and whether we lived within the limitations of that anointing. The reason is this: we will not be rewarded because of a gift God gave us.

> *For we must all appear before the judgment seat of Christ, that each one may receive what is due him for the things done while in the body, whether good or bad.*
> —2 Corinthians 5:10

Whether or not we receive a reward will be determined by our *accepting* our anointing (which requires obedience) and *living within its limitations* (which means not disobeying), whatever the profile that follows.

We will also be blessed here below on the basis of how we lived within the grace given to us. We may or may not be pleased with the profile that comes with that anointing. But the greatest thing that can happen to you or me at the judgment seat of Christ is to hear Jesus say, "Well done."

To the degree that we accept and live within our anointing we can sense God saying even now, "Well done." It brings a wonderful feeling that comes from knowing you are pleasing God. Not man. God. And it is within the grasp of every single one of us.

Excerpted from *The Anointing: Yesterday, Today, Tomorrow* (Charisma House, 2003).

Unique Possibilities of Faith

Hebrews 11 gives us three unique possibilities of what true faith looks like:

1. *True faith is always original.* It sets its own pace and loves to treat existing molds with contempt. It mocks precedents and transcends our own projections. The same God who loves each person as though there were no one else to love also challenges each person as if there were no on else who could succeed. True faith challenges us to be unique and to set our own pace.

2. *True faith is unlimited in its potential.* Faith refuses to accept the "inevitable"; it marches to a different beat of the drum than what the masses hear. To grasp the nature of true faith is to *understand its opposition to nature* and the way we naturally think. In the natural, we say, "It cannot be done." But faith says, "It *can*." Faith builds its domain with the stone that the "builders rejected" (Matt. 21:42). Faith is not threatened by the solitude of seeing what others are blind to.

> *Who through faith conquered kingdoms, administered justice…quenched the fury of the flames…whose weakness was turned to strength…. Women received back their dead, raised to life again.*
> —HEBREWS 11:33–35

3. *True faith is unrewarded obedience.* Faith is obedient to the God who gave it. This obedience is not contingent upon results or calculated success. It is not at work because it "works"; it is at work because its motivation is pleasing God. Faith is not motivated to do what it does because it anticipates a certain payment in this life in return; it just does it.

What emerges as a common thread in the events described in Hebrews 11:33–35 is that they were *unprecedented*. When Shadrach, Meshach, and Abednego were bound and cast into the fiery furnace, there was no precedent that they would be seen walking loose with the Fourth Man. But their faith "quenched the violence of fire" (v. 34, KJV). This is the essence of true faith.

Excerpted from *Believing God* (MorningStar Publications & Ministries, 1997).

Yesterday's Man

Although I've read 1 Samuel 16:1 many times, one day it was as though a laser beam flashing from three different directions illuminated the verse with a clarity that shook me rigid. In one verse I saw three types of ministry: yesterday's man or woman, represented by King Saul; today's man or woman, represented by Samuel, to whom God was speaking; and tomorrow's man or woman, represented by David, whom Samuel was led to anoint.

> The LORD said to Samuel, "How long will you mourn for Saul, since I have rejected him as king over Israel? Fill your horn with oil and be on your way; I am sending you to Jesse of Bethlehem. I have chosen one of his sons to be king."
>
> —1 SAMUEL 16:1

King Saul, yesterday's man, lost God's approval but still wore the crown. Tomorrow's man, David, got the anointing but without the crown. Today's man had to break with yesterday's man and cast his lot with tomorrow's man.

In recent years I have found myself using the expression "yesterday's man." It refers to a person who ceases to be relevant. He or she may continue to minister and say things. But such a person has somehow "lost" it—he is out of touch.

He is saying the same old thing he has uttered in years gone by when it probably had impact, if not power. But it has ceased to carry weight today. Such a person often struggles to prove himself, trying to show his relevance, but the power has gone. In other words, such a person is a has-been in God's sight, thriving on his natural skills, grace-gifts, strong personality, or influential platform, and may lead many people. But God has secretly passed the greater anointing to his or her replacement—tomorrow's man or woman.

Excerpted from *The Anointing: Yesterday, Today, Tomorrow* (Charisma House, 2003).

Today's Anointing

Most of us do not want the feeling of being irrelevant. We want to feel that what we have to say relates to the present scene, that we are equipped for what is needed today—in short, that we have today's anointing. The most horrible feeling in the world must be that one is yesterday's man or woman, once used but not relevant now.

The task of every generation is to discover in which direction our sovereign Redeemer is moving, then to move in that direction. I can think of nothing worse than for God to be at work and for me not to see it, for His anointing to be on someone's ministry and for me not to recognize it.

> *I bear on my body the marks [stigma] of Jesus.*
>
> —GALATIANS 6:17

The trouble is that we all have an inclination to believe "the old [wine] is better" (Luke 5:39). For example, we like what is familiar, the old hymns or songs we became accustomed to, the old style of preaching we grew up with. In a word: where there is no stigma (offense)—no mark of the Lord.

The first church I pastored was in Palmer, Tennessee. Although I came from the hills of Kentucky, where the preaching style was often loud and emotional, I did not develop a preaching style that was popular then. It didn't matter whether there was any content in your sermon; a certain style largely determined whether you were acceptable. They called it the "holy tone."

When I took the pastorate, that is the style the people were used to—and wanted. They honestly equated the style with the anointing. It was the "old wine" to which they were accustomed. For all I knew, perhaps in a previous era, truly anointed men developed that manner of preaching. But by the time I was around it was only a form of godliness with no power. And no stigma.

Many of us are very happy if God is so kind as to "do it again" as He has done it before. In this we are happy. For this we are quite ready. Why? Because there is little stigma here.

We want to avoid any stigma when it is outside our comfort zone. "What will *they* think? What will *they* say?" But today's anointing is totally *missed* by looking over our shoulders, probably more than by any other factor.

Excerpted from *The Anointing: Yesterday, Today, Tomorrow* (Charisma House, 2003).

The Holy Spirit Brings Joy

Joy is not a happiness that comes from outside things—like a pay raise, a new job, vindication, a letter with good news, or receiving a coveted invitation. It is the Spirit's *own* witness, indeed the person of the Holy Spirit Himself, coming right inside of you that brings joy. This is why it is called immediate and direct. Joy comes from within. With syllogistic reasoning the Holy Spirit applies the word; we use our minds to apply what we have heard and are thus able safely to conclude that we are going to heaven. But our minds applied the word and *then* it touched the heart. But this *rest of soul*—the result of the immediate and direct witness of the Spirit—comes without any reasoning, applying, thinking, deducting, or reflecting. It is the Spirit overruling our minds and going directly to the heart—straight from heaven to the soul. It is an act of God, sovereignly bestowed, and there is not one thing you can do to *make* it happen. And yet Jesus tells us it is what the Father delights to do for those who ask Him.

> *For the kingdom of God is not a matter of eating and drinking, but of righteousness, peace and joy in the Holy Spirit.*
> —ROMANS 14:17

One further fruit of this is how the Bible comes alive—you know more than ever that the Bible is the very Word of God. I do not believe one needs the baptism of the Spirit to believe that the Bible is the Word of God, but I am certainly saying that it enables you to believe it more than ever! All of it! You know you have not been deceived. You see clearly and without doubt that Christianity is true, the Christian faith is real, and Jesus is real. His resurrection is real.

Joy is knowing you've got it right, not because of how much you have read or how much teaching you have received, but by the presence of the Holy Spirit in power. Nothing at all compares with this.

Excerpted from *Pure Joy* (Charisma House, 2006).

What's in a Name?

Shakespeare's question "What's in a name?" would have been taken very seriously in the ancient Hebraic world, for the name was an indispensable part of the personality. It has been said, "Man is constituted of body, soul, and name." "As a man is named, so is he," so it was often claimed.

Often in the Bible we see the appropriate use of names. When Abigail sought mercy from David she said, "May my lord pay no attention to that wicked man Nabal. He is like his name—his name is Fool, and folly goes with him" (1 Sam. 25:25). The word *Nabal* means "fool." Abram was given a new name, Abraham, "the Father of Many Nations." Isaac literally means "laughter," because when Sarah overheard that she was going to have a child of her own, she laughed. Jacob means "supplanter," or "one who takes by the heel," but God changed his name to Israel, which means "one who perseveres with God."

> *A good name is more desirable than great riches; to be esteemed is better than silver or gold.*
>
> —PROVERBS 22:1

Paul said that God has highly exalted Jesus and given to Him *the* name which is above every name. (See Philippians 2:9.)

There are certain questions that the use of this name raises, and the first of these is, "What precisely is that name that is above every name?" Now a very strong hint toward the answer to this is found by examining the actual phrase, "exalted to the highest place."

The meaning is "one who is" or "one who causes to be." "I AM" means the "one who is;" "I AM WHO I AM" is the "one who causes to be." It was the ultimate revelation of God's name; a name than which no greater could be conceived. It was the name above all names.

Excerpted from *Meekness and Majesty* (Christian Focus Publications Ltd., 1992, 2000).

Prepare to Be Misunderstood

The paramount stigma of being today's man or woman is probably that of being misunderstood. Nothing is more painful than this. We can cope with a lot that people say against us—as long as they are fully in the picture and still disagree. But what *hurts* is when they *aren't* in the picture and they form judgments and perceptions that are based on limited information.

I sometimes think that much of Jesus' pain at His crucifixion was a result of His being misunderstood. Nothing made sense. It didn't add up that the same man who raised Lazarus from the dead a few days before was now hanging on a cross. Why didn't Jesus *stop* the proceedings that led to His crucifixion? Anybody who could control the wind and storm on the Sea of Galilee could surely have intervened before Herod or Pilate.

> *Then all the disciples deserted him [Jesus] and fled.*
>
> —MATTHEW 26:56

There were any number of ways in which He could have stopped being crucified. Common sense told everybody this. So why was He being crucified?

The disciples couldn't figure it out—they all forsook Him and fled (Matt. 26:56). Never once did Jesus explain Himself.

It must have been almost unbearable emotional pain for Jesus to see Mary Magdalene sobbing her heart out at the scene of the cross and not be allowed to whisper to her, "It's OK, Mary; all is going according to plan. I'm atoning for the sins of the world by My blood." But there was no hint of this. He had to bear the further stigma of being misunderstood, even by those closest to Him.

Whether others understood or not, He did the right thing—He listened to God.

Excerpted from *The Anointing: Yesterday, Today, Tomorrow* (Charisma House, 2003).

Don't Beat Yourself Up Over a Mistake

There are some actions of the past in some of us that we will probably never, never, never know for sure whether they were right or wrong. That is, we will never know until we get to heaven. God also lets some things remain in suspension to keep us from taking ourselves too seriously!

And what is the best attitude to adopt from then on? I answer: we learn to laugh at ourselves. Leave it to God. Have a laugh! The truth is, God for the moment has chosen not to tell us whether what we said or did was right! We might as well laugh, because crying about it won't help! If you make a choice whether to laugh or cry, why punish yourself?

> *If we are out of our mind, it is for the sake of God; if we are in our right mind, it is for you.*
>
> —2 Corinthians 5:13

Giving something over to God is a great privilege. We cast our anxiety upon Him because He cares for us (1 Pet. 5:7). Once we cast our care on Him—leaving our burden to the Lord, we should not look back. The highest level of proof that we really have cast our care upon the Lord is to forget the whole thing and just laugh!

People who take themselves too seriously cannot laugh at themselves. They certainly cannot bear to be laughed at. But when we don't take ourselves too seriously, we will not take it so hard when we are laughed at, and therefore we can enjoy laughing with them—at ourselves!

God is in no hurry to give us the shaking of the shoulders or the slap on the wrist—or whatever we may need. I just know one thing: God tends to deal with me sooner or later, and often sooner—especially if it has to do with a cross word with Louise, my children, or a close friend. I am just thankful that He doesn't let me get away with things!

Excerpted from *Controlling the Tongue* (Charisma House, 2007).

Put God First

All relationships must ever be subservient to God's greater glory. No matter how close people get to each other, they must be closer to God. The irony is, the closer people are to God, the more they will love each other. The more they put the voice of God prior to their commitment to each other, the more they really respect each other.

I think of some of my close friends. The dynamic that holds us together is that we love God more than we do each other. If I stopped listening to God and turned away from Him, I would expect my friends to warn me—then lovingly rebuke me if I did not come to my senses.

Anyone who loves his father or mother more than me is not worthy of me; anyone who loves his son or daughter more than me is not worthy of me.
—MATTHEW 10:37

No friendship or relationship is worth its salt if it does not have an inflexible commitment to God's glory first and to one another second. It would break my heart if I had to break with any of my friends—for any reason. But I would do it if I had to because of my greater love for God's honor.

It is a severe test to one's mettle whether God will always be put first—and obeyed. Today's man or woman must get his or her approval from God only. "How can you believe if you accept praise from one another, yet make no effort to obtain the praise that comes from the only God?" (John 5:44).

It is a way today's servant of Christ must bear the cross. But the more I bear this cross, the more I put God's voice first, and the more I am jealous of God's glory, then the more will I be respected, appreciated, and loved by these friends. That, in fact, is what makes real friendship.

Excerpted from *The Anointing: Yesterday, Today, Tomorrow* (Charisma House, 2003).

I Am Loved!

How does it make you feel to know that someone loves you? Many people are just a little uneasy when someone comes up to them and says, "I love you." Sometimes I say it to people I know really well. As I am about to get off the telephone, I say, "Love you," and they don't know how to respond. "Right, oh well, um…" is often all I get in return. Once in a while, if they are used to me telling them I love them, they say, "Oh well, same to you." But it is a good feeling to know that you are loved. I want to hear it from my wife every day, and I guess she wants to hear it from me every day, too. Victor Hugo, the nineteenth-century French writer, said, "The supreme happiness in life is the conviction that we are loved."

> *"I have loved you," says the* LORD.
> —MALACHI 1:2

We all have a need to be loved. When people are difficult to understand, when I wonder what makes them tick, I find that what they most need, and what they most want, is to be loved. There is nothing that breaks the hardest heart like the feeling of being loved. All of us can face terrible opposition and suffering if we feel approved of, accepted, and loved by someone whose opinion matters to us.

There is an even greater feeling than knowing another person loves you, and that is knowing that God loves you. There is no greater feeling than that. When I feel that God loves me and approves of me, I can face a thousand foes. And the message of Malachi is just that, *You are loved*. We all have skeletons in our closets, and God knows every one of them, yet He still says, "I love you."

Excerpted from *Between the Times* (Christian Focus Publications Ltd., 2003).

What Really Matters

Sometimes the hardest thing in the world is to accept yourself. I have struggled immeasurably at this point. To be myself has been about the hardest thing I've sought to do in ministry. My consolation is this: God will use me only to the extent to which I am true to what I know. This means I must not pretend to understand a verse in the Bible that remains hidden at the moment.

But in the early years I began to take myself a bit seriously, especially if I had preached a good sermon. While compliments can be encouraging, they almost ruined me in some ways because I tried to come up to a standard that some said I met. It wasn't my standard but theirs.

> *We, however, will not boast beyond proper limits, but will confine our boasting to the field God has assigned to us, a field that reaches even to you.*
> —2 Corinthians 10:13

It hadn't been that way at first. I was merely myself. But my preaching began to change. Some said I had been shouting too loudly when I first preached, so could I please stop it. Still others said, "Don't tell anecdotes or refer to yourself when you preach." When I managed to remember these things, I would get praise from certain people who hinted that, just maybe, I came up to their standard!

But I was miserable. Before I knew it, I was bordering on moving outside my anointing. If I was truly myself, I was afraid people would think, *Yuck*. But if I was not myself, God would think it! I eventually came to terms with my limits—which is probably the hardest thing I have ever done. It became a matter of sheer obedience to God. I had to affirm Him for making me as I am and affirm myself, even if people didn't like it. After all, I began to see with ever-increasing conviction that what matters is what God thinks and the way I will be regarded on the Final Day.

Excerpted from *The Anointing: Yesterday, Today, Tomorrow* (Charisma House, 2003).

As God Forgave You

There are a lot of things God knows about me that I wouldn't want anyone else to know. God has enough on me to bury me! But you will never know any of it because God won't tell.

This is precisely how you and I are forgiven: "As far as the east is from the west, so far has he removed our transgressions from us" (Ps. 103:12). Our sins are "wiped out" (Acts 3:19). It is as though our sins don't exist anymore—they are gone, gone, gone, gone! Insofar as our standing and security with God are concerned, they will never be held against us.

Joseph is sometimes referred to as a type of Christ—a person in the Old Testament who, long before Jesus came along, displayed characteristics of Jesus Himself. Despite his imperfections, Joseph was indeed a type of Christ in many ways. His ability to forgive his brothers as he did foreshadows Jesus' actions toward His disciples. Scared to death and ashamed over the way they had deserted Jesus when He was arrested, they were huddled behind closed doors when the resurrected Jesus turned up unexpectedly and declared, "Peace be with you!" (John 20:21). The disciples were totally forgiven—and they knew it.

> *Be kind and compassionate to one another, forgiving each other, just as in Christ God forgave you.*
> —Ephesians 4:32

We all have skeletons in our closets; some are known to others, many are unknown. It is comforting to know that God freely and totally forgives all of our sins and will never tell what He knows. That is the way Joseph forgave. And that is the why we are urged, "Be kind and compassionate to one another, forgiving each other, just as in Christ God forgave you" (Eph. 4:32).

Excerpted from *Total Forgiveness* (Charisma House, 2002).

Remedy for Burnout

God never promotes us to the level of our incompetence. What He truly calls us to do, we can do. As St. Augustine prayed, "Command what Thou wilt; give what Thou commandest." God *always* provides grace for what He has called us to do. "Your strength will equal your days" (Deut. 33:25). If you or I are operating at a level that brings fatigue and leads to what we now call "burnout," then something has gone wrong; we moved outside our anointing at some stage. It should never happen.

> *The bolts of your gates will be iron and bronze, and your strength will equal your days.*
>
> —DEUTERONOMY 33:25

This is not to deny that God may hide His face from us. It is not uncommon to experience the "dark night of the soul." But this is not necessarily the same thing as burnout. God may leave us to test us, as He did Hezekiah, "to know everything that was in his heart" (2 Chron. 32:31). But burnout is what we bring on ourselves by taking on what God did not command.

The apostle Paul came to terms with his limitations and strengths. When his enemies scoffed, "His letters are weighty and forceful, but in person he is unimpressive and his speaking amounts to nothing" (2 Cor. 10:10), it stung. It hurt. But he spoke with disarming frankness when he implicitly acknowledged nonetheless that his public speaking probably did not flow with the eloquence of a trained orator. "I may not be a trained speaker, but I do have knowledge" (1 Cor. 11:6).

"But I do have knowledge," he could say. He may not have been a trained speaker, but he knew what he was talking about. And as it happened, his expertise touched on the *very issue* that had become the focus at the time. So his anointing came through where it counted. It turned out he *had* training that mattered. To Paul's opponents, the issue was *how* you said it; to Paul, the issue was *what* you said. In other words, Paul's anointing of knowledge more than compensated for his deficiency in public speaking.

There are some lessons here for you and me. First, as I said already, nobody has everything. That is enough to keep all of us humble. But there is another lesson: For every limit there is a compensation. You may not have the gift you envy in another, but God has given you an anointing that person probably does not have.

Excerpted from *The Anointing: Yesterday, Today, Tomorrow* (Charisma House, 2003).

How to Recognize God

The most wonderful thing that can happen to anybody is for God to turn up. The problem is that we don't always recognize Him at the time, and we only see later that it was God.

The trouble is, we think God can only come in one particular way, and that's the way we've met Him. The question is this: If He turned up in an unexpected way, would we affirm Him?

The sooner we learn to recognize the Lord, the better. For some, it may take years to see that God has been in a situation with them; for others, it may take only a few seconds. But the narrower the time gap, the better, for it shows our hearts are in tune with what God is doing. I can think of nothing worse in the world than for something that God is in to be happening and I not recognize it.

If you're not a Christian, then it's also true for you that the sooner you realize when God is there, the better, because the Bible says, "My Spirit will not contend with man forever" (Gen. 6:3). Let me put it like this. It may be that whenever you hear preaching, you sense that the Holy Spirit is dealing with you, that God is on your case. You know that the preacher wouldn't know much about you, if anything at all,

> *When Jacob awoke from his sleep, he thought, "Surely the LORD is in this place, and I was not aware of it."*
> —GENESIS 28:16

and the only way he could speak in this manner was if God had led him to do so.

If you are a Christian and the Lord turns up and you don't recognize Him, you are impoverished since you miss seeing God for who He is, then. I guarantee you will wish later you had seen it was the Lord sooner.

Be open to the unexpected time. Be open to the unexpected manner in which God might turn up. He came to Jacob in a dream. God can do that.

Jacob affirmed God. Fortunately for him, it didn't take him long. The question is, how long will it take you?

Excerpted from *All's Well That Ends Well* (Authentic Media, 2005).

God's Gifts and Callings are Irrevocable

Because the gifts and calling of God are "irrevocable," a person who had a tremendous anointing yesterday can continue to see the momentum of that anointing continuing to manifest itself. He or she may hastily conclude that "the anointing is still with me" when it is but the momentum of yesterday's anointing.

This is sobering. I could be a hypocrite in my personal life, and yet my gift could continue to function. I could even deceive myself by telling myself, *I must be right with God, or I couldn't preach.* The truth is, God's calling and gifts are irrevocable. That means that God will not withdraw my preaching gift simply because

> *For God's gifts and his call are irrevocable.*
>
> —ROMANS 11:29

I have not been a loyal, obedient son. He gave me certain abilities when He made me and called me into the ministry. By study and hard work I can improve upon those gifts—*without* a fresh anointing that comes *only* from continued intimacy with God. And when people say, "That was a good word," or "God spoke to me through you today," I could assume that God is very pleased with me indeed. One of the worst things we can do is to take compliments too seriously.

It is possible that there are those who sincerely don't know better. They are well equipped, high powered, eloquent, and charismatic; people are blessed by their ministries. These people who are thus used by God may sincerely believe they are pleasing God because their anointing is functioning so well. "I am under God's anointing," they may well say. True. But it could be yesterday's anointing. There may be nothing fresh about it.

The fresh anointing is the essential thing. It is what replenishes the irrevocable. If our irrevocable anointing is not replenished by a fresh touch of God, we are depending on yesterday's anointing.

Excerpted from *The Anointing: Yesterday, Today, Tomorrow* (Charisma House, 2003).

A Life in the Spirit

Flowing in the Spirit is the best way to live. This is not to say that one is conscious all the time that he or she is flowing in the Spirit. But one can be fairly certain whether the Holy Spirit resides in a person *ungrieved*, and when we know this is the case, there is a great peace and an absence of tension and anxiety.

A marvelous example of flowing in the Spirit was the way Paul reacted to a demon-possessed girl who had a gift for predicting the future and kept pursuing him. For days, she kept mocking Paul and his companions and shouting, "These men are servants of the Most High God, who are telling you the way to be saved." The funny thing was, she was telling the truth. Finally, Paul became so troubled that he turned around and said to the malicious spirit, "In the name of Jesus Christ I command you to come out of her!" At that

> *But as for me, I am filled with power, with the Spirit of the Lord…*
> —Micah 3:8

moment the spirit left her (Acts 16:16–18). When we flow in the Spirit we reflect God's timing: never too late, never too early, but always right on time.

There are, however, unusual times of flowing in the Spirit. That is when God is up to something that is not your usual everyday happening. Most of life is lived not on the mountaintop, but in the valley. We must learn to flow in the Spirit in the valley as well as during those times when God does the unusual.

God has never—ever—let me down or left me with the feeling I had been deceived when I experienced flowing in the Spirit. It was pure joy, although sometimes it can be costly. You may lose some friends because you are misunderstood, but God will never desert you.

Excerpted from *The Anointing: Yesterday, Today, Tomorrow* (Charisma House, 2003).

Joy Is Coming

Has something ever broken your heart? Have you ever felt that because your heart is breaking, all you can do is weep? Some people can cry at the drop of a hat, but I'm not referring to that kind of tears. Some men are afraid to cry, because they feel that it is not manly. But the greatest man that ever was, Jesus of Nazareth, wept (John 11:35).

Psalm 126 refers to the end of a nightmare: "When the LORD brought back the captives to Zion, we were like men who dreamed" (v. 1). In other words, it seemed too good to be true. But while the nightmare was on, they thought it would never end.

> *Those who sow in tears will reap with songs of joy. He who goes out weeping, carrying seed to sow, will return with songs of joy, carrying sheaves with him.*
> —PSALM 126:5–6

A nightmare is an awful thing. I think that some of them may be caused by the devil. The last thing I do before I fall asleep is to pray for the sprinkling of the blood of Jesus upon my family and myself. I pray so every night, because I know the devil likes to seize upon us in our sleep, when we cannot control what is happening.

The nightmare referred to in Psalm 126 was that of Israel living in captivity in Babylon, a captivity that lasted for seventy years. Many died there, and others were born there. The whole time they lived in Babylon, all they could think about was going home.

You may be enduring a psychological or emotional nightmare, where you think you are losing your mind because the depression is so severe and the anxiety so intense.

Maybe you are facing a financial nightmare, being deep in debt. I think of those in our society who are elderly and have to survive on small incomes. It is very sad to think of them being put under that kind of pressure.

Perhaps it is a physical nightmare that you face, where something has gone wrong inside your body and the outlook is bleak.

Perhaps you are going through a social nightmare. You have been ostracized because of the color of your skin or because of your accent.

Here is a promise that is based on a condition. The promise is joy, even success, but the condition is tears.

Excerpted from *Higher Ground* (Christian Focus Publications Ltd., 1995).

Wait to Succeed

In early 1956 I felt that God gave me a fresh message to preach. I saw things in Scripture that I had not heard preached anywhere. I saw teaching, doctrine, and insight that I thought had been revealed to nobody but the apostle Paul! I foolishly left college since I felt I had no more to learn there. I also was convinced that the Second Coming of Jesus was so near that I was wasting my time with further preparation.

My dad was distraught that his only son had come to this. Dad begged for proof that I was in God's will. I assured him God was going to use me—powerfully and *internationally!* I had been given visions from the Lord that showed me clearly that I would see great revival. Dad had one question: When? I replied with absolute confidence, "Within one year." He asked me to write it down so he could have it to show me one year later! I wrote it down. One year later I was selling Stroll-O-Chairs, a portable assortment of baby equipment. I had no opportunities to preach.

Dr. Lloyd-Jones once said to me, "The worst thing that can happen to a man is to

> *Perseverance must finish its work so that you may be mature and complete, not lacking anything.*
>
> —JAMES 1:4

succeed before he is ready." That statement was probably the most powerful word he ever gave me. I believe it to be true, and I can only conclude that I was withheld the success I had hoped for by God's gracious will. One reason I took myself too seriously back in 1956 was that I received visions that indicated I would be used of God. I assumed these visions would be fulfilled soon. They weren't. But because I had them and believed they were truly from the Holy Spirit, I assumed I was special. I became arrogant. I was not ready.

I am so thankful God is still peeling away those layers of arrogance and presumption. I'd rather not be greatly used at all than be given a greater anointing that I would abuse. God has withheld the success for which I have hoped for my own good—to keep me from being successful before I am ready.

Excerpted from *The Anointing: Yesterday, Today, Tomorrow* (Charisma House, 2003).

How to Handle Jealousy

There are few people who have not been either the subject or the object of jealousy at some time in their lives. Someone has said that jealousy is the sin nobody talks about; I think it is the sin nobody admits to—at least, readily. We do not like admitting to being jealous because this exposes our insecurity and weakness; the last thing we want another person to know is that we are insecure. Yet the chances are, our jealousy is one malady everybody else can see but us, and although we cannot deny that there are also psychological implications, fundamentally, jealousy is sin.

For since there is jealousy and quarreling among you, are you not worldly?...The man who plants and the man who waters have one purpose, and each will be rewarded according to his own labor.
—1 CORINTHIANS 3:3, 8

We may define jealousy as an attitude of envy or resentment toward a more successful rival. Sometimes it results from frustrated attempts to achieve an ambition, and sometimes it results from seeing somebody who has more talent, greater social advantages, more money, better looks, or a better personality than we have. It may also arise when we see another succeeding where we have failed and we allow our resentment to grow into jealousy.

The reason it is easy to detect jealousy in others is they inevitably behave in a way that betrays their feelings. However, being the object of jealousy is also problematic. Most of us know what it is to have somebody jealous of us.

Yet what if another's jealousy of you is *real*? How do you handle a situation like this? You need to identify the *real* enemy. Paul identified the real enemy: the devil. So if you are the target of unjust criticism aimed to hurt you by attacking your character or by diminishing your influence, know that Satan is behind it all. However, you should also realize that you are no different, and in similar circumstances the chances are that you would react in the same way.

Only God can deal with jealousy, and only God can forgive it. But the Bible says, "If we confess our sins, he is faithful and just and will forgive us our sins" (1 John 1:9).

Excerpted from *A Vision of Jesus* (Christian Focus Publications Ltd., 1999).

Today's Servant of Christ

Part of the sacrifice of being today's servant of Christ is that vindication usually comes tomorrow, possibly after we are in heaven. Partly what made those in Hebrews 11 "today's" servants in their day was that they were willing to have the fruits of their labors borne by a successive generation. "These were all commended for their faith, yet none of them received what had been promised. God had planned something better for us so that only together with us would they be made perfect" (Heb. 11:39–40).

Peter reminded his readers that, as for the prophets of the Old Testament, "it was revealed to them that they were not serving themselves but you, when they spoke of the things that have now been told you by those who have preached the gospel to you by the Holy Spirit sent from heaven. Even angels long to look into these things" (1 Pet. 1:12).

> God is not unjust; he will not forget your work and the love you have shown him as you have helped his people and continue to help them.
>
> —Hebrews 6:10

This is an example when those *with the Lord* continue to be today's men and women. Those Hebrew Christians who did not succumb to the pressures of their day would never be forgotten.

We are all guilty of thinking of ourselves and how we will be remembered. But the irony of church history is that those who prepared most for tomorrow's church were the most remembered; those who wanted to build their own empires became yesterday's men and women while they were still alive—and hardly remembered afterwards.

The late President Ronald Reagan kept a little plaque on his desk that read, "There is no limit to how far one can go as long as he doesn't care who gets the credit." That to me is profound. If you and I can bring that into our own lives, I suspect it would make a considerable difference—not only in our usefulness, but also in how we are remembered. It would mean wanting, first of all, the honor that comes from God only, then to affirm His servants, no matter who they are. That is the challenge of being today's man or woman.

Excerpted from *The Anointing: Yesterday, Today, Tomorrow* (Charisma House, 2003).

Snuff Out Gossip

Gossip. What an ugly word. I hate the word. It is what sells millions of cheap and tawdry magazines at the checkout line in a supermarket. I so despise them that I like to think I am above this stuff.

I may not read these magazines, but I am just as guilty as those who do read them when I myself hear with glee that a person I don't like has been found out—and I pass it on; or I repeat news of something unflattering about an enemy or a person who has wanted to hurt me in some way; or I make a person feel good that I know would relish news of their enemy's difficulty. James says the tongue is a fire (James 3:6), and when I enter into conversations like this, *I grieve the Holy Spirit.*

> *Without wood a fire goes out; without gossip a quarrel dies down.*
> —PROVERBS 26:20

Gossip is a defense mechanism to preserve our self-esteem. It arises out of an inferiority complex; we build ourselves up by tearing others down—or enjoying hearing that they are in trouble of some kind. It is a poisonous habit that betrays our insecurity and lack of spirituality. If gossip makes us feel better, we are self-deceived.

We may claim to be Spirit-filled, sound in our theology, faithful in our commitment to the church, zealous in worship, and have devotional lives that are highly admirable. But when we grieve the Spirit by saying what comes to mind that is not honoring to God, we become the very examples James laments: we praise the Lord and curse men.

James asks, "Can both fresh water and salt water flow from the same spring?" (James 3:11). If the well in us—the Holy Spirit (John 7:38–39)—overflows, one expects the fruits of the Spirit (Gal. 5:22–23). But when the Spirit begins to speak through us, and instead of love, joy, and peace, suddenly there emerges anger, vengeance, and envy, something has gone terribly wrong.

The Holy Spirit will not produce gossip, anger, revenge, or any other fleshly reaction any more than a fig tree can bear an olive or a grapevine bear a fig (James 3:12–16). It is impossible for the Holy Spirit to produce other than the fruit such as love, joy, peace, and self-control. If we say we are Spirit-filled, then let us display the fruit of the Spirit.

Excerpted from *Controlling the Tongue* (Charisma House, 2007).

The Power of the Word

God cares about the honor of His name. But He cares even more about His integrity, which is His Word. This is why Psalm 138:2 says that God has magnified His Word over all His name.

Signs, wonders, and miracles were first unveiled in the Bible when God revealed His name to Moses (Exod. 6:2–3). Yet God wants His Word to be magnified above signs and wonders. Salvation is more important than miracles. Salvation was thus unveiled to Abraham four hundred years before the era of signs and wonders. We are not saved by signs and wonders but by the gospel.

We must be careful, therefore, to walk in obedience to all the Word. Jesus said, "Everything must be fulfilled that is written about me in the Law of Moses, the Prophets and the Psalms" (Luke 24:44). "Not the least stroke of a pen" would be omitted from the fulfillment of the Law (Matt. 5:18). This shows how clearly and carefully God regards *every word* He utters.

> *When Jesus had finished saying these things, the crowds were amazed at his teaching, because he taught as one who had authority, and not as their teachers of the law.*
>
> —MATTHEW 7:28–29

When Jesus healed a boy with an evil spirit, "they were all *amazed* at the greatness of God" (Luke 9:43, emphasis added). And yet the exact same word, *ekplesso*, is used to describe the affect of Jesus' words when He finished the Sermon on the Mount.

This shows that Jesus could *amaze* people by His *word* as easily as by signs and wonders! Indeed, when He put the Sadducees in their place, the crowds "were *astonished* [same Greek word] at his *teaching*" (Matt. 22:33, emphasis added).

If Jesus could amaze and astonish either by His word or by miracles, it seems to me that this should happen today as well. But we apparently have lost faith in the power of the Word and fancy that miraculous healings alone can restore God's honor. In my opinion, either should do this.

Excerpted from *The Anointing: Yesterday, Today, Tomorrow* (Charisma House, 2003).

God's Math

There are two operative words in this text: the first is the word *one*; the second is the word *own*. The two roles of planting and watering when added up are one. It is what God does, no matter how many plant and how many water. God makes things grow. One plus one equals one—that is God's mathematics! Ten plus ten equals one; one hundred plus one hundred equals one: God, who makes things grow.

There are a number of points I want to explore in this text.

The first is *teamwork*. The Oxford English Dictionary defines team as "a set of people working together." Why? They are one. This will mean that *each member surrenders a high profile*. For those who have an ego problem this is quite a task! You say, "Well, this won't apply to me; I don't have a problem with ego." Don't you? Let me ask you a question: If you look at a group photograph you are in, whose face do you look for first?

> *The man who plants and the man who waters have one purpose, and each will be rewarded according to his own labor.*
> —1 CORINTHIANS 3:8

So the operative word, *one*, leads to another word, *surrender*—of seven things:

1. Identity
2. Independence
3. Individuality
4. Inflexibility
5. Indifference
6. Inequality
7. Personal interest

Incidentally, it is not a question whether or not we will result in one, because God will see to that. What is sobering is how this oneness will happen. Either we will do it voluntarily and get a reward, or we do it involuntarily and suffer loss.

The second point in this verse is *talent*. The man who plants—is that your talent? The man who waters—is that your talent? Planting and watering are metaphors that refer to the kind of ministry that God gives to particular Christians. Now that does not mean that they have to be one or the other, for Paul was both. The point is that each Christian has a gift, and all of these combined together add up to one.

Excerpted from *When God Says "Well Done!"* (Christian Focus Publications Ltd., 1993).

Openness to the Spirit

Some of us find it easier to be open to the Word than to the Holy Spirit. Being open to the Word directly is to be open to the Spirit indirectly—as the Spirit applies that Word. But being open to the Spirit is when He manifests Himself in an *immediate and direct* manner.

We feel *safe* with the Word but fearful that the Holy Spirit may lead us out of our comfort zone. But the Holy Spirit to whom we should be open is the Author of the Bible, and He will not lead us in any way that is contrary to what He has written through His sovereign instruments. We are as safe with the Spirit as we are with the Word. And yet if we are not open to the Spirit, we will likely never experience some of the very same things described in the Word.

> *And blessed is he, whosoever shall not be offended in me.*
>
> —MATTHEW 11:6, KJV

When one is offended by the Spirit, it is because he is offended by God. It is not possible to find God pleasant and to find the Holy Spirit offensive. It is incongruous to affirm all that Jesus Christ was and did, then turn around and reject the Holy Spirit. The persons of the Godhead are united. Equally, each has His own stigma. The Holy Spirit mirrors the other persons of the Godhead; therefore, how we respond to the person of the Spirit may show what we really feel about either the Father or the Son.

We must affirm God as He is—the Holy Spirit is God. When our hearts are truly right with God, we will find that God is not offensive at all! We will instead find Him glorious! But we must take God as He is and be prepared to affirm the presence of the Holy Spirit—however God may sovereignly choose to reveal Himself.

Excerpted from *The Anointing: Yesterday, Today, Tomorrow* (Charisma House, 2003).

R. T. KENDALL

Do You Want It Now or Later?

Who doesn't appreciate an accolade or two, but are you willing to become a small fish in a big pond? In other words, when all you have done has gone unnoticed and you do not get recognition, what matters most to you—receiving an immediate reward (man's recognition) or a heavenly reward (God's recognition)?

If Paul had said, "I have planted and God gave the increase," there would be room for self-importance. How humbling it is that God uses more than one person in another's conversion! There is not a single one of us who owes his or her conversion and growth just to one person. In my case I could speak not of a dozen but of fifty, maybe a hundred, all of whom have had a powerful influence on me. The test is the willingness to be a small fish in a big pond.

> Be careful not to do your "acts of righteousness" before men, to be seen by them. If you do, you will have no reward from your Father in heaven.
>
> —MATTHEW 6:1

What if I am not noticed for all the hard work I do? My effectiveness must be determined by (a) my willingness to be insignificant and have an insignificant part, and (b) my willingness to have an unnoticed part. Great men show themselves small when they become too worried about their place in history.

But what does it matter? In a short time we will all stand before the judgment seat of Christ, where it will all come out. People who are so eager to have their biographies say this or that about themselves will find out that one day we will *all* know the real truth anyway! The question is, if I am a peacemaker, will I keep quiet about it? If I am persecuted, will I keep quiet about it? If I am pious, if I pray, fast, and give sacrificially, will I keep quiet about it? If I am determined to get noticed, well, I will probably get it, but that means I get paid *now*, but recognition in this life is a very low pay indeed.

Excerpted from *When God Says "Well Done!"* (Christian Focus Publications Ltd., 1993).

When Someone Lies About You

A re you in distress at the moment because someone has falsely accused you? Whatever the cause, perhaps you have never realized that God has permitted the distress, and, because you lack this perspective, you fear that you will break under the strain. But God is saying, "I am behind all that is going on right now; I am the Architect of the distress. And do you know why? It is the only way I could get your attention."

One form of distress that God uses to get our attention is caused by the *deceit of others*. This was the origin of the psalmist's distress, because he had been criticized unfairly. (See verse 2.)

Maybe part of the reason you are in distress is that you have been criticized, and it hurts. Criticism is painful. In fact, sometimes the criticism that we don't want to hear is the hardest to take because *it is true*. "Faithful are the wounds of a friend" (Prov. 27:6, KJV).

But the psalmist was the victim of a deceitful tongue. The psalmist had either

> *In my distress I cried unto the LORD, and he heard me. Deliver my soul, O LORD, from lying lips, and from a deceitful tongue.*
>
> —PSALM 120:1–2, KJV

been lied *to* or lied *about*. What is a lie? A lie is an untrue statement with the intent to deceive. If you have been lied about, eventually the truth will come out. I guarantee it.

It can be very painful, however, during that time of postponement. Maybe that's where you are. Perhaps you have lost your job because someone lied about you; perhaps you have lost a friendship because something was said that wasn't true; perhaps you have lost influence because somebody lied about you, and there is not a thing you can do to defend yourself.

Remember who is on your side: God. God is truth; it is impossible for him to lie (Heb. 6:18). The day is coming when God will clear not only His own name, but your name, too.

Excerpted from *Higher Ground* (Christian Focus Publications Ltd., 1995).

Grace to Keep Quiet

Not just apostles, not just ministers, not just deacons, but the totality of the body of Christ shall be judged: every person shall receive his own reward according to his own labor. Every man, every woman, every function, every gift, every talent, all we ever did will be projected on God's gigantic screen. Even that time you got hurt and kept quiet about it. Those years you paid your tithes and it hurt, but you kept quiet about it; those moments when you dignified the trial but kept quiet about it; that person you totally forgave, but you kept quiet about it; or the one you stayed up all night and helped but kept quiet about it. Each will be rewarded according to his own labor.

> ...his work will be shown for what it is, because the Day will bring it to light. It will be revealed with fire, and the fire will test the quality of each man's work. If what he has built survives, he will receive his reward.
>
> —1 Corinthians 3:13–14

When will this happen? And what does *each will be rewarded* mean? This refers to the future, and perhaps this disappoints you. We all want to be paid now! Yet every man *will* receive. We may wish it had said, "Every man *receives* his own reward" in the present tense. That way I am guaranteed recognition now; that way I am guaranteed dividends now. But must we get our pay today?

Do you only get involved in a particular activity of the church if you think it is working? Do you do something because immediately you get results? God can, and often does, bless obedience now, but our motive may betray that we cannot wait for the judgment seat of Christ. How much better that you continually remember that you will yet stand before God and give an account of the things you did throughout life. It will be worth it all to hear two words from Jesus: "Well done." What I did in life that was swallowed up and unnoticed will be found out and blazed in headlines and discovered *then*.

Excerpted from *When God Says "Well Done!"* (Christian Focus Publications Ltd., 1993).

Forgiveness Is a Lifelong Commitment

When I consider the fact that our Lord Jesus Christ knows all about my sin but promises to keep what He has forgiven a carefully guarded secret, it increases my gratitude to Him. God does not blackmail us. And when a person is guilty of blackmailing someone else, it gets God's attention. He won't stand for it. To hold another person in perpetual fear by threatening, "I'll tell on you," will quickly bring down the wrath of God. When I ponder the sins for which I have been forgiven, it is enough to shut my mouth for the rest of my life.

Making a lifelong commitment to total forgiveness means that you keep on doing it—for as long as you live. It isn't enough to forgive today and then return to the offense tomorrow. I heard of a person whose wife said, "I thought you forgave me." He replied, "That was yesterday." Total forgiveness is a lifelong commitment, and you may need to practice it

> *Against you, you only, have I sinned and done what is evil in your sight, so that you are proved right when you speak and justified when you judge.*
>
> —PSALM 51:4

every single day of your life until you die. No one said it would be easy.

I have seen some people cave in and return to the offense after they extended their forgiveness to someone. But it is not total forgiveness unless it lasts—no matter how great the temptation is to turn back.

If you are prepared to make a covenant to forgive—and to forgive totally—you must realize you will have to renew that covenant tomorrow. And it may be even harder to do tomorrow than it is today. It could even be harder next week—or next year. But this is a lifetime commitment.

Excerpted from *Higher Ground* (Christian Focus Publications Ltd., 1995).

Receive the Highest Treasure

All who are saved *are* going to heaven, but not all who go to heaven will receive a reward. This may be new theology to you, but you need to understand that. You may have thought, *Well, if I am saved, I am saved, and I am not going to worry about anything else.* When you stand before the judgment seat of Christ, even though you are not going to go to hell, you will see then why Paul stressed it again and again.

When workers get their paycheck they decide whether to spend it all now or put some in the bank. So when you are tempted to take recognition, you can put it on deposit or you can just spend it. There is a chance to get your spiritual recognition pay now, for instance, by getting even with that person by snapping back, by reminding people that what they did was wrong. Although you are right, and you "win" and receive your pay, that is it. You withdrew what could have been on deposit in heaven. Only it is low pay. You really lost.

> *Do not store up for yourselves treasures on earth, where moth and rust destroy, and where thieves break in and steal. But store up for yourselves treasures in heaven, where moth and rust do not destroy, and where thieves do not break in and steal.*
>
> —MATTHEW 6:19–20

What is the high pay? I do not really know. Paul uses three words, as far as I know, to describe it: reward, praise, crown. Peter also uses the expression: "you will receive a rich welcome" into the kingdom when you die (2 Pet. 1:11). But this assumes a certain conduct (2 Pet. 1:5–8). Not all will receive this welcome.

What is a high pay? What is the reward? What is the crown? As I have said, I do not know for sure what that is, but I am sure it is worth waiting for. And I am sure I am not alone. Many of you will want to hear from the lips of Jesus Himself: "Well done." I call that high pay!

Excerpted from *When God Says "Well Done!"* (Christian Focus Publications Ltd., 1993).

Taking God for Granted

The expression "to take for granted" means to be so sure of having something that we no longer appreciate it. That is what this passage is about.

The thing that particularly grips me about this passage is that God notices. These professional clergymen had actually given God animals they couldn't use themselves. They thought that God wouldn't notice and didn't care. But He did notice. He sees everything we do.

> *Instead of honoring me, you profane me. You profane me when you say, "Worship is not important, and what we bring to worship is of no account."*
> —MALACHI 1:12, THE MESSAGE

This word is not just for preachers; it is for every believer, because every believer is part of the body of Christ. God not only noticed what was happening, but He also was angry about it. He didn't let the priests get away with what they were doing, and He won't let us get away with taking Him for granted either.

How do we know God was upset with them for taking Him for granted? He felt so strongly about it that He said He would prefer that the doors of the church were closed than for this mockery to continue. "Oh, that one of you would shut the temple doors, so that you would not light useless fires upon my altar!" (Mal. 1:10).

If you are engaged in ministry, whether you are a deacon or involved in children's work, doing the flowers or sweeping the floors, and you are saying, "What a burden," and you are bored with it, don't you realize what a privilege God has given to you to do anything in His name?

You will never be a Christian until you come to the place where you recognize that, far from being able to do anything for God, you don't deserve the least of His grace. As long as you feel you deserve better from God than He has given you, you are not saved. The people who are saved are those who realize they were lost and on their road to hell when God stopped them in their tracks and showed them that Jesus died for them. When the Holy Spirit showed them their sin, the last thought in their minds was that they could do God a favor! And what a warning to us.

Excerpted from *Between the Times* (Christian Focus Publications Ltd., 2003).

How to Develop Active Listening

If we are going to learn how to develop active listening to the voice of the Spirit, there are a few characteristics that we need.

The first characteristic required for active listening is an open mind. That means, a mind closed to nothing that coheres with holiness. Paul says about this, "Finally, brethren, whatsoever things are true, whatsoever things are honest, whatsoever things are just, whatsoever things are pure…" (Phil. 4:8, KJV).

The second characteristic for active listening is a willingness to let go of our pride, a willingness to be vulnerable.

The third characteristic is that we are always listening out for God's voice, even when this involves a telling off. God may speak to us through a friend or a stranger; through unanswered prayer or through the withholding of vindication. It may be through disappointment. It can be simply because we see the need. If we are really walking in the light, we will look anywhere for God's way of speaking.

> He who has an ear, let him hear what the Spirit says to the churches.
> —REVELATION 2:7

So often we expect God to speak to us in one way, when all the time He is approaching us differently. Someone has put it like this: God gives hints rather than directions. He lets you come to the conclusion for yourself.

The fourth characteristic to hearing God is that we deal with any impediment that militates against the Spirit, for example, any personal bias that we superimpose upon God, calling it His will when it's actually our own prejudice, and any grudge or unforgiving attitude.

Again, we must beware of any fleshly appetite that dulls our spiritual outlook: it may be a television program, our choice of reading or of friends. Some things may not be bad in themselves, but we know that they dull our desire for God.

When we learn to develop a lifestyle of active listening, we will hear God's voice much more frequently than before, because now we are beginning to recognize when He speaks.

Excerpted from *Worshipping God* (Hodder & Stoughton, 2004).

Discover Your Gift

It is imperative that you discover what God wants you to do and go ahead with it in the church and in your life. Dr. Clyde Narramore says, "Your natural gift is God's hint what to do with your life." Let me pose three questions to help you explore ways in which your gifts can be recognized.

This first is: *What do you enjoy?* Your gift is often what you like to do. And you say, "Well, I couldn't have imagined that to be something *God* would want me to do." I never will forget, back in 1954, when God used a Scotsman, Dr. John Logan, who was ministering in America, to make me come to terms with the fact that God had called me to preach because I loved talking about the Bible. And I think it was one of the reasons I had postponed recognizing a call to preach, because I almost felt guilty that it was what I loved more than anything.

> *Do not neglect your gift, which was given you through a prophetic message when the body of elders laid their hands on you.*
> —1 TIMOTHY 4:14

The second question is: *What do you feel is right for you?* I often quote Romans 14:19: "Do what leads to peace." That does refer to church unity, of course, but I think equally it refers to *internal* peace. A person who operates at the level of his incompetence is tired all the time. This is what causes a nervous breakdown. And sometimes his pride won't let him admit to himself, "I can't do this." When this happens you need to step back, admit that this is not your gift, and do what leads to peace. You need to ask yourself, *What is right for me?* You do what gives you peace inside.

The third question is: *What do others recognize in you?* If God has called you to preach, there will be open doors; people will want you. We must live within the limit of our gift, but also up to the level of responsibility that our gift requires. Do not covet another person's gift, but admit what you know is *your* own gift and responsibility.

Excerpted from *When God Says "Well Done!"* (Christian Focus Publications Ltd., 1993).

The Esteem of God

I heard Gigi Tchividjian give a talk in which she admitted to low self-esteem. She said, "Whenever I was introduced, I was referred to as Billy Graham's daughter, the wife of a Swiss psychiatrist, or the mother of six children." She concluded that she had no identity of her own, but she sought it and found it in Christ.

As God earmarked you for a work in the future, I would urge you to get your sense of self-esteem from knowing you please God alone. Just Him. He isn't hard to please. First, the blood of Jesus washed all sin and imperfection away. Second, Jesus is at the Father's right hand and is moved with compassion over our weaknesses. Third, the Father, in any case, "knows how we are formed, he remembers that we are dust" (Ps. 103:14).

It is true that God will refine you so that when your time has come you will be ready and trustworthy of a greater anointing. But you won't be perfect. "If we claim to be without sin, we deceive ourselves and the truth is not in us" (1 John 1:8). God isn't waiting for you to get perfect before

I know you by name and you have found favor with me.
—Exodus 33:12

He can use you. Otherwise He wouldn't use anybody—ever.

Do you have a heart after God? Do you yearn to honor Him? Do you aspire to seek not honor and glory from your peers but the honor that God alone can bestow? If so, God will find you. Your parents may not see in you what is there, however well they think they know you, but God does. He will find you. He will discover you. Someone said, "It takes fifteen years to become an overnight success." God's time has come when someone who knows all that is needed to know about you steps in without your raising a finger.

Excerpted from *The Anointing: Yesterday, Today, Tomorrow* (Charisma House, 2003).

Build on the Right Foundation

What we are told in this verse is that when Paul laid the foundation in Corinth some four years earlier, he was doing nothing more than following God's architectural blueprint.

Peter says that foundation was predestined; the Lamb that takes away the sin of the world, who died on the cross, was slain from the foundation of the world. What happened at Calvary two thousand years ago was simply the following of a blueprint that had been predestined in eternity.

It is provided, or as Jude puts it, "... the faith that was once for all entrusted to the saints" (Jude 3). We do not need to go looking for this blueprint in the archives building as though no one knows what the faith is. We have it in the Bible, given by inspiration of God.

This foundation is an unchangeable foundation, not just from place to place as in Ephesus, Corinth, or Thessalonica, but

> *For no one can lay any foundation other than the one already laid, which is Jesus Christ.*
>
> —1 Corinthians 3:11

also from generation to generation. This is why Jude says, "I...urge you to contend for the faith that was once for all entrusted to the saints." It is not received *from* the saints; it is delivered *to* the saints.

> But if anybody does sin, we have one who speaks to the Father in our defense—Jesus Christ, the Righteous One. He is the atoning sacrifice [propitiation] for our sins.
>
> —1 John 2:1–2

What does John mean? For God to be propitious toward us means that He is favorable toward us, because when Jesus died He *was* the propitiation who satisfied the justice of God! Thus, calling this foundation propitious simply means that all who rest on it are saved. The superstructure may go wrong, but all who rest upon the foundation are saved.

Excerpted from *When God Says "Well Done!"* (Christian Focus Publications Ltd., 1993).

Of What Am I Made?

How do we know whether our own individual superstructure is comprised of gold, silver, and costly stones?

First, our *application of teaching*. We must first understand it. Then we must receive it for ourselves. Thereafter, we must make it change us.

Second, our *approach to temptation*. What do we do when we are tempted? Maybe we are going to face real temptation, but it is up to us whether we resist it or succumb to it.

Third, our *attitude toward trials*. We cannot avoid trials. Jesus said, "In this world you will have trouble" (John 16:33). As Christians we will face trouble and trials, perhaps even worse than we have known before. Our attitude toward trials will often largely determine what comprises our superstructure. You can look at trials as God's invitation on a silver platter to move up higher, or you can discredit it, show contempt for the trial, and after it is over be no better off because you refused to dignify it.

> *If any man builds on this foundation using gold, silver, costly stones, wood, hay or straw, his work will be shown for what it is...*
> —1 Corinthians 3:12–13

There is a fourth way of finding out what you are made of, and it is probably the main one: *our ability with the tongue*. In Matthew 12:36–37, Jesus described the day of judgment:

> But I tell you that men will have to give account on the day of judgment for every careless word they have spoken. For by your words you will be acquitted, and by your words you will be condemned.

That does not refer to whether you are saved or lost, because in the context the person has already been assumed to be saved. Here He is talking about our words. What you and I actually *say* will in all probability be what gets us into trouble and will grieve the Holy Spirit. I guarantee you, gold, silver, and costly stones will be our own superstructure largely to the degree to which you and I control our tongues.

Excerpted from *When God Says "Well Done!"* (Christian Focus Publications Ltd., 1993).

Allow God to Be God

Everyone, at some point in their lives, feels that God has betrayed them and let them down. They find He seems more like an enemy than a friend. Nine out of ten people say, "Well, God, if that's how You want it to be, then I'll go my way and You go Yours." Only one out of ten, I reckon, breaks that betrayal barrier and holds on, like Jacob who wrestled with the angel and said, "I won't let go unless you bless Me."

The same kind of thing happened to Abraham. We read in Genesis 22:2 how God tested Abraham by asking him to sacrifice his son—his *only* son. That made no sense to Abraham. But Abraham showed he was willing to obey God, and God honored him for what he was prepared to do.

Sooner or later, God will ask you to do something that makes no sense at the time. Perhaps the barrier you have to break is the one that doesn't make sense at the time, but you must give God the benefit of the doubt. Abraham obeyed God and was never sorry.

We want God to be partial for us, but we have to come to the place where we allow God to be God. Would we affirm Him if He were to work powerfully in another church, in another denomination? Would we say, "That is God"?

> *What then? If some did not believe, their unbelief will not nullify the faithfulness of God, will it? May it never be! Rather, let God be found true, though every man be found a liar.*
>
> —ROMANS 3:3–4, NAS

During the American Civil War, someone came up to President Lincoln and asked, "Is God on our side or their side?" Lincoln's reply was, "All I want to know is whether we are on God's side." That is what we need to learn. When it comes to understanding God, we need to be on God's side and let God be God.

Excerpted from *All's Well That Ends Well* (Authentic Media, 2005).

Entertaining Angels

When we get to heaven, I have no doubt that we will get to see the angel who was sent to be with us from the moment of our birth. Not just from the moment of our conversion, but from the moment of our birth. Because "are not all angels ministering spirits sent to serve *those who will inherit salvation?*" (Heb. 1:14, emphasis added). Could we not all testify to an awareness of God looking after us before we came to faith?

> *Do not forget to entertain strangers, for by so doing some people have entertained angels without knowing it.*
> —HEBREWS 13:2

Would you like to entertain an angel? Three suggestions:

- *Be open to anybody at any time.* You never know if God will send someone who will give you a word that is life changing. I have had it happen to me more than once—by being open to just anybody. God spoke, and the person through whom He spoke may, for all I know, have been an angel.

- *Look in the direction of those you think could not possibly help you.* Listen to what Jesus said: "When you give a banquet, invite the poor, the crippled, the lame, the blind, and you will be blessed. Although they cannot repay you, you will be repaid at the resurrection of the righteous" (Luke 14:13–14). If you want to know how you could possibly entertain an angel, look to people who could not possibly pay you back. God may speak through one of them.

- *Remember that the angel, or agent that God uses, may be quite nondescript.* He or she may not have wings; there may be no glistening brilliance. You may look at a particular person and think, *Well, no angel here.* Be careful. You never know!

Do you want God to appear? What if, by being gracious to someone you didn't think could help you, you got a word that was life changing in return? What an honor! It could happen to you even today.

Excerpted from *When God Shows Up* (Renew Books, 1998).

Save Me From Self-Righteousness

Do you know that self-righteous people are the hardest people in the world to reach?

I would rather deal with anybody rather than a self-righteous Christian. I have begun praying, "God, save *me* from self-righteousness." It is the easiest trait in the world to enter into my own life when I literally think I'm in the right and it's the other person that is in the wrong.

When you are dealing with a self-righteous person, you have a battle on your hands. And this is why smugness is so dangerous.

We can recognize smugness in other people although seldom can we see it in ourselves; yet it is one of those things that is hard to prove. You find it wherever you go; they all believe that they are the ones that have got it right: "We are the ones God is blessing; we are saying this, this, this…" Where is that one who will say, "There is something wrong with *us!*"

> *You were taught, with regard to your former way of life, to put off your old self…to be made new in the attitude of your minds; and to put on the new self, created to be like God in true righteousness and holiness.*
>
> —EPHESIANS 4:22–24

In order not to have to listen to what God may be saying through someone else, we justify ourselves as being the ones through whom God is going to work; if blessing comes, it will come through us! We do not like to think that God could be doing a work somewhere else with someone of whom we do not approve.

Perhaps you do not like this teaching. But if this sounds like you, then if you go on that way I guarantee you, one day your superstructure of smugness will come out. The truth is that smug people have no objectivity about themselves; they live in a dream world. They do not think, for they know they are right!

The rule of thumb, therefore, is stay smug, and you will erect a superstructure of straw. Be broken, and you will erect a superstructure of gold.

Excerpted from *When God Says "Well Done!"* (Christian Focus Publications Ltd., 1993).

Where Is Your Heart?

There are Christians who are marked by worldliness. I believe worldliness comes down to three things: sensuality, sophistication, and secularization.

Sensuality is the lust of the flesh: people obsessed with sex, as opposed to a lifestyle of self-denial. *Sophistication* can be thought of as the lust of the eyes: people obsessed with culture, learning, and refinement as opposed to simplicity. *Secularization*—John calls it "pride of life"—is the obsession with material things as opposed to spirituality.

Worldly Christians who would rather stay home and watch television on Sunday night are nevertheless often the first to criticize things. They appear godly and righteous when they are, in fact, hypocrites.

This is why Christians do not tithe! They can look for every reason in the world why they should not have to do it. It is the worldly spirit that looks for a way not to tithe.

> *Do not love the world or anything in the world. If anyone loves the world, the love of the Father is not in him. For everything in the world—the cravings of sinful man, the lust of his eyes and the boasting of what he has and does—comes not from the Father but from the world.*
> —1 John 2:15–16

This is why they do not pray. I was talking to someone not long ago whose marriage is on the rocks. I just said to them, "How much do each of you pray?" I was not surprised to hear, "Not at all." How much time *do* we spend in prayer, by ourselves? How much time do *you* take to be alone with God? Thirty minutes a day should be the minimum for each of us. I do not care how busy we are. It will give me no pleasure to stand beside you at the judgment seat of Christ and watch a videotape of these words flashed before you, when in fact you justified how busy you were at the time.

Rule of thumb: get immediate gratification because you want to enjoy the things of the world now, and you will erect a superstructure of straw; but if you have the love of the Father in you, it will be a superstructure of gold.

Excerpted from *When God Says "Well Done!"* (Christian Focus Publications Ltd., 1993).

Flow in the Spirit

What does flowing in the Spirit mean? It is moving along with Him, keeping in step with Him, and missing nothing He may be wanting to do through us. There is such a thrill in flowing in the Spirit. You feel what you are doing is worthwhile; you feel authenticated, you feel loved; you feel you are part of something very important—the kingdom of God. You feel this when visiting a sick person or resisting temptation, when you walk to work or do work in the office. It is a twenty-four-hour-a-day possibility.

> *Since we live by the Spirit, let us keep in step with the Spirit.*
>
> —GALATIANS 5:25

This is what Peter and John were doing when they were walking toward the temple one afternoon but were unexpectedly stopped—only to see the healing of a forty-year-old man who had never walked. (See Acts 3:1–10.) There are two questions that emerge: (1) Why were these disciples led at this particular time to administer healing to this man? (2) How did they know this man would suddenly be healed?

The Holy Spirit was sovereignly at work, carrying out the Father's will, when Peter and John came upon this man at the temple gate. That is the only explanation for the healing right then and not before.

But the question still remains: how did they know that God was going to heal this man? It was because they were walking in the *ungrieved* Spirit; the heavenly Dove was remaining on them. The easiest thing in the world to do is to grieve the Spirit, and the extent of His sensitivity cannot be exaggerated. But Peter and John were enjoying sweet fellowship with the Spirit and with each other, so they did not miss out on what God was prepared to do. It gave them great joy to be involved in this miracle. Since we live in the Spirit, let us keep in step with the Spirit.

Excerpted from *Pure Joy* (Charisma House, 2006).

Trials Have a Purpose

Everybody is either in a trial now or between trials. You have either just had one, you are going to have one, or you are having one. But why call it a "fiery" trial as Peter does? This is because by its light the fire reveals precisely what we are spiritually.

It is apparent, of course, that this only appeals to those who have a desire to be godly.

For example, our endurance can be tested during a trial by how we respond to it. If we begin complaining and murmuring, we will acknowledge later that we did not stand up to the trial very well for we did not display a godly nature. Thus trials will test our ability to manifest all the fruit of the Spirit. They test our work whether we have been walking in the light, and they expose how spiritual we really are, which is the sum of all that has gone on before.

These have come so that your faith—of greater worth than gold, which perishes even though refined by fire—may be proved genuine and may result in praise, glory and honor when Jesus Christ is revealed.

—1 Peter 1:7

What makes a trial a trial is that God, as it were, leaves us, and we feel deserted and betrayed. We say, "God, I don't believe this; why would You do this to me? Why desert me at a moment when I needed You the most?" Is that not the way you have felt? That's why it is called a "fiery" trial; God leaves you to test you, to see what is there. And so, this is the thing about the trial by fire: it exposes how spiritual we really are—which is the sum total of all our Christian living so far. We are forced to see ourselves, and we can find out how Christlike we truly are.

Excerpted from *When God Says "Well Done!"* (Christian Focus Publications Ltd., 1993).

Love to Cope

Why be filled with the love of God? In the time of testing, in the time of trial, does it work? And the apostle Paul pauses, almost dramatically, to show that this love of God will not only enable us to be like Jesus, but also will support us in the time of severest trial. We can put up with anything if we have this love.

The verse contains four descriptions of love: love trusts, hopes, protects, and perseveres. And these four descriptions stand alongside four envisaged situations. They are four negative situations that you and I face all the time. Paul shows how love meets each particular situation. These situations are listed in ascending order with regard to the amount of pressure that they have on us. So the minimal level, or the minor pressure, is where a wrong has been done to us. Alongside this Paul says, "Love always protects."

> *[Love] always protects, always trusts, always hopes, always perseveres.*
> —1 Corinthians 13:7

Then there is the next level, that of moderate pressure where there is an external want in our lives. Alongside that Paul says love "always trusts." Then there is a higher level, that of major pressure, where a worry totally dominates us. Alongside that Paul says love "always hopes." But the highest level, that of maximum pressure, is spiritual warfare. Addressing this situation, Paul says love "always perseveres." So, at each level of pressure, we are given descriptions of love, but there is more. We need to see that the grace that equips us for the situation is that which also enables us to protect, trust, hope, and persevere.

Paul is showing us the benefits that are ours that enable us to cope in the time of pressure. He says that we protect, we trust, we hope, we persevere. He doesn't say we will be shouting "Glory! Hallelujah!" all the time. He doesn't say, "Oh, this is wonderful!" Nothing like that. But what he does say is that it works.

Excerpted from *Just Love* (Christian Focus Publications Ltd., 1997).

R. T. Kendall

God Loves Failures

Jacob is one of the most important characters in the Old Testament. He was the grandson of Abraham, the son of Isaac, and the third of the patriarchs: Abraham, Isaac, and Jacob. If we look at Jacob's life, we soon recognize that the Bible does not cover up the weaknesses and frailty of its heroes. Jacob, whose name was later changed to Israel, was not a particularly attractive person.

If ever there was anyone who knew the guilt of failure, then Jacob is your man. The name *Jacob* means "heel" (or possibly "deceiver"). Jacob was the world's greatest manipulator. He wanted to control people. He was a terrible parent and brother. He stole his twin brother Esau's blessing, and, by cunning, he tricked him into selling his birthright.

> *For the foolishness of God is wiser than man's wisdom, and the weakness of God is stronger than man's strength.*
> —1 CORINTHIANS 1:25

Jacob may have been a complainer, a controller, but God loved him. "Jacob I loved, but Esau I hated" (Rom. 9:13). Jacob, though not a very nice guy and not a very attractive person, was loved by God. When it came to the end of Jacob's life, the writer of the Epistle to the Hebrews chose one event, which says that "Jacob...worshiped as he leaned on the top of his staff" (Heb. 11:21). It shows him in his old age before he died, looking back on his life, a life riddled with guilt, but a life that, when it was all over, turned out as if it were perfect. He got his son back. He learned to appreciate Leah and the things God had done for him.

The "Jacobs" of this world aren't very pleasant, but God loves them.

God loves failures. Do you know why? It's because He wants to take your life, turn it into a trophy of grace, and bring you to the place where you see that His hand has always been on you. He wants to turn that failure into a blessing.

Excerpted from *All's Well That Ends Well* (Authentic Media, 2005).

What Brings Us Under Judgment?

This verse is important for Christian living. Three things lie behind this verse. The first is undiscovered sin. God focuses on sin that has not been brought to your attention. It has always been there, but, for some reason, you did not realize it.

For years I did not see it, but I was such a murmurer and such a complainer. I am sure everyone else who knew me saw it, because others always see our faults! We just cannot see them in ourselves. But there came a time when, thank God, He just grabbed me and showed me.

But why was I not aware of that sin before? The simple answer is that I was not listening to God. I was not spiritual enough to recognize it. It is no coincidence that great spirituality always carries with it a great sense of sin.

The second is unconfessed sin. Why does anybody confess sin? It is because we are ashamed. We can confess sin because

> *But if we judged ourselves, we would not come under judgment.*
> —1 Corinthians 11:31

we are truly sorry, and when we are sorry we turn from it. That does not mean we will be perfect, but we will loathe ourselves for our imperfection and try by the grace of God not to repeat it.

The third point is unrestituted sin, which is when you refuse to make things right. So why would you make restitution? There are two simple reasons to do so. First, you will give another person peace. The second reason is that you will get peace yourself by doing it. Not all confessed sin requires this, of course, but there comes a time when you have no choice but to make things right with a fellow Christian. And when you make restitution, it will give him peace, and you will be at peace.

If you deal with the sin now, it will not show up then. Sweep it under the carpet now, and it will come out then.

Excerpted from *When God Says "Well Done!"* (Christian Focus Publications Ltd., 1993).

Forgiveness Begins in the Heart

Total forgiveness must take place in the heart or it is worthless. If forgiveness truly takes place in the heart, one does not need to know whether one's enemy will reconcile. If I have forgiven him in my heart of hearts, but he still doesn't want to speak to me, I can still have the inner victory. It may be far easier to forgive when we know that those who maligned or betrayed us are sorry for what they did, but if I must have this knowledge before I can forgive, I may never have the victory over my bitterness.

> *Dear friends, if our hearts do not condemn us, we have confidence before God.*
> —1 JOHN 3:21

If Jesus had waited until His enemies felt some guilt or shame for their words and actions, He would never have forgiven them.

It is my experience that most people we must forgive do not believe they have done anything wrong at all, or if they know that they did something wrong, they believe it was justified. I would even go so far as to say that at least 90 percent of all the people I've had to forgive would be indignant at the thought that they had done something wrong.

Total forgiveness, therefore, must take place in the heart. If I have a genuine heart experience, I will not be devastated if there is no reconciliation. If those who hurt me don't want to continue a relationship with me, it isn't my problem because I have forgiven them. This is also why a person can achieve inner peace even when forgiving someone who has died.

Confidence toward God is ultimately what total forgiveness is all about; He is the one I want to please at the end of the day. He cares and knows whether I have truly and totally forgiven, and when I *know* I have His love and approval, I am one very happy and contented servant of Christ.

Excerpted from *Total Forgiveness* (Charisma House, 2002).

Ultimate Joy

Jesus drew His strength from His obedience; it was His sustenance. That is what excited Him, just being obedient.

Similarly, what makes a Christian a consistently committed person is that he gets his joy in doing what he knows pleases the Father. When he is obedient, that is his joy.

When we are obedient, too often it is because we say, "Well, later on I'll get something out of this." But what happens when this is our motivation is that we give up when the going is rough; we give up if things do not work out. We want some evidence that this obedience counts for something. We must come to the place where we get our joy from obedience. Joy is the unlooked-for reward that Jesus certainly knew was the outcome of His humility.

> "My food," said Jesus, "is to do the will of him who sent me and to finish his work."
> —JOHN 4:34–35

Although we know that Jesus is God, He allowed Himself to be considered as other than God: He allowed Himself to have another identity in peoples' eyes.

We will sometimes use the expression *projecting an image*. Everyone has an image. Sometimes it is an image we want; sometimes it is one we dislike. What image did Jesus project? There was one identity, and it was one that if they said it, He considered it a compliment. Do you know what it was? It was the identification as a *prophet*. In truth, Jesus is said to be prophet, priest, and king.

Jesus embraced the role of a prophet, and this is the image He conveyed. It is interesting that the one undoubted characteristic of a prophet is that vindication always comes later, after death, when they get to heaven.

This is the problem. Jesus was a prophet, and to be a prophet means no vindication until you are dead, and then, when you are safely out of the way, the next generation will praise you. My fellow Christians, we are called today to become prophets. Expect no recognition; do not even expect a decent burial. But great will your reward be in heaven!

Excerpted from *Meekness and Majesty* (Christian Focus Publications Ltd., 1992, 2000).

Even the Weakest Can Still Build for Eternity

Even the weakest Christian can build a lasting superstructure. You may say, "Well now, look here, I am not able to do this or that, and I just feel I must be the weakest Christian that ever lived." It is worth remembering the Old Testament character Barak.

Barak was the equivalent of an Israeli general in the days of Judges. Deborah, a judge in Israel during that period, was told by the Lord that the time had come to defeat the enemy. So she turned to Barak and said, "Take ten thousand of your men and meet on Mount Nebo, and the Lord is going to deliver the enemy into your hand."

But store up for yourselves treasures in heaven...
—MATTHEW 6:20

Barak said, "No, I just do not think I want to do that. I'm not ready." But then he said, "Deborah, if you'll go with me, I'll go."

She said, "Well, now, just a minute; if I go, you are not going to get any glory; it will go to a woman."

He said, "It's all right."

Now why did Barak do that? He did that because he wanted to see Israel win, but he was afraid they would not win by himself, and he asked for Deborah to go with him. And a woman, Jael, in fact, got the glory, and we have the song of Deborah in Judges 5:24; it is not about Barak. He felt like he was a nobody; nevertheless, in Hebrews 11, when the writer comes down the Old Testament, whom does he choose to mention as having faith? Barak. And I find that so encouraging—that the weakest Christian can do it. The reason Barak was given that glory was that he did not want the glory then.

Excerpted from *When God Says "Well Done!"* (Christian Focus Publications Ltd., 1993).

Let Go and Let God

As long as others are looking over our shoulders to see what we are doing or saying, we will cling to our reputation. But we will not see God's best fulfilled in us.

What will be the consequences if we do live like this? First, the other side of emptying yourself is really trusting God for the outcome. When we let go of ourselves, we affirm God's manner of working things out. As long as you hold on to yourself, you may not be impoverished, but you lose the fruitful outcome. Indeed, this verse says that you do not even aspire to it. But when you let it go, surprise, surprise, you get it back a hundredfold! It means, therefore, that you trust God for the outcome.

> *The man who loves his life will lose it, while the man who hates his life in this world will keep it for eternal life.*
> —JOHN 12:25

It may not be the way you would have done it, but remember that, as Christians, we have a loving heavenly Father who is all powerful and able to give what is best.

He still speaks to us. Give up your Isaac; give up your valued possession…your uncertain future…your ego…your reputation…and trust God for the outcome. It will be fun to see what He does!

Second, having looked to God for the outcome, what is that outcome going to be? In the short term there is peace and the presence of God. Peter advocated that we "cast all [our] anxiety on him, because he cares for [us]" (1 Pet. 5:7). That is what will give you such a release within. In the long term, there is a reward worth waiting for—to hear from the lips of God Himself, "Well done."

Let go of yourself, empty yourself, and be filled with all the fullness of God. Leave the outcome to God, and you will know joy beyond compare.

Excerpted from *Meekness and Majesty* (Christian Focus Publications Ltd., 1992, 2000).

Your Silence Is Golden

Do you know what it is to take your stand in a particular situation and have nobody agree with you? Unvindicated righteousness occurs when a righteous deed was criticized or misunderstood. Now it could be you were wrong. You may not know. At the end of the day the righteous Judge will do the vindicating.

However, perhaps you were right. Let us say you have taken your stand because you were honoring God and following the Holy Spirit, and there was not a vestige of ego or pride in it. You were just doing it for the honor of God alone, and as a result you were lied about and people believed those lies. You made no attempt to put the record straight. You could have cleared your name, but you did not. That is what God likes. Had you cleared your name, you would have built a superstructure of straw, but you kept quiet, and God's heart was moved. Your silence was golden—pure gold in fact. In 2 Thessalonians 1:6, in the very same paragraph when Paul talks about the Second Coming of Jesus in blazing fire, he also said, "It is a righteous thing with God to recompense tribulation to them that trouble you" (KJV).

> *Do not worry about how you will defend yourselves or what you will say, for the Holy Spirit will teach you at that time what you should say.*
>
> —LUKE 12:11–12

But we want to know when this will happen. The NIV is very clear: this will happen when Jesus comes in fire, in glory. There is no promise of vindication this side of heaven. You may get it, but there is no promise of it. Maybe you were tempted to speak out and clear your own name, but on that day you will be glad you kept your mouth shut, because God loves to clear the name of those who have been mistreated.

Excerpted from *When God Says "Well Done!"* (Christian Focus Publications Ltd., 1993).

Resilient Love

There have been those of us who felt we had done something so wonderful because we totally forgave somebody who did something bad to us. We did it once, and we were so proud of it. It was such an unusual thing, you can never forget it! But that is not resilient love; resilient love is when love is not an ordeal but a habit, so that when they lie about you next week, you just bounce back and you do not try to clear your name or try to set the record straight. It is when you are not even aware anymore that you do it.

In his first letter, John states a truth about resilient love. He says, "There is no fear in love" (1 John 4:18). In this instance the NIV translation improves on the King James Version, for it goes on to say, "But perfect love drives out fear, because fear has to do with punishment." It means you want to punish somebody who has hurt you; you want to make them look bad; you want to give them the cold shoulder; you want to tell them what they did to

> *I have loved you with an everlasting love;*
> *I have drawn you with loving-kindness.*
> —JEREMIAH 31:3

you. And do you see why is it that we are afraid? We are insecure.

The best illustration is the story of how Joseph revealed himself to his brothers in Egypt. He spoke to them in private, with no one listening, so nobody would know who had hurt him or what had been done to him. He wanted to protect his brothers. This was resilient love.

It is when there is such absence of fear that you do not want anybody to know what they did to you. I want to ask you a question: Has somebody hurt you, and have you told anybody that the person hurt you? Why did you tell them? You wanted to punish the one who hurt you; you wanted to make the person look bad. But there is no fear in love.

Another thing about Joseph was that he did not want his brothers to be afraid of him. If you want to keep somebody afraid of you, it is because you are afraid and insecure, and you want to be able to control them. But fear has no place here.

Excerpted from *When God Says "Well Done!"* (Christian Focus Publications Ltd., 1993).

Pray in the Spirit

There will be no praying in heaven. We may regret many things at the judgment seat of Christ—how we used our time, how we spent our money, the friends we chose, the decisions we made; but I can safely promise you one thing you will not regret: the time you spent alone with the Lord. If Jesus, who was the Son of God and was filled with the Spirit without limit (John 3:34), felt the need to do this, how much more do you and I need it?

Praying in the Spirit is a vital part of spiritual warfare. This seems to be what Paul means in Romans 8:26: "The Spirit helps us in our weakness. We do not know what we ought to pray for, but the Spirit himself intercedes for us with groans that words cannot express."

> *Build yourselves up in your most holy faith and pray in the Holy Spirit.*
> —JUDE 20

Praying in the Spirit is praying in the will of God. It is the only kind of praying that matters, because it is only when we ask in God's will that we are heard. We are fools if we think we can upstage God's will, as if our idea would be better than His.

Here is a principle you can count on for the rest of your life: God always gives His best to those who leave the choice with Him. The reason is this. He already has a plan for you. It has been carefully thought out. The same wisdom that entered into God's plan for creation and redemption is the brilliance and care that lay behind His thoughts toward you. This is why only a fool would try to come up with a better idea than the one already conceived in God's heart and mind. Therefore to pray the will of God is the best thing we can do when it comes to prayer.

So I ask you, "How much do you pray?"

Excerpted from *Pure Joy* (Charisma House, 2006).

How to Handle Criticism

This message is a word that is relevant for anybody who has difficulty in *handling criticism*. Maybe you know what it is to be criticized. Maybe you have had enough. Maybe it was by parents, and others are still doing it even though you have grown up. Maybe you know what it is to live with a nagging wife who is always putting you down. Maybe it is your husband criticizing you. Maybe somebody at the office. Perhaps somebody at university, in college, maybe a friend. Maybe a Christian with some stature criticized you, and because of who it is, you take it seriously. Whatever the situation, Paul shows us how to handle it.

Many of us just fall apart when somebody criticizes us or sits in judgment on anything we have done. We just cannot handle it. But Paul was not afraid; he was unintimidated.

The reason is he knew what they were trying to do. They were trying somehow to punish him verbally. Do you know what it is to be punished verbally? Have you ever punished anyone in this way? You are putting them down. Perhaps you are wanting them to feel guilty.

But the fact of the matter is that whenever you concede that the other person is trying to punish you, you immediately

> *I care very little if I am judged by you or by any human court; indeed, I do not even judge myself. My conscience is clear, but that does not make me innocent. It is the Lord who judges me.*
> —1 CORINTHIANS 4:3–4

know that they are acting in fear. This does not mean, however, that we should not listen to criticism. We need each other. But it is sheer judgmentalism such as Paul was receiving that we must throw off.

That means that when anybody criticizes you and you are afraid that what they are saying about you is going to hurt you, remember the words of Peter: "Be self-controlled and alert" (1 Pet. 5:8). Do you know that the way to get the devil to leave you alone is to let him see that it just does not bother you? You resist him and refuse to let him intimidate you. That is the first thing to do in response to criticism.

Excerpted from *When God Says "Well Done!"* (Christian Focus Publications Ltd., 1993).

How to Cope With the Past

When it comes to our past, God knows everything. God wants to bring us to the place where we can be ourselves. We do not have to pretend, because God knows us. We also know that He has forgiven us. What is certain is that we must not let past failure or our lack of spiritual progress immobilize us.

This psalm is a reminder that some have a past full of hurts. Perhaps that describes you. If that is the case, remember two things: in the Christian family there will be fellow believers who have suffered in a way similar to you, who can sympathize with you; best of all, Jesus will sympathize with you.

> *Many a time have they afflicted me from my youth, may Israel now say: Many a time have they afflicted me from my youth: yet they have not prevailed against me.*
>
> —PSALM 129:1–2

There are some people who have such a keen sense of rejection that they just can't handle a situation where someone tries to love them. They believe somehow it won't be true.

But even though you have known rejection and hurt or have damaged emotions, these experiences will not save you. You may think that because of these experiences you deserve a special break and somehow God will let you into heaven. But He will not.

A lot of people, if they have had some kind of hurt, have not received the victory over their attitude toward the problem. Instead they let the situation have the victory over them.

We must deal with the anger and bitterness toward those who caused the hurt or toward God for allowing it. If we do, God grants us a sweetness of spirit that will lead us actually to pray for those who caused the hurt.

Let me tell you how to cope with your past. It is not to say, "This is the way I am"; it is to say with the psalmist, "But they have not gained the victory."

Excerpted from *Higher Ground* (Christian Focus Publications Ltd., 1995).

Judge and You Will Be Judged

Here is something always to remember about what we should know about those who judge us. There are three things: the first is that *they do not have all of the evidence.* We know that God is not finished with us yet in any case. In addition, they do not know everything, even in the area where they think that they are in a position to say this or that. They do not have all of the evidence, so they do not really know at the end of the day what they are talking about.

We also should remember that when anybody judges us, *they have disobeyed Jesus.* We are just not given permission by Jesus to judge anybody. And when anybody judges me, I know he has disobeyed Jesus.

The third thing is, *the opinion people have of us is temporary.* It is only a matter of time before they will change their tune; they

> *Do not judge, or you too will be judged.*
> —MATTHEW 7:1

will have to, eventually. Remember, however, that this works both ways. When you judge someone, you will be ill-informed, disobedient, and eventually judged by God.

The next time you are prepared to criticize another person, and you wonder why God does not deal with that person, I want you to ask yourself this question: *Has not God been patient with me?* Can you recall that time when you were not the perfect example and God continued to bless you? He supplied your needs, He helped you, He was with you, He answered prayer. Things were happening, and you can look back later and think, *Oh, God was good to me; I didn't deserve that.* Always remember, maybe another person does not deserve it either, but God is being good to them just as He was being good to you.

Excerpted from *When God Says "Well Done!"* (Christian Focus Publications Ltd., 1993).

Right or Wrong, Leave It to God

Years ago I talked to a minister who came to me at a place where I was preaching in the northern part of England. He said, "I'm in the worst bondage. I think I've married the wrong woman."

I asked, "How long have you been married?"

He replied, "Twenty-five years!"

"Well," I said, "what if you have married the wrong one? What are you going to do?"

He did not know. But he was all torn up about it.

Looking back, many of us have doubts about this or that, wondering whether we did do the right thing. The apostle Paul would say, "But it doesn't matter. What is in the past is in the past. You don't have to decide."

> *For it is God who is at work in you, both to will and to work for His good pleasure.*
> —Philippians 2:13, nas

I think one of the most interesting discussions is whether or not Paul was right to go to Jerusalem in Acts 21. We read that different people warned him, and even Agabus prophesied in the Spirit and said, "You shouldn't go to Jerusalem!" But Paul still went.

You may say that Paul would not make a mistake, but Luke says they spoke "in the Spirit" and said he should not go. So it looks to me like Paul disobeyed. Now I do not think Paul gave it that much thought; he just said, "I'm going to go." Looking back on it, however, he could say in Philippians 1:12, "Now I want you to know, brothers, that what has happened to me has really served to advance the gospel." So he was not concerned whether he had been right or wrong. He was concerned that the gospel kept going, and that is what he was happy about.

Many of us are not concerned whether the gospel goes on but rather, "Was I right?" and "What about me?" Paul said it does not matter. Because who knows? The outcome is unknown. One does not have to know whether one is totally right or totally wrong. Leave it to God to order all your ways!

Excerpted from *When God Says "Well Done!"* (Christian Focus Publications Ltd., 1993).

The Blessing of Having an Enemy

When you know that a person is obsessed with you and is out to discredit you, you are very, very blessed indeed. This doesn't happen to everyone. You are chosen, for behind your enemy is the hand of God. God has raised up your enemy—possibly just for you! King Saul's pursuit of David was the best thing that could have happened to David at the time. God did David a very special favor: he raised up Saul to keep him on his toes, to teach him to be sensitive to the Spirit (1 Sam. 24:5), and to teach him total forgiveness. Saul was David's passport to a greater anointing.

When you totally forgive your enemy, you have crossed over into a supernatural realm. Perhaps you are like me and wish you could excel in all the gifts of the Spirit; you wish you could have a hand in signs and wonders; you'd love to see your usefulness intensified and extended by a double anointing. The gifts are *supernatural*; that is, they are above and beyond the

> *Afterward, David was conscience-stricken for having cut off a corner of his robe.*
> —1 Samuel 24:5

natural order of things. There is no natural explanation for the truly miraculous. But if you and I totally forgive someone who is truly an enemy, believe me, we have just crossed over into the realm of the supernatural.

I believe this is the highest level of spirituality that exists. This is as good as it gets. Totally forgiving an enemy is as spectacular as any miracle. No one may even know, though. You quietly intercede for them in solitude. Only God, the angels, and the devil know.

You and I can do something exceedingly rare: forgive an enemy (if we have one). Loving an enemy defies natural explanation.

It begins with having sufficient motivation. I am literally seeking to motivate you in these lines to do what very few do—but which all *can* do: totally forgive anyone who has hurt you. And the blessing is beyond words to describe.

Excerpted from *Total Forgiveness* (Charisma House, 2002).

Run for the Prize

In the Olympics an athlete was subject to disqualification if he did not go through ten months of strict training. It is interesting that in those ten months the athlete had to do away with lawful pleasures. The Greek word that is used here is *agnoidzo*; it means "to agonize." It means self-control in all things, and so the implication is that if the athlete has to have self-control for ten months prior to the games, so this Christian race is to be run throughout a lifetime of self-control. This refers, of course, not merely to the body, but to the whole man—body, mind, spirit.

> *Everyone who competes in the games goes into strict training. They do it to get a crown that will not last; but we do it to get a crown that will last forever.*
> —1 Corinthians 9:25

The prize won at the Olympics was a wreath, sometimes made of pine, and strangely enough, sometimes made of celery! That's right! Can you imagine wearing a wreath of pieces of celery? Perhaps if it is fresh and you give me some salt with it I could enjoy it.

The wreath was already beginning to wither when they put it on the winner's head. So when Paul says they do it to get a crown that will not last, that sounds like an understatement. But what it looked like was not the point. The winner had no thought of the composition of the crown. As with modern athletes, victory meant fame; it was for prestige and sometimes fortune, so that the crown was simply a symbol of victory.

Paul says that crown was nothing in the light of the believer's prize. Who knows what it will look like? Who knows whether it is a symbolic gold crown or if it is literal? Who knows? But just to hear the words of Jesus, "Well done!" will give to that person a self-consciousness that will last forever.

Excerpted from *When God Says "Well Done!"* (Christian Focus Publications Ltd., 1993).

Refining the Anointing

Aman or woman with a secret anointing always needs further preparation. We do not get the necessary refinement by merely praying for more of the Holy Spirit. Jesus had all the Holy Spirit that there was—the Spirit without limit (John 3:34). Yet, "although he was a son, he learned obedience from what he suffered" (Heb. 5:8).

I find this truly amazing. To think that Jesus, the God-man, needed suffering to be perfected. He was man *as though* He were not God—and was filled with the Spirit without any measure or limit set on that filling. He was *completely* filled with the Spirit. He was also God *as though* He were not man! And yet, "in bringing many sons to glory, it was fitting that God, for whom and through whom everything exists, should make the author of their sal-

> *Although he was a son, he learned obedience from what he suffered.*
>
> —Hebrews 5:8

vation perfect through suffering" (Heb. 2:10). All I can say is, if our Lord Jesus Christ needed to suffer before He could be all that God the Father envisaged for Him, how much more do we need to suffer before God can trust us with the full extent of the anointing?

Suffering was David's passport to a greater anointing. Though the Spirit came upon him in power (1 Sam. 16:13), little did David know that, rather than being crowned king in the next week or two, he would have years and years of fleeing Saul—for one reason: to guarantee that the secret anointing in him was refined.

The secret anointing in you, though you are kept from a high profile, will still be a threat to the enemy God chooses for your refinement. David could not hide his anointing. He wasn't ambitious. He simply did what he was asked to do and did it too well. David thought the preparation would never end. You may feel the same way. But thank God for the secret anointing in you. Thank God for friends. And thank God for your enemies. They will probably mean more to you, at the end of the day, than your friends!

Excerpted from *The Anointing: Yesterday, Today, Tomorrow* (Charisma House, 2003).

Beware of Your Competitor—the Body

We are all in a race—are we are trying to outdo one another? No. Not at all. In this race every single one of us can receive that prize. So our competition, Paul says, is our bodies. He says, "I beat it and make it my slave." The word *slave* is the translation of the Greek word *doulos*.

Paul is not meaning here that we get to heaven because we beat our bodies black and blue, but according to Paul we could miss the prize if we do not. And the prize was very important to him. So he regards his body as a slave of the spirit.

> *No, I beat my body and make it my slave so that after I have preached to others, I myself will not be disqualified for the prize.*
>
> —1 CORINTHIANS 9:27

Behind Paul's thinking are three principles. First, Paul knew that being an apostle, being a preacher, did not *guarantee* him the prize. In fact, according to James 3:1, it makes it worse. So the higher profile you have, the greater gift, the more you are called to do, the harder it is to get the prize.

Paul knew also that God is *no respecter of persons* and therefore will not bend the rules for anybody. Now if there were ever a soul whom you would think God would bend the rule for, it was the apostle Paul. Look at the way he suffered. Surely that ought to move the heart of God to say, "Well, Paul, because you have worked so hard, when it comes to the prize I'm not going to be so strict with you." But it is the opposite.

And last, Paul knew his greatest competitors were not his fellow Christians—but his own body. Like Paul, we ought to be aware that our greatest competitor is not our fellow Christians but our very own bodies. In other words, it is possible to be a success as a preacher, but that success could be under a cloud, not because the preaching lacked eloquence, or truth, or converts, but because of a *failure in personal holiness*.

Excerpted from *When God Says "Well Done!"* (Christian Focus Publications Ltd., 1993).

God's Inflexible Impartiality

I find it interesting that in 1 Corinthians 9:25 Paul refers to strict training and in verse 27 to the body being tamed: he says, "I beat my body and make it my slave." So our bodies are given to us as a trust from God. Our bodies are also a spiritual temple (1 Cor. 6:19). They are also referred to as "instruments of wickedness" (Rom. 6:13). And last, the source of the tongue (James 3:6), which is considered "a world of evil among the parts of the body."

The Corinthians were in danger of missing out on the prize. The question is: Are we? What grips me, and I pray it will grip you, is that Paul believed in God's ruthless impartiality. Let that grip you. At the judgment seat of Christ Paul knew that his own present intimacy with God did not mean that he could tell God what

> *God is not one to show partiality, but in every nation the man who fears Him and does what is right, is welcome to Him.*
> —ACTS 10:34–35, NAS

to do. Paul's intimacy with God did not result in an over-familiarity with Him, whereby he says, "Well, it can't happen to me." Paul did not have indemnity because he was an apostle; preachers do not have indemnity because they seek conversions; high-profile Christians have no indemnity; your years of Christian service are not going to guarantee that you get the prize.

Martin Luther said, "When I get to heaven, I expect to be surprised three times. There will be those in heaven I thought wouldn't be there, and there will be some missing I thought would be there, but the greatest surprise will be that I am there myself." But could I paraphrase that one more time? I suspect there will be three surprises: some will receive the prize I thought would not, some will not be rewarded that I thought would, but the greatest surprise will be if I receive it.

And I pray that we all do.

Excerpted from *When God Says "Well Done!"* (Christian Focus Publications Ltd., 1993).

Getting God's Attention

Y ou and I are like Samaritans. We don't deserve to be saved. God notices gratitude—and ingratitude.

The truth is, we need to realize that we should be deeply thankful for what God has done for us—whatever it is—as was that Samaritan who was healed of his leprosy. We must remind ourselves that we are simply unworthy and in no position to bargain with God.

The longer I live, the more amazed I am over God's goodness and mercy to me. For too long I was like the nine who went on their way. God has given me the chance to choose to be like the one leper who returned to say, "Thank You."

> *And Jesus answered and said, "Were there not ten cleansed? But the nine—where are they? Was no one found who turned back to give glory to God, except this foreigner?"*
> —LUKE 17:17–18, NAS

That Jesus would say "Where are the other nine?" tells me how much God notices gratitude and ingratitude. It certainly encourages me to show thankfulness to Him, and it truly scares me—now that I seem to know better—when I think of how ungrateful I have been for too many years.

The moment we say "thank you" to the Most High God, we have His undivided attention. Therefore, whenever we sense God is hiding His face from us, it is a precious opportunity not only to get His attention but also to please Him more than ever. It is truly a "sacrifice of praise" (Heb. 13:15) when we manage to praise Him in adverse circumstances. Moreover, it is then when we make the greatest spiritual progress in our Christian life.

So, do you want to get God's attention? Have you had difficulty getting His attention? Here are two things you can do: (1) Ask for mercy when you approach the throne of grace, and (2) say "thank You" when God answers prayer.

Excerpted from *Just Say Thanks!* (Charisma House, 2005).

Sometimes God Is Silent

Oswald Chambers once asked a provoking question: "Am I close enough to God to feel secure when He is silent?" In other words, must I have constant two-way communication with God to feel approved and loved by Him? We must develop a maturity that does not panic "between the times"—to use a helpful phrase from Richard Bewes. *In season* is a time of refreshing when God clearly manifests Himself. *Out of season* is when He seems to hide His face from us, those times when He is silent.

God wants us to learn as much from His silence as we learn from His absence. For example, often we learn more about ourselves when God hides Himself than in times of conscious blessing. His silence is like taking an examination in which we must demonstrate how much we have learned about His "ways."

An intimate, unique experience of some kind with God is important for each of us to have. It can be the best thing that can happen to us—but it can also be dangerous. After such an experience we can express a spiritual arrogance and pride that exalt us, in our own eyes, above other "less special" believers. If that happens, perhaps the only thing that can bring us back to a humble awareness of our spiritual position is for God Himself to desert us momentarily.

> *God, do not keep silent; be not quiet, O God, be not still.*
> —Psalm 83:1

People who suppose they have this sort of relationship with God lack in both teachability and accountability. They sometimes think they are spiritually superior to all who try to help them. The only thing that will possibly help them is for God Himself to "stay behind" while they carry on in their presumption.

It happened to me as I described above. It hurt very much, and I couldn't understand it for a while. God appeared to betray me. Not that I noticed it at first.

It happens, I believe, to nearly every person who has had an authentic experience with the Holy Spirit. God hides His face—suddenly without notice. No apology. Just silence. The explanation comes (usually) much, much later.

Excerpted from *The Sensitivity of the Spirit* (Charisma House, 2002).

"But If Not" Faith

A sweet old lady stood up in a prayer meeting in Alabama, only to exhort: "Do you have the 'but if not' faith?"

It is absolutely true that we must be willing to serve God whether or not He blesses us. That was part of the reason for the Book of Job. Satan questioned whether Job, a wealthy man, would serve God if he wasn't blessed materially: "Does Job fear God for nothing?" (Job 1:9). Job's suffering soon followed—with God's permission and purpose. Job later said: "Though he slay me, yet will I hope in him; I will surely defend my ways to his face" (Job 13:15).

> *Our God whom we serve is able to deliver us from the burning fiery furnace, and he will deliver us out of thine hand, O king. But if not, be it known unto thee, O king, that we will not serve thy gods, nor worship the golden image which thou hast set up.*
>
> —DANIEL 3:17–18, KJV

Likewise Shadrach, Meshach, and Abednego—the three Hebrew young men living in Babylon—were commanded to worship King Nebuchadnezzar's image of gold under the threat of being thrown into a furnace. They wouldn't bend. They wouldn't bow. And they didn't burn. But they were *willing* to die. Nebuchadnezzar wanted to know why would people like these three men refuse to do a simple thing like falling down before his image of gold.

The "but if not" faith! God is able to bless us, but if not, we will not bow down to idols. God will bless us when we give, but if not, we will give anyway. God will bless us when we worship and praise Him, but if not, we will worship and praise Him anyway.

We must not only be willing to be vocal in our thanking God, but we must also do it all the time—whether we feel like it or not. Whether He blesses us or not.

Excerpted from *Just Say Thanks!* (Charisma House, 2005).

The Need to Remember

God has a perfect memory, and yet, if we are to believe the psychologists, so have we. Psychologists say we never really forget. Well, you could have fooled me, but that's what they say. We do forget, however. When we look back on our past we remember things that were pleasant. Yet it is one thing consciously to *remember things*; the sad thing is there are some things we don't forget, especially if something is pointed out to us. One of the things that will make hell, hell is that you will have a memory in hell. In Luke 16:25, Abraham said to the man who was in hell, "Son, remember that in your lifetime you received your good things, while Lazarus received bad things, but now he is comforted here and you are in agony."

> *I thank my God every time I remember you.*
>
> —Philippians 1:3

But even on this planet, sometimes even as Christians our memories have to be jogged. At the Last Supper Jesus said, "Do this in remembrance of me" (Luke 22:19). One of the reasons for the Lord's Supper is to jog our memories, to remind us how we know we are going to go to heaven. For when we eat the bread and drink the cup, there before us are symbolized the body and the blood of Jesus.

The first time the word *remember* appears in the Bible is in Genesis 9:15–16, where God said to Noah, "I will remember my covenant.... Whenever the rainbow appears in the clouds, I will see it and remember the everlasting covenant." Sometimes it seems as if God is slow to remember. Sometimes we come to Him and cry, "O God, remember!" The question is, we ask God to remember, but do *we* remember? There is one thing God appreciates, and I cannot stress this too much, He appreciates being thanked. Remember to thank Him.

Excerpted from *All's Well That Ends Well* (Authentic Media, 2005).

Praising God When You're Feeling Low

Praising God when I am sad pleases Him. It shows I trust His Word and that I love Him without His doing everything that pleases me. It is a wonderful opportunity for blessing—just to believe!

It is also called a "sacrifice of praise" (Heb. 13:15). We sacrifice feelings, we sacrifice pleasure, we sacrifice time—just to praise God. And when we don't feel like it—when we are at a low point, we then really show a sacrifice of praise. In fact, the lower we are, the greater the opportunity to demonstrate a sacrifice of praise to God.

> *Through Jesus, therefore, let us continually offer to God a sacrifice of praise— the fruit of lips that confess his name.*
> —HEBREWS 13:15

The Epistle to the Hebrews has a lot to say about sacrifices. They mostly refer to the sacrifice of animals. This is because the sacrifice of animals in the Old Testament pointed to the Ultimate Sacrifice— when God gave His one and only Son to die on a cross (John 3:16).

But sometimes the word *sacrifice* is used with regard to what *we* give up. Although the primary meaning of sacrifice refers to the slaughter of animals to appease God's justice, it also means to give up something for the sake of something more important. Hence Paul said, "Therefore, I urge you, brothers, in view of God's mercy, to offer your bodies as living sacrifices, holy and pleasing to God—this is your spiritual act of worship" (Rom. 12:1). David said, "I will sacrifice a thank offering to you and call on the name of the LORD" (Ps. 116:17).

When we take the time to praise God, we sacrifice time. We all can think of things we ought to be doing. It is easier to watch television than it is to take the equal amount of time to praise God. To praise God for thirty minutes is a sacrifice of time, of pleasure, of our basic wishes, and, possibly, of our temperament.

Excerpted from *Just Say Thanks!* (Charisma House, 2005).

"I Appreciate You"

Showing gratitude must not be done only to God. We all need to remember to show appreciation to people. Paul said, "I am obligated to both Greeks and non-Greeks, both to the wise and the foolish. That is why I am so eager to preach the gospel also to you who are at Rome" (Rom. 1:14–15). He showed gratitude by what he did. His ultimate gratitude was, of course, to God, but he was not unaware of how God used people to bless him. Read Romans 16. It is largely written to thank people! Paul wanted to show how grateful he was by his actions. We are all obligated to people who have helped us. We may not always be able to show it to the very people, however much we would like to, but we can act upon what they have given us and do good to others.

> Now we ask you, brothers, to respect those who work hard among you, who are over you in the Lord and who admonish you.
>
> —1 THESSALONIANS 5:12

I am very grateful to preachers and teachers in my past. My first pastor was Rev. Gene Phillips. He could not know how his life impacted me during the first few years of my life. I could go on and on naming people whose lives made me want to pray more. And yet I thank these men best by living a life that honors them.

It has been my practice to thank people, then, if I can, when they are still alive. People like compliments. I know I do. Do you? Tell people when they are a blessing to you. It may be the first time anyone has taken the time to speak a blessing to them. Your kind word of appreciation may come to them when they have had a bad day and lift them up!

Excerpted from *Just Say Thanks!* (Charisma House, 2005).

No Place for Gloating

If you wish to be today's servant, then you must also resist gloating when you have been vindicated. If Samuel had been small-minded, he would have been glad Saul had failed the test. Samuel was the only one who warned against the kingship. We therefore might expect him to shout to the housetops, "I told you so." How do we know he didn't do that? Because God said to Samuel, "How long will you *mourn* for Saul, since I have rejected him as king over Israel?" (1 Sam. 16:1, emphasis added). There was no gloating, only mourning.

> Do not gloat when your enemy falls; when he stumbles, do not let your heart rejoice...
>
> —PROVERBS 24:17

A good evidence that we can be trusted with today's anointing and today's stigma is that we mourn when a brother or sister slips or falls. Cain said, "Am I my brother's keeper?" (Gen. 4:9). The answer is *yes*. I fear that the anointing many of us desire is largely delayed because of a rival spirit. We look over our shoulders and, consciously or unconsciously, compete with one another. Virtually no consideration at all is given to seeking the glory that comes only from God. We want mutual adulation more.

Today's man or woman ought also to be on the lookout for tomorrow's man. Jonathan Edwards said that the one thing Satan cannot successfully counterfeit is a love for the glory of God. As long as you and I truly love God's honor, including the reputation of *His* church today and tomorrow, it is good evidence we haven't been duped by the devil. But if it is my own reputation I worry most about, there is no proof I am today's man. In fact, it's quite the opposite.

Excerpted from *The Anointing: Yesterday, Today, Tomorrow* (Charisma House, 2003).

Remember the Benefits

Can you remember a time God was angry at you? I can. The unveiling of His anger is the scariest thing under the sun. I know what is it is to receive a wake-up call from God. I know what it is to feel His "hot displeasure" (Ps. 6:1, KJV). It is a severe kind of chastening one does not want to experience. But I have, and I pray I will never be foolish enough to forget it.

Prosperity may have the consequence of making us forget. Good health is something many accept without thinking. A job, a place to work, having a good income are things one can begin to take for granted.

Praise the LORD, O my soul, and forget not all his benefits.

—PSALM 103:2

The message of this is: don't forget to be thankful. Thank God for the air you breathe. Thank Him for sunshine. Thank Him for rain. Thank Him for food to eat. Thank Him for clothes, for a warm bed at night, and for shelter.

If God prospers you, He is putting you on your honor—to be thankful. And to show it. So tell Him!

David lists all the benefits: forgiveness for all his sins, the healing of all his diseases, redeeming his life from the pit, crowning him with love and compassion, satisfying his desires with good things, his youth being renewed like the eagle's (Ps. 103:3–5).

One of the irrefutable evidences for the divine inspiration of the psalms is the repeated praises to God and admonition to praise. Only God could lead a human being to pen psalms like that. The most natural tendency in the world is to forget to be thankful.

Remembering can sometimes come to us without any effort—should God bring it to our attention. What God wants from us, however, is that we remember because we *choose* to remember.

Excerpted from *Just Say Thanks!* (Charisma House, 2005).

Stop Judging!

I think the hardest thing in the world that I have had to learn is to stop judging. I cannot say that I have learned it completely. God is not finished with me yet, and He is still dealing with me in this respect. I have discovered that the less judging I do, the more peace I get.

Paul is not talking here about hating sin, because that is something we should all do. He is talking about finding fault with someone who is threatening you, someone who is giving you problems, or perhaps someone who just "gets your goat."

> *Therefore judge nothing before the appointed time; wait till the Lord comes. He will bring to light what is hidden in darkness and will expose the motives of men's hearts. At that time each will receive his praise from God.*
>
> —1 CORINTHIANS 4:5

Sometimes it is a personality clash and you make it into some big issue when it is really a personal one. Many times what is posed as a theological issue is nothing more than a problem of jealousy, envy, or pride, which are purely personal problems. Failing to recognize that, we get embroiled in it and say, "God's with me," and He is not. It is too common a mistake.

There are five things we ought to know about being judgmental, and the first is that judging is *speculation*. We simply do not have all the evidence.

Second, judging is *schismatic*. It will always cause division; you cannot avoid it. Whenever you begin to judge, the church will be divided.

Third, judging is *selfish*. Primarily it is a sign of our self-righteousness. We do not think so, but it is, and it is self-serving.

Fourth, judging is *spineless*. No strength of character is required for you to be judgmental, and it shows no taste.

Fifth, judging is *superseding* because you are doing not only what God says not to do, but you are actually doing what God says belongs to Him: "To me belongeth vengeance. Vengeance is mine." Five good reasons, then, for taking this verse seriously: stop judging!

Excerpted from *When God Says "Well Done!"* (Christian Focus Publications Ltd., 1993).

Just Tell Him

When Louise and I go through the old prayer list (I've kept it—lest we ever forget), we now run through the same petitions only to say, "Thank You, Lord, for the way You have worked." Most of these petitions have been answered. Never have we felt so grateful to God. And yet we make sure that we never, never, never forget but always remember to tell Him how thankful we are.

Again and again comes the injunction: give thanks.

> Give thanks to the LORD, call on his name; make known among the nations what he has done.
>
> —1 CHRONICLES 16:8

> Give thanks to the LORD, for he is good; his love endures forever.
>
> —1 CHRONICLES 16:34

> With them were Heman and Jeduthun and the rest of those chosen and designated by name to give thanks to the LORD, "for his love endures forever."
>
> —1 CHRONICLES 16:41

One of the great kings of the Old Testament was Hezekiah. "Hezekiah trusted in the LORD, the God of Israel. There was no one like him among all the kings of Judah, either before him or after him" (2 Kings 18:5). It is said that "he succeeded in everything he undertook" (2 Chron. 32:30). Part of the explanation for Hezekiah's greatness and prosperity was that he assigned priests and Levites to offer burnt offerings and "to give thanks" (2 Chron. 31:2).

> *Praise the LORD. Give thanks to the LORD, for he is good; his love endures forever.*
>
> —PSALM 106:1

It is a matter of remembering. It is so easy to forget, but I for one do not want to come to the end of my years with blushing over not remembering to give thanks to the Lord. Just tell Him! He likes to hear it. We will never be sorry, and doing it promises that one day we will hear from the lips of Jesus Himself, "Well done." Be assured *He* will remember to say it.

Excerpted from *Just Say Thanks!* (Charisma House, 2005).

The Choice to Rejoice

What separates Christians from non-Christians is not whether bad things happen to them but whether we can make the choice to rejoice in all circumstances.

In Philippians 4:4 we are given a command to rejoice: "Rejoice in the Lord always. I will say it again: Rejoice!" It is a command because joy isn't always spontaneous. Sometimes it comes unexpectedly, but it is wrong to wait only for the spontaneous joy. Many years ago I used to sing, "Every time I feel the Spirit moving in my heart I will pray." The problem with that old spiritual is that, speaking personally, if I waited until I felt the Spirit moving in my heart, I fear I would not pray all that much. Paul said to "be instant in season, out of season" (2 Tim. 4:2, KJV). "In season" is when the Spirit is consciously at work; "out of season" is when we feel nothing.

> *Rejoice in the Lord always. I will say it again: Rejoice!*
> —PHILIPPIANS 4:4

We are to rejoice *always*. Why? Because circumstances change. If we are found rejoicing at all times, we are showing gratitude. If we make a commitment to gratitude, it means we must be prepared for the unexpected trial and dignify that trial when it comes. Dignifying the trial means:

- Refusing to complain
- Accepting that the trial is from God
- Letting God end the trial His way

Every trial has a built-in time scale. It *will* end! God will see to that. God knows how much we can bear. If we will truly believe that, we can keep our commitment to be grateful—and show it by the choice to rejoice no matter what the circumstances.

Excerpted from *Just Say Thanks!* (Charisma House, 2005).

Ask for Mercy

Have you ever asked God for mercy? Have you ever come to that point where you have realized that God doesn't owe you a favor? He doesn't owe you an explanation; rather, what you need is mercy.

One definition of mercy is "refraining from inflicting punishment or pain on an offender or enemy who is in one's power." Here is a person who has the right to punish and also the power to do so. He has the right to punish, because the offender deserves justice and deserves to be punished. Mercy occurs when the person who could punish shows leniency instead. In short, God's mercy is not getting what we, as sinners, deserve.

The writer of this psalm (we don't know who he was) understood that God can give or withhold mercy. It was written by one who understood God and who also understood himself. He had come to terms with what he was like. He realized he had no right to snap his fingers and say, "God, You have to do this!" He knew that *God doesn't have to do anything.* Therefore he said, "We will just look to God. We will wait for Him. As the eyes of slaves look to the hands of their master, as the eyes of a maid look to the hands of the mistress, so our eyes look to the Lord."

> *Behold, as the eyes of servants look unto the hand of their masters, and as the eyes of a maiden unto the hand of her mistress; so our eyes wait upon the LORD our God, until that he have mercy upon us. Have mercy upon us, O LORD, have mercy upon us: for we are exceedingly filled with contempt. Our soul is exceedingly filled with the scorning of those that are at ease, and with the contempt of the proud.*
> —PSALM 123:2–4, KJV

Have you ever talked to God like that? If you haven't, you are not a Christian. A Christian is a person who has come to realize that he has no bargaining power. He sees himself as having sinned against God, offended His holiness, broken His law, and shown contempt for His Word. When a person realizes that he is a sinner, all he can do is ask for mercy.

Excerpted from *Higher Ground* (Christian Focus Publications Ltd., 1995).

Ways of Showing Gratitude

We show God gratitude by not only telling Him, but we show gratitude also by living a holy life. Never forget that we are not saved by being holy; we are holy because we have been saved. But because we are still sinners, we easily forget and become careless.

Gratitude is demonstrated furthermore by our giving Him one-tenth of our income. Now tithing was made legal under the law. We, however, are not under the law but under grace. We are not required to tithe as a condition to salvation. But God promises to bless those who do.

> *Rooted and built up in him, strengthened in the faith as you were taught, and overflowing with thankfulness.*
> —Colossians 2:7

We show our thanks to God for saving us by sharing our faith with others. What if our gratitude to God were summed up entirely by our witnessing to others? What gratitude to God would *you* have manifested until now?

We thank God by the amount of time we spend alone with God. We reveal how important another person is to us by the actual amount of time we give to them. How much time do you give solely to God by being utterly alone with Him and talking only to Him?

We thank the Lord by discovering what pleases the Lord. This comes by experiencing two things: (1) walking in the light (1 John 1:7) and (2) becoming acquainted with the ungrieved Spirit of God (Eph. 4:30). When we discern *what* pleases Him, we know better *how* to please Him!

We show gratitude also by our church attendance. It is no small insult to God's name when His people are not found regularly meeting together. "Let us not give up meeting together, as some are in the habit of doing, but let us encourage one another—and all the more as you see the Day approaching" (Heb. 10:25).

Excerpted from *Just Say Thanks!* (Charisma House, 2005).

It's About Heaven

Is there any news more wonderful than this: we are going to heaven! There is a sense in which the bottom line of the Christian faith is this: those who trust in Christ's death on the cross are going to heaven and not to hell. Martin Luther regarded John 3:16 as the "Bible in a nutshell." Those who believe in the Son will not perish, that is, will not go to hell. Those who believe in the Son will have everlasting life, that is, will go to heaven.

Too often the heart of the Christian message becomes clouded with what in fact are but secondary benefits of the gospel. For example, "We are so much better off here below." Or, "Our lives have changed. We are much happier than before. Even society is all the better when the gospel has made an impact." True. I know what people mean by that.

But the main reason Jesus died on the cross was to make it possible for us to go to heaven when we die. Believe it or not, Christianity is essentially about our death. The wages of sin is death (Rom.

> *If only for this life we have hope in Christ, we are to be pitied more than all men.*
>
> —1 Corinthians 15:19

6:23). Jesus came to reverse what Adam lost in the Garden of Eden. The gospel is essentially about this great reversal.

We will know a lot more about heaven five minutes after we've been there than all the speculation this side of heaven! We all have questions, such as: Will there be literal streets of gold? Will there be literal mansions in which we will live? How will we spend our time, that is, if time as we know it exists in some way? In a word: What will we be doing in heaven?

Whatever else is true, I am sure of this: among many other things, we will all spend a great deal of "time" in eternity thanking God for His goodness.

Excerpted from *Just Say Thanks!* (Charisma House, 2005).

Grieving the Spirit

In over fifty years of studying the Bible, one truth has alarmed me more than any other. You might think it has to do with standing before God at the final judgment. But, surprising as it may seem, it isn't that. The truth that alarms me most is the possibility of grieving or quenching the Holy Spirit without knowing it—the painless way in which the anointing can be lifted from me. When this occurs, because I know nothing whatever at first, I carry on as though nothing has happened.

It is possible for one who has experienced the precious anointing of the Holy Spirit to swiftly, painlessly, lose that anointing. I can displease the Lord and feel nothing.

> *And do not grieve the Holy Spirit of God, with whom you were sealed for the day of redemption.*
> —EPHESIANS 4:30

It is very possible that I could spend years doing what I presumed was God's will—preaching, teaching, witnessing, and being involved in church work—when God was hardly present in my efforts at all. I may even have the applause and respect of people the whole time, and they not have a clue I have moved ahead of Jesus.

It is a great mystery of the anointing of which one may be unaware—even though it is working most powerfully. On the other hand, one also may not be conscious that it has been lifted! When Moses came down from Mount Sinai, "he was not aware that his face was radiant" (Exod. 34:29). Yet Samson, who could tear a lion apart with his bare hands, was as weak as a kitten when the anointing left him—but he was unconscious of this until he tried to do what had seemed so natural the day before. (See Judges 14:6; 16:20–22.) The supernatural often seems natural to the anointed man or woman.

When the Holy Spirit is grieved, the anointing lifts. We usually feel nothing at the time. It isn't until some time later that we notice we have carried on out of habit or through the momentum of a natural gift.

Excerpted from *The Sensitivity of the Spirit* (Charisma House, 2002).

Confess It!

When we speak of unconfessed sin, what do we mean? It will be useful to consider David, the Old Testament king, and his adulterous relationship with Bathsheba.

We should note that, had David died during the two years before the prophet Nathan exposed his sin of adultery and murder, David would have been saved so as by fire. You cannot tell me that David was only saved *after* the prophet Nathan came to him. No, David was a saved man before.

David, you see, thought he had gotten away with it. Two years is rather a long time, but then he was sleeping well at nights. All was going well. But one day, there came a knock on his door, and the prophet Nathan exposed the whole thing. Nothing was ever to be the same again for David.

> *That if you confess with your mouth, "Jesus is Lord," and believe in your heart that God raised him from the dead, you will be saved.*
>
> —ROMANS 10:9

But God gave David a second chance, that is to say, his life was not finished. Had David been taken away during those two years after he sinned as he did, he would have gone to heaven without a reward. But God says, "David, would you like to start over?" and David, though it was the downward side of his life, began to trust the Lord again and God used him. Mark it: David will not be saved by fire on that Day. He showed himself to be a man of God after his repentance.

Maybe you feel that there is a skeleton in your closet and there is no hope of a reward in your case. You must deal with that; confess it. Do not go around telling people, but get it right. Stop it! There is time left; thank God you were not taken, for had you been, you would have been saved so as by fire. God has given you time. Thank Him for it.

Excerpted from *When God Says "Well Done!"* (Christian Focus Publications Ltd., 1993).

Losing His Presence

In this story, we are looking at young Jesus while He lived here on earth with His earthly parents. Nevertheless, this illustration from the life of Jesus illustrates the way in which the sovereign Holy Spirit may test our sensitivity to Him by not moving with us when we choose to carry on with our plans.

The occasion was not only the observance of the Feast of Passover, but it was also the *Bar Mitzvah* of Jesus. Although from birth Jesus was God as though He were not man, and man as though He were not God, Jesus was now being truly authenticated as the God-man—especially by Joseph and Mary, who knew the facts.

> *After the Feast was over, while his parents were returning home, the boy Jesus stayed behind in Jerusalem, but they were unaware of it.... When they did not find him, they went back to Jerusalem to look for him.*
>
> —LUKE 2:43, 45

But Joseph and Mary missed it. Apparently, the dialogue with Jesus and the teachers in the temple continued for three days—all without the knowledge of Joseph and Mary. Jesus was doing His Father's business.

What a pity that Joseph and Mary missed it. When the Feast was over, Joseph and Mary returned home. Jesus stayed behind, but "they were unaware of it" (v. 43). In other words, they sincerely thought Jesus was right there with them. Why? They presumed He would adjust to their thinking and plans. After all, it was—as far as they were concerned—time to go home. They did not see a need to adjust to Him. But He chose to stay behind.

Joseph and Mary moved on as if nothing had happened. Unaware that Jesus had stayed behind, they sincerely thought He was with them. If we discover that we have moved ahead of God and have left Him behind, we must go looking for Him. That is what Joseph and Mary had to do.

Once we have lost God's special presence, we can only find Him by initially returning to the place where we lost Him.

Excerpted from *The Sensitivity of the Spirit* (Charisma House, 2002).

Give Thanks to the One Who Remembers

God made a choice to remember, and He wants us to *choose* to remember! He wants us to hold Him to His own Word. Nehemiah prayed this way (Neh. 1:8). The psalmist prayed the same way: "Remember your word to your servant, for you have given me hope" (Ps. 119:49). Hezekiah prayed much the same way (Isa. 38:2). With His own Word we can pray so as to give God "no rest" until He grants our request. (See Isaiah 62:7.) We likewise pray with Habakkuk: "In wrath remember mercy" (Hab. 3:2).

> *Give thanks…to the One who remembered us in our low estate.*
> —Psalm 136:3, 23

The most depressing book in the Bible (to me) is the Book of Judges. The unthinkable things that are described in this book show that there is a precedent for the worst kinds of sin and wickedness. The bottom line of the Book of Judges is, "In those days Israel had no king; everyone did as he saw fit" (Judg. 21:25). But there is an ominous explanation that lay behind this folly—an even greater folly: (1) They "did not remember the Lord their God, who had rescued them from the hands of all their enemies," and (2) they "failed to show kindness" (Judg. 8:34–35).

God's promise to remember His Word is recounted again and again:

God remembered Rachel.

—Genesis 30:22

God…remembered his covenant.

—Exodus 2:24

For he remembered his holy promise given to his servant Abraham.

—Psalm 105:42

In other words, God keeps His promise to remember. He puts us on our honor to remember to be grateful. God kindly cautions us not to forget to be grateful. He puts it succinctly: give thanks.

Excerpted from *Just Say Thanks!* (Charisma House, 2005).

Find What Pleases the Lord

We learn what pleases those closest to us primarily by spending time with them. By trial and error we also discover things they like and dislike. When it is a relationship we really desire to develop, it becomes fun to make the other person happy.

But this is not always easy—even when we have known someone for years. For example, although my wife, Louise, has repeatedly said she doesn't like surprises, I never really believed it because *I* do like surprises. But after countless blunders I came to realize that she really means it! She wants to know the plans I have in mind for birthday or anniversary celebrations *in advance*, and I now adjust to her wishes. She has also had to adjust to many of my eccentricities—like having no heavy discussions late in the evening or in the morning before two cups of coffee!

> *Find out what pleases the Lord. Have nothing to do with the fruitless deeds of darkness, but rather expose them.*
> —EPHESIANS 5:10–11

The Lord has His own ways, too, and He wants us to know them and adjust to them.

We may think they are odd—at first—but the benefits of accepting Him as He is and adjusting to what pleases Him will result in great blessing and peace.

We have the wonderful advantage of having the whole Bible at our fingertips. This surely leaves us without excuse. And yet if we let the Bible replace the immediate witness, guidance, and voice of the Spirit, we quench Him in one stroke.

Unless we are careful, we will not only begin to take ourselves too seriously, but we will also fail to tune into the ways of the Spirit—simply because we already presume that we know them so well.

For we too must learn—by experience—what pleases the Lord. This means spending time with the Lord and developing a sensitivity to His ways. We must find out what pleases Him.

Excerpted from *The Sensitivity of the Spirit* (Charisma House, 2002).

Don't Quit

Can you think of any moment lately when you were glad Jesus had not come? If He had come, would He have found you complaining, criticizing, or ready to give up? Perhaps you know what it is to be lonely; perhaps you were passed over; perhaps you feel that life has passed you by; perhaps you feel it is unfair that you had to have the lousy wife or husband you have or the illness. Endure the trial with dignity.

But what is enduring with dignity? It means that at the Second Coming of Jesus, beware that you are not *questioning* God. Beware of bitterness against Him.

It also means do not be found *quenching*. That is trying to abort a God-ordained trial. Every trial has a timescale, and it will end. There is no trial given to you that is not common to man from which God will

> *Our God whom we serve is able to deliver us from the furnace of blazing fire...*
> —DANIEL 3:17, NAS

not make a way of escape. Now that is God's promise. It does not matter what the trial is. You may say, "This one is too big for me"—it is not. The devil will make you think it is too big for you, and you may think that you have found a loophole so you can complain. The trial will end, but if you try to end it before it is over, you will build a superstructure of straw.

As you read this you may be undergoing a trial greater than you imagined, and maybe no one has a clue what you are going through. You are almost ready to quit. *Don't!* Your endurance in this trial of your faith will bring praise, honor, and glory to Jesus Christ on His appearing. Dignify the trial even though your faith is tried by fire. *Do not* quit! You are the one who has an opportunity to have what Paul calls "reward."

Excerpted from *When God Says "Well Done!"* (Christian Focus Publications Ltd., 1993).

God's Ultimate Plan

Being born into a Christian home has its advantages, but it is no guarantee that a person will become a Christian. One of the saddest things I know is to be born into a Christian home where you have heard it all, and you let those precious years pass by without responding in your heart. What can you be sure of once you're a Christian? The first thing is this: God has a plan.

God has a plan for your life, and He knows what is good and what is right for you. It's easy for us to get impatient. All of us have something we want, and when we don't get it, we become impatient. Now what God may lead one person to do, He may not lead another to do. The worldly may call this "luck," but for the Christian, it just means God sorts things out.

> *"For my thoughts are not your thoughts, neither are your ways my ways," declares the* Lord.
>
> —Isaiah 55:8

God has a purpose. He has a plan for you; He has a providence for you. That means things will happen in your life where, unknown to you, God will be at work. There is an explanation for everything that happens. If you are a Christian, nothing happens to you without a purpose. You may not know the reason by tomorrow afternoon. You may begin scratching your head and asking, "Why did God allow this to happen?" Don't become bitter about anything, for one day you will see God had everything under total control.

Excerpted from *All's Well That Ends Well* (Authentic Media, 2005).

A Sensitive Spirit

If I am to be today's man or tomorrow's man—should I not want to ensure my anointing by focusing not only on the winds and fire, but also upon the sensitivity of the Spirit? Yes, we long to experience the fire as well as a mighty rushing wind in our church. But I believe that the way to power and more anointing is by being more sensitive to the Holy Spirit. I suspect that the Dove is the link to the fire.

The word *sensitivity* has two meanings. In essence, one meaning is "the capacity of being easily hurt." The other meaning is "the capacity for being aware of the needs and emotions of others."

> *The Spirit of the LORD will rest on him.*
> —ISAIAH 11:2

The second meaning, being sensitive to another's feelings, is a strength. We all need to develop in this area.

But when we speak of the sensitivity of the Holy Spirit, we must refer to *both* of these meanings. We may or may not think these qualities are very attractive in the Holy Spirit's personality, but like it or not, the Holy Spirit is like a turtledove—and flutters away where peace does not prevail. However, the Holy Spirit is equally sensitive to *our* feelings. The Holy Spirit is a gentleman.

There are two main truths I want to make clear. The first relates to the *sensitivity of the Holy Spirit*. This refers to how sensitive He is when He is grieved. If we can tune in to the sensitivity of the Spirit, we learn what grieves Him, how to avoid grieving Him, and how we must adjust to Him if we want His intimate company.

The second truth is the importance of developing a *sensitivity to the Spirit*. We must be tuned in to His active will, or voice. If we develop a sensitivity to the Spirit, we will hear Him when He speaks and thus avoid quenching the Spirit. In that way we can see the glory of God manifested in our lives and, hopefully, in the church.

Excerpted from *The Sensitivity of the Spirit* (Charisma House, 2002).

The God of Glory

If we want to see the glory of God, we should know something of the God of glory. I fear that an unhappy difference with so many of us, compared to Stephen, is that we are experts in speaking of the glory of God but not in seeing it.

What do you suppose was the first thing that crossed Stephen's mind when it came to describing God? Jesus said that out of the abundance of the heart, the mouth speaks. If you had to fill in the blank and come up with the one word, above all, that best describes the God of the Bible, what word would you use? The best single word to describe the God of the Bible is *glory*, and that is what Stephen said.

There is so much that we could say about this word. But the glory of God is the sum total of all His attributes, and I think after all is said and done, it comes down to two things:

- His mind: that is His will, what He wants, what He is up to—you could say the glory of God is the dignity of His will.

- It's the very way He manifests Himself, the way He chooses to reveal Himself.

When we get to know God, we discover that the greatest thing about Him is His glory, and we want to see that glory. What a sight it was that this man who could begin talking about the God of glory would in the end see the glory of God. He fell asleep. He lost his life over it. He lost the battle, but he won the war.

Excerpted from *The God of the Bible* (Authentic Media, 2002).

Adjusting to the Holy Spirit, Part I

Adjusting to the Dove is not easy. It is inconvenient. It requires making major changes in some of the habits that have never bothered us before. The question is, how far are you and I prepared to go in developing an acute sensitivity to the Holy Spirit's ways? I pray it will not be said of us, "They have not known my ways," as God said of ancient Israel (Ps. 95:10). By not knowing His ways, Israel forfeited her inheritance.

Adjusting to the Dove is welcoming His presence. It is also giving Him no cause to leave.

Let your gentleness be evident to all.
—Philippians 4:5

How do we welcome Him? For one thing, tell Him! Have you often addressed the Holy Spirit with these words, "Holy Spirit, I welcome You"? Do this. Tell Him He is most welcome. Doing this is, in my opinion, virtually the first thing we must utter to God—together with the prayer for the sprinkling of Christ's blood on us—every single morning of our lives.

You may say, "He already knows He is welcome." Really? Do you not think He would love to hear you tell Him this? When you visit someone, and that person says to you, "You are most welcome here," doesn't it make you feel good?

Is the Holy Spirit so sensitive that He needs to be told He is welcome? Perhaps. Most people, sadly, want little or nothing to do with Him. You can prove you are different by welcoming Him! You can develop a deeper intimacy with the Lord by talking to Him about the most obvious and simple things—just as you would do with a friend.

But welcome Him to come in the manner He chooses.

Excerpted from *The Sensitivity of the Spirit* (Charisma House, 2002).

Adjusting to the Holy Spirit, Part II

There are several ways in which He may test our willingness to welcome Him. He may gently suggest that your attitude toward someone is not right. If you push this thought to one side, the chances are that the Spirit may well unobtrusively slip away. You cannot be selective in the manner He may choose to come. When the Spirit departs like this, as I have been saying, you usually feel nothing at first. And yet you *do* feel something—righteousness in yourself that your attitude is justified.

> **The Lord is near.**
>
> —Philippians 4:5

I've been in that position a thousand times. I know what it is to feel so upset that *they* could do such a thing! Often I have conversations with myself, imagining what I will say to the other person. I rehearse what the other person did. "That can't be right," I keep saying. I even imagine that I hear God saying, "Of course that's not right." I start feeling good, as if God is on *my* side—*not theirs*. I tell myself that I sense the presence of the heavenly Dove. Wrong! If anything, it's a pigeon.

When I welcome the Holy Spirit I must take Him as *He* wants to come. He may flood my soul with joy and peace. He may highlight a verse as I read the Bible, showing me something I hadn't seen before. I love it when He applies the Word to a current situation in such a manner that I *know* what to do that day. I don't like it, however, when that Word instructs me to apologize to my wife—or a deacon, friend, or fellow minister—before I can feel great peace again.

Of one thing we can be sure, however. The *end result* of the Holy Spirit's manifestation provides considerable inner peace. Peace.

Excerpted from *The Sensitivity of the Spirit* (Charisma House, 2002).

Value the Kindness of God

Gratitude may be defined simply as showing that one values the kindness of God. It is a feeling, but it is more than a feeling. Gratitude is also demonstrated by what we *do*; it may be a sacrifice in that we don't have an overwhelming feeling. Sometimes we *feel* grateful; sometimes we do not. But we must always *be* grateful, whether or not we feel like it. We must *do* it, that is, demonstrate gratitude not only by words but also by deeds.

> *But when the kindness and love of God our Savior appeared, he saved us, not because of righteous things we had done, but because of his mercy.*
>
> —Titus 3:4–5

Gratitude shows that we set a value on God's kindness. "In order that in the coming ages he might show the incomparable riches of his grace, expressed in his kindness to us in Christ Jesus" (Eph. 2:7).

Sanctification is thus the process by which we are made holy. It is both a process and an experience. It is used in the New Testament, however, in more than one way. Sanctification is something that happens to *every* Christian.

Sanctification is progressive and is never completed until we are glorified. As Paul said, "Therefore, I urge you, brothers, in view of God's mercy, to offer your bodies as living sacrifices, holy and pleasing to God—this is your spiritual act of worship. Do not conform any longer to the pattern of this world, but be transformed by the renewing of your mind. Then you will be able to test and approve what God's will is—his good, pleasing and perfect will" (Rom. 12:1–2).

Moreover, sanctification is a never-ending commitment. If we "got it" completely along the way, we could forget about it from then on! But only glorification will mark the end of this life commitment. In the meantime, we demonstrate our gratitude to God for His sheer grace by holy living, self-denial, and walking in the light. Not in order to make it to heaven, but in thankfulness because heaven is assured.

Excerpted from *Just Say Thanks!* (Charisma House, 2005).

Becoming Vulnerable

Being vulnerable is not cowardice or being a "wimp." In fact, it is the opposite—it is being a tower of strength. It is what Paul means by becoming a *man* (1 Cor. 13:11). It is when you are so strong inside that you do not take yourself so seri-

> *For to be sure, he was crucified in weakness, yet he lives by God's power. Likewise, we are weak in him, yet by God's power we will live with him to serve you.*
>
> —2 CORINTHIANS 13:4

ously. *Vulnerability* means the ability to be hurt, being unprotected. Our friend Alan Bell says that love is "moving forward without protecting yourself." Becoming vulnerable is therefore the opposite of the sin of self-protection.

Jesus was the strongest man who ever lived. He had the power to stop the entire crucifixion proceedings. He proved that by manifesting only a degree of His power when the chief priests and soldiers came to arrest Him. The Word tells us that when the soldiers surrounded Him in the garden, suddenly dozens (some scholars think it was hundreds) all "fell to the ground" (John 18:6). But Jesus *chose* to be vulnerable.

Many marriages on the rocks could be healed overnight if both husband and wife would become vulnerable, stop protecting himself or herself, and stop pointing the finger.

Taking myself too seriously grieves the Spirit and robs me of anointing. The issue of "who gets the credit" paralyzes many ministers today—so many want to be noticed and given due recognition.

Many a person forfeits greater usefulness because he or she can't bear the thought of not getting deserved credit for something. Neither can many people tolerate someone else's getting credit for something they did themselves. I can understand this. But it is a wonderful inner release—and glorifying to God—to be utterly self-effacing and to abandon the praise of people. God can trust such a person with a wider ministry.

Excerpted from *The Sensitivity of the Spirit* (Charisma House, 2002).

Setting People Free

The ministry of emancipation is what Jesus and the Holy Spirit are all about. The problem is, we want to control things. I doubt there is a much greater sin than deliberately leaving a person in the bondage of guilt when it lies within our power to emancipate that person.

Emancipating another person requires several steps. We must:

- Forgive that person totally by refusing to tell what we know.

- Keep the person from feeling intimidated.

- Enable the person to forgive himself or herself.

- Let the person save face.

If you want to make a friend forever, let that person *save face*. Allow another a sense of self-esteem, a sense of dignity and self-worth. When Prime Minister Joseph of Egypt looked at his eleven scared brothers and said, "It was not you who sent me here, but God," he was letting each of them save face (Gen. 45:8). They had tried to destroy him twenty-two years before, and their guilt was unthinkably deep.

> *Welcome him as you would welcome me. If he has done you any wrong or owes you anything, charge it to me.*
> —PHILEMON 17–18

Joseph knew that. He set them free. "God intended it for good," he told them (Gen. 50:20). How that must have felt!

We can control people not only by guilt, but also by keeping them under our thumb in order to manipulate them. The Holy Spirit does not manipulate us—He sets us free. Many strong leaders (owing largely to their own insecurity) keep their followers under control by making them feel disloyal if they do not dot every *i* and cross every *t* as *they* would do. Such leaders, I believe, are in danger of quenching the Holy Spirit and robbing people of freedom. The Holy Spirit is in the business of emancipating, and when we enjoy His ungrieved and unquenched presence, we will *keep* it by giving up personal control of people.

We have the high privilege of *being Jesus to others*—setting them free.

Excerpted from *The Sensitivity of the Spirit* (Charisma House, 2002).

Be Faithful in Season or Out

If we collapse the moment the Lord withdraws His special presence, it suggests we haven't learned much. Whereas we dare not proceed without Him, sometimes we have no choice but to get on with our calling and make the most of the situation.

Preach the Word; be prepared in season and out of season; correct, rebuke and encourage—with great patience and careful instruction.

—2 TIMOTHY 4:2

I try to spend a certain amount of time every day in quiet before the Lord. In the perfect world I will feel His presence, read His Word with full assurance of understanding, and go out to do my job with great confidence. But it isn't always like that. In fact, it is not very often that I feel a great sense of God in my quiet time.

It is "in season" when God's special presence is *felt*; "out of season" is when He chooses to stay behind—to see if we will put into the practice the things we learned in His presence.

It takes greater faith and devotion to pray, trust, and obey when God is absent than when He is present. I suspect we please God more by being faithful "out of season" than by being faithful "in season." More faith is required "out of season."

There is a sense in which we can get emotionally tied to the Lord in an unhealthy manner. Jesus sent out the Twelve (Matt. 10:5–15). Later He sent out seventy-two others, during which He was not personally at hand for those who went out (Luke 10:1–12). They needed to be on their own, as it were, to put into practice what they had learned from Jesus.

The special anointing of the Spirit is much the same. I am required to carry on whether or not I *feel* Him present. If I didn't carry on, I would never go out much at all. I would also be demonstrating that I had not learned much from His presence and His Word at all.

Excerpted from *The Sensitivity of the Spirit* (Charisma House, 2002).

Are You Somebody's Thorn?

It is sobering to realize that *you* may be a thorn in the flesh to someone else. Has it dawned on you that you are another person's problem because of your particular personality? The problem is, of course, yours, but you unfortunately make it somebody else's as well. It may be the person who has to live with you, work with you, or deal with you from time to time. You force that person to have to walk on eggshells around you. He or she loses sleep because of you. How does that make you feel? Well, it sobers me to my fingertips, knowing that I may very well be another person's thorn in the flesh.

> *As iron sharpens iron, so one man sharpens another.*
>
> —Proverbs 27:17

Perhaps you are aware of your problem, but you say, "I can't help it. This is who I am." You have prayed about it often. But have you really tried to get help? You are never too old to learn as long as you want your problems solved.

So when you don't have a balanced personality, you have difficulty in getting along with people. You keep sticking your foot in your mouth. You keep rubbing people the wrong way. Only Jesus had the perfect personality. He also has the perfect combination of self-confidence and care for others. That is the ideal person: having the balance of self-confidence, concern, and care for others.

If your personality is your thorn in the flesh, then you should admit it. Be thankful if you can see that you have a problem.

A personality problem is not necessarily sin. It is because you are a sinner that you have it, yes, for nobody is perfect. And yet there is a point at which a personality problem becomes sin: when you excuse it and justify it. If you say, "Well, that's just me," that's when it becomes sin. It is sinful when you excuse yourself and do nothing about it.

Excerpted from *The Thorn in the Flesh* (Charisma House, 2004).

Seek Him in Big and Small Things

This is a wonderful proverb and a wonderful promise. "All your ways" refers to anything pertaining to us. Some people worry that they should not bother God with small things. But as Pastor Jim Cymbala puts it, "Don't worry about bringing small things to God, for with God everything is small!" It is much easier to bring the more difficult requests to God when we are in a daily habit of bringing *everything* to Him already.

> *In all thy ways acknowledge him, and he shall direct thy paths.*
>
> —Proverbs 3:6, kjv

One of the saddest moments in the life of Joshua came when the Gibeonites lied to and deceived Joshua and the Israelites. (See Joshua 9.) Before he died, Moses had warned the Israelites: "Make no treaty" with any of the inhabitants of Canaan (Deut. 7:1–2). But the Gibeonites ingeniously manipulated their way into Joshua's good graces, and before he realized what was happening, "Joshua made a treaty of peace with them to let them live, and the leaders of the assembly ratified it by oath" (Josh. 9:15). Soon afterward they realized they had been tricked. "But all the leaders answered, 'We have given them our oath by the Lord, the God of Israel, and we cannot touch them now'" (v. 19). Israel had the problem of the Gibeonites on their hands for years and years.

These difficulties happened because the Israelites "did not inquire of the Lord" (v. 14). Although they had the faithful means of knowing God's will at their fingertips, they bypassed this process and moved on without Him.

We do the same thing when we do not talk to God about everything. *Everything.* I have done things like accepting invitations and engagements I should have declined—all because I said yes too rashly. Often, when the time came to fulfill these obligations, I had to say, "Why did I agree to this?" I now pray more carefully over every little opportunity that comes my way.

It does not follow that every single time I fail to know God's will clearly, He lets me do something stupid. He has graciously overruled my haste thousands of times and bailed me out—or mercifully led me along. But I have now lived long enough to take seriously the matter of seeking the Lord earnestly and constantly in the big things and the small things.

Excerpted from *The Sensitivity of the Spirit* (Charisma House, 2002).

Do You Live by Feelings or the Word?

Feelings can be so deceptive. They are the product of all our wishes, fears, prejudices, and past experiences. We may develop a "sixth sense" of what is right and wrong that can be very misleading. Even worse, we can truly be led of the Holy Spirit one day and *think* we are the next—and be wrong.

Had you asked me prior to May 1982 whether we were trying to reach the poor, I would have honestly said, "Yes, but I don't feel *led* to emphasize that aspect of evangelism." My subjective feelings made me uncomfortable with reaching out to people like that.

But today I know I wasn't listening to the Holy Spirit. The Holy Spirit has spoken objectively in His Word—whether I liked it or felt drawn in that direction or not.

> *Those who are led by the Spirit of God are sons of God.*
>
> —Romans 8:14

I know what it is to give my subjective feelings priority over God's objective Word—and feel good about it. For a period of time, I, for the most part, dismissed having to concentrate on the poor. I justified my thinking on the basis that *others* have a special calling in that area of ministry—and I didn't. In one sense my thinking was correct, of course. However, because I was not listening to the Holy Spirit's desires in this matter, I was not making a sufficient effort to reach every kind of person, regardless of culture or background, with the gospel.

Our subjective feelings—more commonly known as our comfort zones—may camouflage as God's voice.

Regardless of whether we are helping the hurting, paying our tithes, or not keeping a record of wrongs, so often we make decisions based on what we feel or think. And we do this without realizing we have done anything contrary to God's thinking.

Excerpted from *The Sensitivity of the Spirit* (Charisma House, 2002).

Remedy for an Unhappy Marriage

An unhappy marriage hardly needs defining. We are talking about when you are stuck with spending the rest of your life with someone with whom you are not happy. It is a thorn in the flesh; it is painful. Paul said he prayed three times for his particular situation to be resolved. Perhaps *you* have prayed thirty-three times, or even three thousand thirty-three times, for your situation to improve. In your dreams, you saw only marital bliss. But, no, it has been anything but bliss. You have watched others separate, and you have envied them. Others get divorced and you think, *I wish that could happen to me*, but you have stuck it out. You are not happy.

> *Each one of you also must love his wife as he loves himself, and the wife must respect her husband.*
>
> —Ephesians 5:33

Can this actually describe a Christian? Yes. Does God truly want this in a Christian marriage? No. Have you said to yourself, *Is this all there is?* It is like going to that place on vacation when you say, "Is this it? I have looked forward to *this?*" So it is with marriage. Yet, if you put Jesus Christ first, this nightmare of a marriage can be the greatest source of blessing.

A wife must submit to a husband who is not very nice, and a husband must love his wife even if she, at the moment, may not seem lovable. This is the pattern. Husbands, love your wives. That means you must respect her, build her up, and care for her. This is the challenge to see whether you are a real man. Do you think you are a man merely because you can attract women? Or because of how strong or how good-looking you are? Do you want to be a real man? Then love your wife! That is what builds character.

No marriage is perfect. Most marriages can be saved, and you can fall in love all over again. Love Jesus Christ more than you love each other. Don't wait for the other person to get it right, and you may one day realize that that thorn is part of a rose, beautiful and fragrant.

Excerpted from *The Thorn in the Flesh* (Charisma House, 2004).

Doing Righteous Deeds but Disobeying God

I t is easy to get so busy in doing "righteous" things such as being active in church matters—and think that God must be thrilled. He may be nowhere near, but we carry on.

I think it is possible for God to be with us in one area and absent in another area at the same time. For example, He dealt with me in two significant areas: complaining and bitterness. The result was a fresh renewal of the Spirit in my personal life and public ministry.

But there is another area of my life where I was, I fear, a failure. It had to do with my role as a father. I was doing "righteous deeds"—preaching, praying, and,

> *And all our righteous deeds are like a filthy garment.... For Thou hast hidden Thy face from us ... But now, O Lord, Thou art our Father, we are the clay, and Thou our potter; and all of us are the work of Thy hand.*
>
> —Isaiah 64:6–8, nas

yes, fasting once in a while. Books emerged from the press. Some people claimed to be blessed by my preaching and writing. But I overlooked my family.

This illustrates why I believe it is possible to experience the presence of Christ and His absence at the same time. Strange as it may seem, God can show His face and hide His face at the same time. He can be with me powerfully in one aspect of my life, yet allow the Dove to flutter away in another.

You may ask me, "Why didn't God *tell* you to spend time with your family?" He did. I didn't listen. I carried on. And yet He has proved to be with me in my ministry generally. But we must be careful not to presume that God approves of all that we care and do merely because He is gracious to us in a particular area.

God isn't interested in our performance of certain righteous deeds—even though we enjoy doing them. He knows, and we must learn, that we often neglect what should be our priorities while concentrating on righteous deed-doing.

Excerpted from *The Sensitivity of the Spirit* (Charisma House, 2002).

Recognize the "Bruised Reed"

If I were to recount how often I have failed at this point, I fear that the number of times would almost overwhelm me with embarrassment. And yet there was a time in my life when I would not have even thought about this. But one day something happened that caused me to see and realize how insensitive I was to sensitive feelings around me. I am one who has been at home in the fast lane. I seldom suffered fools gladly and often thought, *That should not bother this person.* It was no small breakthrough that forced me to notice a bruised reed before my eyes. Learning to do so changed my life. I discovered that this verse means that God will not hurt the person already hurting—and I must not do so, either.

> *A bruised reed he will not break, and a smoldering wick he will not snuff out, till he leads justice to victory.*
> —MATTHEW 12:20

It's hard for me to think about how many times I caused the Dove to fly away by not being sensitive to the bruised reed. The *bruised reed* is a person who has been severely damaged—let down, deeply offended, deprived of love, misunderstood, neglected, criticized, or abused. These persons may have carried the bruise for many years, or it may only have been there for a short time. But as a result, they are crying out for love—desperate just to be accepted for once.

However, from a fear of not being accepted, they manifest behavior that turns others off. But that is just their way of revealing their bruise. Perhaps they are hypersensitive and not pleasant to be around. The list is endless of ways they may manifest their bruise. There are bruised reeds all around us. The chances are, you can find one when you look in the mirror.

We can become insensitive to the Spirit by not recognizing the bruised reed that God puts in our path. We are all bruised reeds, and when we begin to treat people as such, we will become just a little bit more like Jesus.

Excerpted from *The Sensitivity of the Spirit* (Charisma House, 2002).

Experiencing God's Presence

The manifestation of God's presence can be unveiled in more than one way.

Jacob felt the presence of God at Bethel, and he was *afraid* (Gen. 28:17). For some there is a bias in the direction of the fear of God, which, to them, proves that God is present. Some people are even uneasy with joy. *Fear* is their comfort zone. They have a ready-made theological rationale for not smiling and looking sad instead. When we don't have much joy, we can hide behind the convenient view that God's glory always produces a sense of fear. That feeling of awe was what people experienced as a result of a healing presence in Galilee (Luke 5:17, 26). They felt this immediately after Pentecost (Acts 2:43).

> *You will fill me with joy in your presence.*
> —Psalm 16:11

The angel of the Lord said to the shepherds, "I bring you good news of great joy" (Luke 2:10). As a result of Philip's preaching in Samaria, "there was great joy in that city" (Acts 8:8).

We must try to remain open to the manner in which God chooses to manifest His glory. We can become so firmly entrenched in our specific comfort zone that we fail to recognize the presence of God. At the end of the day, it is impossible to describe adequately the feeling of God's special presence—however it is manifested.

The special presence of God is greater than anything said about it. But you won't miss it if you haven't experienced it. And you can believe it's still present after it has departed. Yesterday's memory of His presence and today's expectancy that it will be present can make you think God is present when He isn't. It is an easy mistake to make.

This is why we should want to be more and more sensitive to the Spirit. As we are more and more sensitive to Him, we will more quickly recognize God's special presence—and His absence.

Excerpted from *The Sensitivity of the Spirit* (Charisma House, 2002).

The Stigma of the Anointing

At the end of the day the anointing will have a stigma. It will offend. John Wesley was offended by George Whitefield's preaching because it was done in the fields instead of in a regular church building.

> *Rejoice that you participate in the sufferings of Christ, so that you may be overjoyed when his glory is revealed.*
>
> —1 Peter 4:13

My congregation at Westminster Chapel was offended when I started our Pilot Light witnessing program on Saturday mornings. I had no idea of ever being a witness on the streets. I was always glad for somebody else to do that. It just wasn't my anointing—or so I thought!

But my thinking changed when I invited Arthur Blessitt to preach at Westminster Chapel in May 1982. The plan was for us to take pamphlets and questionnaires to nearby Page Street, knock on doors, and talk to people about the Lord. But we never made it. Arthur began witnessing to some youth who were standing in front of the chapel, and within a short time, several of them got saved.

Arthur said to me, "Dr. Kendall, I don't know where this Page Street is, but you don't need to leave the steps of your church. The whole world passes by here."

In that moment I had a vision. I saw a pilot light, like that in an oven, that stays lit day and night. I said to Arthur, "Why couldn't we have a ministry talking to passers-by right here outside the Chapel?" In that moment the Pilot Light ministry was born.

I never looked back—but the cost was terrific. All I had preached for the previous five years suddenly came under attack. The invitations to preach, which averaged one every day, came to a halt. Ministerial friends distanced themselves from me. Members of the Chapel began resigning their memberships right and left.

Those were hard days. But I have never been sorry I walked in the light God was giving me then. If you ask me, it was my finest hour. And yet it wasn't easy to have some of my best supporters tiptoe away from me because my obedience embarrassed them. It is part of the stigma.

Excerpted from *The Anointing: Yesterday, Today, Tomorrow* (Charisma House, 2003).

Deal With the Foxes in Your Life

When these things are present in my life, I have discovered that God's special presence is absent:

> ❧ *Self-pity.* Feeling sorry for myself always seems right at first, but I should never give in to it if I cherish the presence of the Dove.

> ❧ *Self-righteousness.* This is the identical twin of self-pity. I reflect on my obedience and imagine that God is giving me a little pat on the back.

> *Catch for us the foxes, the little foxes that ruin the vineyards, our vineyards that are in bloom.*
> —Song of Solomon 2:15

> ❧ *Defensiveness.* This is not merely being "touchy"; it is the natural instinct to resist any criticisms. It is the opposite of turning the other cheek (Matt. 5:39).

> ❧ *Seeking a compliment.* "Let another praise you, and not your own mouth; someone else, and not your own lips" (Prov. 27:2).

> ❧ *Listening to gossip.* I am not sure which is worse—telling another "the latest" or listening to it. It is hard not to listen, especially if it is delicious, bad news about someone I find threatening.

> ❧ *Talking too much.* "When words are many, sin is not absent, but he who holds his tongue is wise" (Prov. 10:19). John Wesley often said that for every hour we spend talking, we should spend two hours in prayer!

> ❧ *Rushing.* Getting in a hurry almost always moves me ahead of the Spirit. The Holy Spirit is not in a hurry.

> ❧ *Pointing the finger.* "Do not judge, or you too will be judged" (Matt. 7:1). Pointing the finger in judgment invariably includes keeping a record of wrongs—which the Bible advises us not to do (1 Cor. 13:5). Doing so will result in the departure of the Spirit's special presence.

When I come to terms honestly with the absence of God's special presence, I am more likely to be in a position to find Him.

Excerpted from *The Sensitivity of the Spirit* (Charisma House, 2002).

Prayer as Worship

If we follow His impulse, the Holy Spirit will always lead us to pray. Consequently, when the Spirit is absent, we will find excuses not to pray: "God understands. He knows I love Him. But I'm tired…I'm so busy…It's just not convenient now."

> *They devoted themselves to the apostles' teaching and to the fellowship, to the breaking of bread and to prayer.*
> —ACTS 2:42

When the Spirit is absent, our excuses always seem right, but in the presence of the Spirit our excuses fade away.

All prayer comes from the Spirit—be it disciplined prayer or spontaneous prayer.

We pray spontaneously, both privately and with other Christians, when we are suddenly aware of a great need in the world or the church. God often uses something external to bring the church to her knees. We ought to see it as the kindness of God when He allows trouble to drive us to prayer. In our individual lives, family tension, financial worries, or illness will do it.

We also pray spontaneously when there is an overwhelming inner pressure from the Spirit resulting in a vivid awareness of the Spirit's presence. When this happens within the church, people come from everywhere to be there.

What are the characteristics of this kind of spontaneous impulse to pray? There are four: time becomes unimportant; there is a caring for others (for example, in Acts 2:44); there is clear guidance; and there is unity (Acts 2:46).

The result of all of this is worship. We need to understand that worship is not just singing hymns, nor even consciously adoring God. Some people think that worship is limited to the moment in which one is saying, "God, I worship You." But this is a wrong idea. Worship is any activity that is carried out under the impulse of the Spirit of God. We are also worshiping God when we are praying for others or witnessing to others.

Excerpted from *Worshipping God* (Hodder & Stoughton, 2004).

The Road to Repentance Leads Back to His Presence

The journey back to where you find the presence of Jesus involves passing through some important stages, one of which is repentance. In part, repentance means admitting you were wrong. Unfortunately, you seldom come to the place of saying "I was wrong" until you are forced to do so. The last thing on earth a person wants to do is admit to being wrong. The natural inclination in all of us is to defend where we are and why. Unless we are forced out of our comfort zone, we will stay in it.

God has to get your attention before you will repent, and He gets it by making you see what you have lost. As long as you can feel you haven't really lost His special presence, you are going to carry on. There are two ways by which you are called to repentance.

> Then Hezekiah repented of the pride of his heart, as did the people of Jerusalem; therefore the LORD's wrath did not come upon them during the days of Hezekiah.
> —2 CHRONICLES 32:26

1. *You admit God's special presence is gone.* Rather than continue as though nothing happened, you repent.

2. *You get caught—exposed.* Someone discovers the truth. Someone "spills the beans." Public shame results.

If you do not admit that God's special presence is gone and repent, God resorts to the second plan—public exposure. When a person is forced to repent because of public exposure, the depth of the repentance remains an open question.

To be granted repentance is a gracious mercy of God. As the Word teaches us, we are "changed…from glory to glory" as a result of repentance (2 Cor. 3:18, KJV). When a renewed measure of His presence reveals your sin and leads to your forgiveness and greater ability to do God's will…you have received insight. The worst thing that can happen to a man or woman is to become stone deaf to the Holy Spirit, losing all sensitivity to His voice.

The way back is the way of repentance. It is admitting that you have lost the special presence of God and have been wrong in your thinking and presumption.

Excerpted from *The Sensitivity of the Spirit* (Charisma House, 2002).

God Is for You, Not Against You

Jesus cared about the sick. One of the first things said about Jesus in the New Testament is His care for the afflicted: "Jesus went throughout Galilee, teaching in their synagogues, preaching the good news of the kingdom, and healing every disease and sickness among the people" (Matt. 4:23). The sick came to Him, and healing them was much of His ministry. Even after He went to heaven, the ministry of healing continued. It is even mentioned in the very last chapter of the Book of Acts that the apostle Paul healed people on the island called Malta. The sick people came to him; he placed his hands on them and healed them, and everybody on the island was cured (Acts 28:9).

> *Is any one of you sick? He should call the elders of the church to pray over him and anoint him with oil in the name of the Lord. And the prayer offered in faith will make the sick person well; the Lord will raise him up. If he has sinned, he will be forgiven.*
>
> —JAMES 5:14–15

James says, "Is any of you sick? He should call the elders of the church to pray over him....If he has sinned, he will be forgiven" (James 5:14–15). Why did James say that? Because the healing ministry of Jesus was not over. God cares about our well-being—spirit, soul, and body. He still wants to heal you.

Sometimes sin and suffering *are* related. Sometimes they are so related that James actually said if one has sinned (meaning that if the illness they are praying for is traceable to sin), when the prayer of faith is offered, then the one who is healed will also have this sin forgiven. So James is showing the *possibility* of the connection with sin. This is why he says *if* one has sinned, he will be forgiven. And that's a big *if*, because it is implying that sin may not be the cause of illness at all. Do not let the devil accuse you or make you believe your illness is because of sin. However, if you have valid suspicion that it is, then, before God, ask for the elders of your church to pray for you.

Excerpted from *The Thorn in the Flesh* (Charisma House, 2004).

Seek His Face

One reason God hides His face is because He wants you to go looking for Him. By seeing what your reaction is when He hides His face, He can test your earnestness to seek Him.

Will you recognize the difference between the flow of your natural giftings and the flow of God's special presence? Will you discern the difference between a gift of the Spirit—which is irrevocable—and the intimacy that kindles holy fire?

> *My heart says of you, "Seek his face!"*
> *Your face, LORD, I will seek.*
> —PSALM 27:8

Are you sensitive to the Dove? Will the counterfeit do? Never! It is only a matter of time until you notice what you have lost when Jesus stays behind. When you see your loss, you must seek His face in repentance. But it's not enough merely to admit you've been wrong. That is only the beginning.

You must go looking for Jesus. It will take you outside your comfort zone to places you've never been. Remember that you can step out of a flowing stream, but you can never step back in at the same place. The flow moves on.

Familiar theology, liturgy, clichés, or styles of worship can be very common comfort zones. You may begin to look for Christ in your comfort zones, but what if He isn't there? Will you admit to this, too?

Seeking the face of the Lord is to settle for nothing but Him. It may require examining teaching you had previously dismissed out of hand. It may mean associating with people you once said you'd have nothing to do with. It may be singing choruses you previously felt were meaningless to you.

Once God has succeeded in getting your attention, you will have to repent and seek God's face without giving up until you find Him. The journey back may require a lot of humbling, sheer embarrassment.

Seeking God's face means settling for nothing but the special presence of God—and not stopping until you know you have found Him wherever He is.

Excerpt from *The Sensitivity of the Spirit* (Charisma House, 2002).

Finding Our Way Back to Him to Move Forward

Do we ever truly recover exactly what we lost? I believe the honest answer is both yes and no. Let me explain.

When we find our way back, the anointing to which we must return is virtually a *new* anointing. It is new because when we find it again, we must adjust to where it is and how it is manifesting now. Adjusting to the Dove is a lifelong process of agony and surprise.

Some of us take longer in our return *to* the anointing because the whole time we are looking for the return *of* the anointing. We are all prone to say, "The old wine is better."

Each of us tends to begin trying to recover the anointing in our most familiar spot—our comfort zone. But God is saying to us, "See, I am doing a new thing!" (Isa. 43:19).

One of the reasons God stays behind and allows us to move on without Him is that we will be forced to see the new and different ways He chooses to manifest His glory.

The Christian life is a continual series of events that lead us out of our comfort zone. These repeated transitions take us from the natural level to that of the Spirit. The irony is that even the new level of the Spirit will eventually become another comfort zone to us. It too will have to be left behind in some sense. Then we will be allowed to become settlers in heaven. Until then we must continue to adjust to the Dove and the surprising and unpredictable ways God challenges our faith.

Excerpted from *The Sensitivity of the Spirit* (Charisma House, 2002).

Fulfilling His Will in Our Lives

Do you believe that you are consciously in the will of God? God wants you to be in His will and to know what His will is. Paul's word followed the previous admonition: "Find out what pleases the Lord" (Eph. 5:10). When you find out what pleases the Lord—and then do it—you may be sure that you are in His will.

The inner testimony of the Spirit, which will always correspond to God's revealed will (the Bible), is sufficient to convey that you are in His will. If you are not in His will it is because you either didn't obey God's explicit Word, like Jonah (Jon. 1:1–3), or you moved ahead of Him, like Joseph and Mary (Luke 2:41–44).

> *Do what is right and good in the LORD's sight, so that it may go well with you.*
> —DEUTERONOMY 6:18

But "all's well that ends well," as Shakespeare put it. At the end of the day, after having a quarrel with the Lord, Jonah let God have the last word (Jon. 4:11). So it was with Joseph and Mary (Luke 2:51).

Both accounts have these ingredients in common—the people referred to were temporarily out of God's will but fully in it in the end. Is it possible to be out of the will of God and yet in the will of God at the same time? Yes. God permits things in your life that sidetrack you for a time. But it is part of His long-term strategy for your life. All that is permitted as to time and circumstance is redeemable.

Whether one has sinned grievously like Jonah or has run ahead of the Lord like Joseph and Mary, God does not desert His own. His aim in each case is to teach you His "ways"—if you will listen. As long as you can hear God's voice and accept His rebukes, it means you are not stone-deaf to the Spirit. Not only is God not finished with you, but the best is just around the corner.

Excerpted from *The Sensitivity of the Spirit* (Charisma House, 2002).

Peace Is Better Than Bitterness

When we are bitter, we delude ourselves into thinking that those who hurt us are more likely to be punished as long as we are set on revenge. We are afraid to let go of those feelings. After all, if we don't make plans to see that justice is done, how will justice be done? We make ourselves believe that it is up to us to keep the offense alive.

Make every effort to live in peace with all men and to be holy; without holiness no one will see the Lord.

—HEBREWS 12:14

That the devil's lie. We only hurt ourselves when we dwell on what has happened to us and fantasize about what it will be like when "they" get punished. Most of all, we grieve the Holy Spirit of God, and this is why we lose our sense of peace.

It is my experience that the quickest way I seem to lose inner peace is when I allow bitterness to reenter my heart. It's not worth it! I made a decision for inner peace. But I found that I had to carry out that decision by a daily commitment to forgive those who hurt me, and to forgive them totally. I therefore let them utterly off the hook and resigned myself to this knowledge:

- They won't get caught or found out.
- Nobody will ever know what they did.
- They will prosper and be blessed as if they had done no wrong.

What's more, I actually began to will this! I prayed for it to happen. I asked God to forgive them. But I have had to do this every day to keep the peace within my heart. Having been on both sides, I can tell you: The peace is better. The bitterness isn't worth it.

I have come to believe that the only way to move beyond the hurt and go forward in life is through total forgiveness.

Excerpted from *Total Forgiveness* (Charisma House, 2002).

Father, Forgive Them

We all have a story to tell. As you read this you may think it is impossible to forgive your unfaithful husband or wife. You may feel you cannot forgive your abusive parent. You may feel you cannot forgive what was done to your son or daughter. How can we forgive the church leader who took advantage of his position? What about the person who lied to us or about us, or the person who believed those lies? The list of potential offenses is end-

> *Jesus said, "Father, forgive them, for they do not know what they are doing."*
> —LUKE 23:34

less. Often closer to home, there are relatives and former close friends who have become enemies.

People experience real pain when they or someone they love is hurt by another person. It is often harder to forgive when the one who has been hurt is someone you love deeply, especially your child. I find it much easier to forgive what people have said or done to me personally than what they say or do to my children.

But it is still very hard to forgive those who have hurt us directly, especially when they do not feel the slightest twinge of conscience.

But remember, at the foot of Jesus' cross no one seemed so sorry. There was no justice at His "trial"—if you could even call it that.

What was Jesus' response? "Father, forgive them, for they do not know what they are doing" (Luke 23:34). This must be our response as well.

Excerpted from *Total Forgiveness* (Charisma House, 2002).

Beware of Yesterday's Anointing

I was brought up in the Church of the Nazarene, a denomination that was born in revival. There was an unusual anointing of convicting power on that church in its early days. They had what its founder, Phineas Bresee, called "the glory."

What was that? It was the anointing—an anointing that transcended their lack of education, money, refinement, and prestige. The presence of God was at times so powerful it seemed almost impossible for lost people to enter their services without getting converted. People who came to laugh and scoff ended up smitten and on their knees in tears before God. The services were frequently characterized by shouts of joy and people waving their handkerchiefs with inexpressible happiness.

> *I have given them the glory that you gave me.*
>
> —JOHN 17:22

In his last days old Dr. Bresee would preach from church to church one message: "Keep the glory down." Why? He knew that if they ever lost it they were finished.

If God had His way in our churches today, what would happen? I don't know. I know how He has worked in the past. The trouble is, our education, culture, and refinement stand in the way of the Spirit having His own way.

When the anointing lifts and the glory fades away, there are always those who sadly won't admit to the withdrawal of the Spirit. They continue trying to "work it up"—creating the shouting and manifestations that become pale imitations.

Once this happens, the glory becomes yesterday's anointing in two ways. First, God may not necessarily want His glory to be manifested in precisely the same way as it had been unveiled in a previous era. Yesterday's anointing was real enough, but it was for yesterday. Second, those who "work it up" are trying to keep yesterday's anointing alive, and the flesh becomes all too obvious. They are trying to relive what God was doing yesterday but may not have chosen to do today.

Excerpted from *The Anointing: Yesterday, Today, Tomorrow* (Charisma House, 2003).

The Ultimate Proof of Total Forgiveness

The ultimate proof of total forgiveness takes place when we sincerely petition the Father to let those who have hurt us off the hook—even if they have hurt not only us, but also those close to us.

I had come face-to-face with this reality, so I prayed for certain people to be forgiven. However, after a few moments, it was as if the Lord said to me, "Do you know what you are asking Me to do?"

I thought I knew the answer to His question, so I said, "Yes."

He then seemed to reply, "Are you now asking Me to set them free as if they had done nothing wrong?"

> That God was reconciling the world to himself in Christ, not counting men's sins against them. And he has committed to us the message of reconciliation.
> —2 CORINTHIANS 5:19

That sobered me! I needed some time to think, but while I pondered His words, the Lord reminded me of the many sins for which He had forgiven *me*. I became frightened of the possibility that He might reveal—or let come out—some of the terrible things I had done.

I then humbly prayed, "Yes, Lord, I ask You to forgive them."

Once more I needed a little time. Then the Lord seemed to say, "What if I forgive and bless *you*, RT, in proportion to how you want Me to forgive and bless *them*?"

By this time I was boxed in a corner, and I surrendered. I began to sincerely pray for them to be forgiven and blessed as though they had caused me no offense. But I cannot truly say that my prayer was particularly godly or unselfish.

This is, after all, the message of the New Testament: "But God demonstrates his own love for us in this: While we were still sinners, Christ died for us" (Rom. 5:8).

What impresses the world most is *changed lives for which there is no natural explanation*.

Excerpted from *Total Forgiveness* (Charisma House, 2002).

The Absence of Bitterness

Bitterness is an inward condition. It is an excessive desire for vengeance that comes from deep resentment. It heads the list of things that grieve the Spirit of God. (See Ephesians 4:30.) And it is one of the most frequent causes of people missing the grace of God. Bitterness will manifest itself in many ways—losing your temper, high blood pressure, irritability, sleeplessness, obsession with getting even, depression, isolation, a constant negative perspective, and generally feeling unwell.

> *See to it that no one misses the grace of God and that no bitter root grows up to cause trouble and defile many.*
>
> —HEBREWS 12:15

We must, therefore, begin to get rid of a bitter and unforgiving spirit; otherwise, the attempt to forgive will fail. It is true that doing the right things, even when you don't feel like it, can eventually lead to having the right feelings. But the very act of trying to do right shows that the bitterness is not as deep as it could be. In other words, if someone feels bitter but begins to put the principle of total forgiveness into action, it shows that he or she is not totally controlled by bitterness. Otherwise he or she wouldn't make a start in doing what is right.

The absence of bitterness allows the Holy Spirit to be Himself in us. This means that I will become like Jesus. When the Spirit is grieved, I am left to myself, and I will struggle with emotions ranging from anger to fear. But when the Holy Spirit is not grieved, He is *at home* with me; He will begin to change me into the person He wants me to be, and I will be able to manifest the gentleness of the Spirit. Relinquishing bitterness is an open invitation for the Holy Spirit to give you His peace, His joy, and the knowledge of His will.

How can we be sure that there is no bitterness left in our hearts? Bitterness is gone when there is no desire to get even or punish the offender, when I do or say nothing that would hurt their reputation or future, and when I truly wish them well in all they seek to do.

Excerpted from *Total Forgiveness* (Charisma House, 2002).

There Is No Fear in Love

Fear can cause us to do silly things. Our insecurity is what causes us to want people to stand in awe of us. We become pretentious; we try to keep other people from knowing who we really are and what we are really like. Sometimes I think the most attractive thing about Jesus as a man was His unpretentiousness. Jesus did not try to create an "aura of mystique"; even common people could relate to Him.

> *There is no fear in love. But perfect love drives out fear, because fear has to do with punishment. The one who fears is not made perfect in love.*
>
> —1 JOHN 4:18

In terms of prestige and power, Joseph had ascended as high as one could get. Had he so desired, he could have kept his brothers at a distance. But, no. That is not what Joseph did. He wanted them to feel no fear in his presence. He wanted to be loved rather than admired.

What Joseph wanted his brothers to feel is what Jesus wants us to feel about Himself and the Father. "Anyone who has seen me has seen the Father," said Jesus (John 14:9). If you had an abusive or absentee father, you may understandably have trouble relating to God as a Father. But there is no law that says we have to have perfect fathers before we can rightly relate to our heavenly Father. The perfect image for us to follow can be found in Jesus Christ—and it is also what Joseph was trying to convey to his brothers. Joseph did not require them to feel a trace of fear or show further how sorry they were before he forgave them; instead, he wanted them to love him and feel his love for them in return.

This is the kind of relationship that Jesus desires with us. He wants us to put us at ease in His presence.

When we have totally forgiven our offenders, we will not want them to be afraid either.

Excerpted from *Total Forgiveness* (Charisma House, 2002).

Dealing With Guilt

I sometimes think guilt is one of the most painful feelings in the world. My own greatest pain over the years has been guilt—and being reminded of my own failure, especially as a parent. If someone wanted to hurt me—to really and truly make me feel awful—all they would have to do is ask, "How much time did you spend with your kids in those critical years as they were growing up?" I am grateful that my children have totally forgiven me for my sins as a parent, but I still struggle with feelings of guilt for the mistakes that I made.

> *And now, do not be distressed and do not be angry with yourselves for selling me here, because it was to save lives that God sent me ahead of you.*
>
> —Genesis 45:5

Joseph wanted to set his brothers free. He did not want them to blame or be angry with themselves; he wanted them to forgive themselves. Forgiveness is worthless to us emotionally if we can't forgive ourselves. And it certainly isn't *total* forgiveness unless we forgive ourselves as well as others.

God knows this. This is why He wants us to forgive ourselves as well as to accept His promises that our past is under the blood of Christ. Joseph was trying to do what Jesus would do: make it easy for his brothers to forgive themselves.

God does that with us as well; He wants to make it easy for us to forgive ourselves.

God doesn't want us to continue to feel guilty, so He says, "Just wait and see. I will cause everything to work together for good to such an extent that you will be tempted to say that even the bad things that happened were good and right." Not that they were, of course, for the fact that all things work together for good doesn't mean necessarily that they were right at the time. But God has a way of making bad things *become* good.

This, then, is total forgiveness: not wanting our offenders to feel guilty or upset with themselves for what they did, and showing them that there is a reason God let it happen.

Excerpted from *Total Forgiveness* (Charisma House, 2002).

Saving Face

Y ou can make a friend for life by letting someone save face. I gather this is an Oriental expression, because for an Oriental the worst thing on earth is to lose face. Some have been known to commit suicide rather than lose face. But I have a suspicion that, deep down, we are all the same when it comes to losing face—none of us want it to happen. God lets us save face by causing our past (however foolish) to work out for our good.

Can you imagine the look on the faces of his brothers when Joseph said to them, "So then, it was not you who sent me here, but God" (Gen 45:8)? Reuben may have said to Judah, "Did we hear him correctly? Did he say that we didn't do what we did, but God did it instead?" To have believed a statement like that would have meant an unimaginable burden of guilt rolled off these men. It would have been news too good to be true.

> *So then, it was not you who sent me here, but God. He made me father to Pharaoh, lord of his entire household and ruler of all Egypt.*
>
> —GENESIS 45:8

For the one who totally forgives from the heart, there is little self-righteousness. Two reasons we are *able* to forgive are:

1. We see what we ourselves have been forgiven of.

2. We see what we are capable of.

When we are indignant over someone else's wickedness, there is the real possibility either that we are self-righteous or that we have no objectivity about ourselves. When we truly see ourselves as we are, we will recognize that we are just as capable of committing any sin as anyone else. We are saved only by God's intervening grace.

When we let people save face, we are doing what is right and just, not being merely magnanimous and gracious.

Excerpted from *Total Forgiveness* (Charisma House, 2002).

Pray for Those Who Hurt You

otal forgiveness involves praying for God's blessings to rain on the lives of your offenders. When you do this as Jesus intends it, you are being set free indeed.

To truly pray for the one who hurt you means to pray that they will be blessed, that God will show favor to them rather than punish them, and they will prosper in every way. In other words, you pray that they will be dealt with as you want God to deal with you. You don't pray, "God, deal with them." You don't pray, "Lord, get them for what they did to me." And neither is it enough to say, "Father, I commend them to You." That's a cop-out. You must pray that they receive total forgiveness, just as you want it for yourself.

> *But I tell you: Love your enemies and pray for those who persecute you.*
> —MATTHEW 5:44

To me the greatest inspiration to live in this manner is found in the life—and death—of Stephen. He is one of my heroes. When I read Acts 6:8–15 and consider the Holy Spirit's touch on his life, his enemies' inability to contradict his wisdom, the miracles he did, and his radiant countenance, I say to myself, *I'd give anything in the world for that kind of anointing.* His secret, however, emerged at the end of his life. While his enemies threw stones at him, he prayed—seconds before his last breath—"Lord, do not hold this sin against them" (Acts 7:60). And therein lies the secret to his unusual anointing.

I must add one caution: Never go to a person you have had to forgive and say, "I forgive you." This will be counterproductive every time unless it is to a person that you know is yearning for you to forgive them. Otherwise, you will create a stir with which you will not be able to cope. They will say to you, "For what?" It is my experience that nine out of ten people I have had to forgive sincerely do not feel they have done anything wrong. It is up to me to forgive them from my *heart*—and then keep quiet about it.

Excerpted from *Total Forgiveness* (Charisma House, 2002).

Mean What You Say When You Pray

I t may seem surprising to some that people who are not Christians can learn to forgive. I believe that there are degrees of forgiveness. A person who is not a Christian could demonstrate what may be called "limited forgiveness" and feel all the better for it. If a person is sufficiently motivated, he or she may achieve a great deal of inner satisfaction by overcoming bitterness. Mahatma Gandhi appealed to a sense of valor and heroism when he said, "The weak can never forgive. Forgiveness is the attribute of the strong." On the other

> Simply let your "Yes" be "Yes," and your "No," "No."
>
> —MATTHEW 5:37

hand, President John F. Kennedy said, "Forgive your enemies, but never forget their names." That is hardly total forgiveness!

The Bible urges us to forgive—totally.

I suppose that the fifth petition of the Lord's Prayer, "Forgive us our debts as we also have forgiven our debtors"—or, as put another way, "Forgive us our trespasses as we forgive those who trespass against us"—has made liars out of more people than any other line in human history. But don't blame Jesus for that. We should mean what we say if we choose to pray the Lord's Prayer. And Jesus did not say we had a choice; He said, "This, then, is how you should pray."

Jesus regarded this as the most important petition in His prayer. "Forgive us our debts" is obviously a plea for forgiveness from God. But then comes the following line (or possibly the big lie): "as we also have forgiven our debtors."

Just after the prayer is finished, Jesus goes on to say, "If you forgive men when they *sin* against you…" Jesus intended the meaning of *sin* when He said the word *debt*. It means "what is owed to God," and because you owe Him pure obedience, falling short of that means you are indebted to Him.

Excerpted from *Total Forgiveness* (Charisma House, 2002).

Being Honest About Bitterness

One way we walk in darkness is by holding bitterness in our hearts toward others—bitterness that creates confusion in our minds and oppression in our hearts. You may say, "Oh, but I *am* having fellowship with God." No, you're not. You just *claim* you are having fellowship with God if there is bitterness in your heart. And if we claim to have fellowship with God but walk in darkness, we lie.

> *If we claim to have fellowship with him yet walk in the darkness, we lie and do not live by the truth.*
>
> —1 John 1:6

Walking in darkness is the consequence of unforgiveness. When I don't forgive, I might spend hours a day in prayer, but I am not having genuine fellowship with God. If I can't forgive the person who hurt someone dear to me, I am walking in darkness. If I can't forgive the person who lied about me to others, I have lost my intimate relationship with the Father. I can even continue to preach, and people can even say, "Oh, what a wonderful sermon! You must be so close to God!" I could put on such an act that you would think that I am the holiest person in the church. But if I have bitterness inside or am holding a grudge against someone else, I am a liar.

Jesus tenderly shows us in the Lord's Prayer that we will be hurt, and we will be hurt by people we never dreamed of. We might think, *Well, yes, I can imagine so-and-so hurting me, but I never thought it would be you!*

Some people do wicked things with their eyes wide open, and these people surely have to know they have done something wrong. You may say, "Do I have to forgive even that?" The answer is yes.

There is a wonderful consolation, however: the greater the sin you must forgive, the greater the measure of the Spirit that will come to you. Welcome the opportunity to forgive the deepest hurt, the greatest injustice, and remember that a greater anointing is waiting for you.

Excerpted from *Total Forgiveness* (Charisma House, 2002).

Tears Will End in Joy

God knows how much we can bear, and even when He chastens in the sense of punishment, He knows how much each of us can take.

It is possible that right now you are going through something awful—a nightmare. Perhaps your nightmare is because you are obedient, and it is God's way of making you more like Jesus. "For it is commendable if a man bears up under the pain of unjust suffering because he is conscious of God" (1 Pet. 2:19). But the nightmare will end.

> *Weeping may remain for a night, but rejoicing comes in the morning.*
> —PSALM 30:5

When the nightmare is over, it could mean a *restoration of honor*. In Psalm 126:4 the psalmist said, "Restore our fortunes, O LORD." It could be that your good name is under a cloud. Maybe you have done something that has caused people to raise their eyebrows, or perhaps you have been falsely accused and you long to have your name cleared.

It could be a *restoration of holiness*. Are you a backslider? Have you been living in sin and just doing anything that your body feels like? It is not worth it.

It could be a *restoration of humility*: "Those who sow in tears, will reap with songs of joy" (Ps. 126:5). Perhaps you have become proud and unmanageable, and God has had to humble you.

Tears get God's attention. Hannah wept because she was barren. God gave her Samuel. The church whose womb has been strategically closed by God may find the answer in sowing in tears, that God could say, "Sing, O barren woman, you who never bore a child....For a brief moment I abandoned you, but with deep compassion I will bring you back" (Isa. 54:1–7).

Do you want to know the way back? It is the way of tears, sorrow that is true repentance. When you are sorry, the way to end the nightmare is to weep. God sees tears.

Excerpted from *Higher Ground* (Christian Focus Publications Ltd., 1995).

Forgiveness Is a Choice

Forgiveness is a choice we must make, and it is not a choice that comes easily. If it were easy, why do you think Jesus would mention it again after He finished the Lord's Prayer? He knows forgiveness is difficult. It wasn't easy for God to do what He did either, but He did it anyway. He sacrificed His Son, and He asks us to make a little sacrifice in return. You must make the choice to let your enemies off the hook and even *pray* that God will let them off the hook. When you do that and really mean it, *you are there.* He looks down from heaven and says good. But then you have to do it again tomorrow. You must make the choice and live it out. Love is an act of the will.

> *And when you stand praying, if you hold anything against anyone, forgive him, so that your Father in heaven may forgive you your sins.*
>
> —MARK 11:25

Making a choice to continue in unforgiveness shows that we aren't sufficiently grateful for God's forgiveness of our own sins. Perhaps we haven't taken seriously enough our own sin or our own redemption. Probably what we all want to say is, "Well, what I did wasn't nearly as bad as what they have done!" And that's where we are wrong! God hates self-righteousness as much as He hates the injustice that you think is so horrible, and He certainly doesn't like it when we judge. So if you must forget the sins of which God has forgiven you, at least remember that one of the most heinous sins of all is self-righteousness.

There is, however, another cause for unforgiveness: that we don't put a high enough value on our relationship with the Father. There should be nothing more important to us than our relationship with God. If you choose to withhold forgiveness from others, you are not putting a high enough value on things today that one day will mean everything to you.

Excerpted from *Total Forgiveness* (Charisma House, 2002).

Graciousness Is Spelled "N-E-E-D"

When Jesus said, "Be perfect, therefore, as your heavenly Father is perfect" (Matt. 5:48), He was setting the stage for a higher level of perfection than many Christians have even thought to strive for. What we see in Jesus' words, "Do not judge, or you too will be judged" (Matt. 7:1), is an example of this level of perfection—not the sinless perfection of Christ, but a level of maturity that allows us to have a true intimacy with God and a

> *Blessed are the merciful, for they will be shown mercy.*
>
> —Matthew 5:7

greater anointing. Being merciful is showing graciousness. Paul said, "Let your gentleness be evident to all" (Phil. 4:5).

The word *gentleness* in this passage comes from a Greek word that literally means "to be gracious." When you could throw the book at somebody but instead you show mercy, you are making the choice to be gracious.

One acrostic that I have found helpful is built on the word NEED. When speaking to or about another person, ask yourself if what you are about to say will meet his need:

Necessary—Is it necessary to say this?

Encourage—Will this encourage him? Will it make him feel better?

Edify—Will it edify? Will what you say build him up and make him stronger?

Dignify—Will it dignify that person? Jesus treated other people with a sense of dignity.

Judging is the opposite of graciousness. Being gracious is the consequence of a choice. Remember that any time you choose to judge, you are not being gracious. Judging someone else is actually uncalled-for criticism. That's what Jesus meant by judging. Criticism that is either unfair or unjust, *even if it is true*, should not be uttered. Remember, be gracious.

Excerpted from *Total Forgiveness* (Charisma House, 2002).

A Little Bit of Spirituality

God *could* throw the book at me at any time. But He *won't*—that is, unless He sees me pointing my finger at somebody else. Then God will say, "Sorry about this, RT, but I must step in and deal with you. You should know better." God Himself will see that I am judged if I judge others.

> *Let your conversation be always full of grace, seasoned with salt, so that you may know how to answer everyone.*
> —Colossians 4:6

It has often been said that a little bit of learning is a dangerous thing. Sometimes a little bit of spirituality is a dangerous thing as well, because one may be just spiritual enough to see what is wrong in others—and to point the finger. The true test of spirituality is being able *not* to point the finger!

You may say, "Well, I have to say something, or nobody else will!" So what if no one else does? The person you are judging doesn't want to hear it, so you are not really helping anyway. When he is judged, he usually will feel worse but not change his behavior.

Consider the atmosphere you live in when it is devoid of criticism. How pleasant it is when we all live in harmony! (See Psalm 133:1.) It is so sweet and so good. Now consider the pain that follows when someone is critical to you. If you don't like being criticized, don't criticize others! A lot of grief could be spared if people would learn to control their tongues.

Jesus Himself said, "But I tell you that men will have to give account on the day of judgment for every careless word they have spoken" (Matt. 12:36). That is enough to scare me into watching what I say!

Excerpted from *Total Forgiveness* (Charisma House, 2002).

God Hates Ingratitude

When Jonah went into Nineveh (a godless nation) with his message, "Forty more days and Nineveh will be overturned" (Jon. 3:4), the eventual result was that the king himself proclaimed a fast.

Is this because the king invited Jonah to his palace? No. Is it because the king left his palace to hear Jonah? No. It was because "the Ninevites believed God. They declared a fast, and all of them, from the greatest to the least, put on sackcloth" (v. 5). It began with the people. Today we use the expression "grass roots"—what ordinary people think and do. It was the people who "believed God." (It doesn't say they believed Jonah.) The consequence was that the news reached the king of Nineveh, and he got involved (v. 6). The fast in turn moved the heart of God, who had sent Jonah to Nineveh in the first place!

> *But Jonah was greatly displeased and became angry. He prayed to the LORD, "O LORD, is this not what I said when I was still at home? That is why I was so quick to flee to Tarshish. I knew that you are a gracious and compassionate God, slow to anger and abounding in love, a God who relents from sending calamity. Now, O LORD, take away my life, for it is better for me to die than to live." But the LORD replied, "Have you any right to be angry?"*
> —JONAH 4:1-4

> When God saw what they did and how they turned from their evil ways, he had compassion and did not bring upon them the destruction he had threatened.
>
> —JONAH 3:10

The whole scenario, then, was God's idea. He had looked upon a godless nation with graciousness by sending Jonah to them. The only ungracious person was Jonah himself who lost face because of his unvindicated prophecy.

God hates ingratitude. His undiluted wrath was displayed in ancient times because people who knew God did not glorify Him as God, "nor gave thanks to him" (Rom. 1:21). God notices our gratitude happily, but He also notices our ingratitude and our not remembering to thank Him.

Excerpted from *Just Say Thanks!* (Charisma House, 2005).

Judging Is God's Prerogative

Judging people is elbowing in on God's exclusive territory. This verse is quoted twice in the New Testament—in Romans 12:19 and Hebrews 10:30. That means that it is not *your* job! "That's my privilege," says God. Judging is God's prerogative, nobody else's. If we move in on His territory, God looks at us and says, "Really? You've got to be kidding." To move in on the territory of the eternal Judge will get His attention—but not the kind of attention we want!

> It is mine to avenge; I will repay.
> —DEUTERONOMY 32:35

The word *godliness* means "being like God," and there are certain aspects of God's character that He commands us to imitate. God wants us to walk in integrity. He wants us to walk in truth and sincerity. But there is an aspect of the character of God where there is *no trespassing allowed*, and the moment we begin to point our fingers at other people, we are on it—we are sinning. That aspect is being a judge.

If you and I are foolish enough to administer uncalled-for criticism, we should remember three things:

1. God is listening.

2. He knows the truth about us.

3. He is ruthlessly fair.

God has a way of exposing us just when we begin to think, *There is no way that could happen to me.* The Lord promises that equitable judgment will be administered. The word *equitable* means "fair" or "just." All of God's judgments are ruthlessly fair. At the judgment seat of Christ, before which we will all stand one day, for once in human history judgment will be fair.

Nearly every day we hear of the courts letting someone off, and we say to ourselves, "Where is the justice?" But God's justice is always fair. The question is, will it occur here in this present life or in the life to come?

Excerpted from *Total Forgiveness* (Charisma House, 2002).

How to Deal With Meddling

Jesus asks, "How can you say to your brother, 'Let me take the speck out of your eye,' when all the time there is a plank in your own eye?" (Matt. 7:4). He is assuming we are rational, sensible people who would immediately see through the inconsistency of meddling in another's affairs. The assumption is this: If we have no plank in our own eyes, it would not be unreasonable for us to offer help. But when we have a plank and still meddle, our fault is far worse than theirs. Meddling is always uninvited and almost always unwelcome.

> *A gentle answer turns away wrath, but a harsh word stirs up anger.*
>
> —PROVERBS 15:1

What if someone meddles in *your* life? How do you respond? Most of us find it hard to respond in a way that pleases God. First, He calls us to maintain a sweet spirit. Never forget: "A gentle answer turns away wrath, but a harsh word stirs up anger" (Prov. 15:1).

Second, we are to agree with them. Usually there is a little bit of truth in what a critic will say to us about us. Even if you can't find a way to agree, you can always say, "I see what you mean."

Third, we should thank them. This will not only defuse their irritation, but it will also enable them to save face should they be up to no good. In addition, we will avoid making an enemy unnecessarily in the process.

What we must never do when being confronted is to defend ourselves or try to impress them with how good or right we are. We must never seek to punish or get even or make them look bad. Ask them to pray for you! But do it in a noncombative manner, never sarcastically. Confess sincerely, "I need all the help I can get." The principles of total forgiveness should enable us to make friends, not lose them.

Excerpted from *Total Forgiveness* (Charisma House, 2002).

The Art of Forgiving and Forgetting

First Corinthians 13, the great love chapter of the Bible, is a perfect demonstration of the cause and effect of total forgiveness. The apex of this wonderful passage is the phrase found in verse 5: Love "keeps no record of wrongs." The Greek word that is translated as "no record" is *logizomai*, which means to not reckon or impute. This word is important to Paul's doctrine of justification by faith.

> [Love] is not rude, it is not self-seeking, it is not easily angered, it keeps no record of wrongs.
>
> —1 CORINTHIANS 13:5

For the person who believes, their faith is "credited" to them as righteousness (Rom. 4:5).

This is the same word used in 1 Corinthians 13:5. It is turned around in Romans 4:8, again using the same word: "Blessed is the man whose sin the Lord will never count against him." Therefore, *not* to reckon, impute, or "count" the wrongs of a loved one is to do for that person what God does for us, namely, choose not to recognize their sin. In God's sight our sin no longer exists. When we totally forgive someone, we too refuse to keep a record of their wrongs.

It must be clearly acknowledged that wrong was done, that evil took place. Total forgiveness obviously sees the evil but chooses to erase it. Before a grudge becomes lodged in the heart, the offense must be willfully forgotten. Resentment must not be given an opportunity to set in. The love described in 1 Corinthians 13 can only come by following a lifestyle of total forgiveness.

Love is a choice. It is an act of the will. When we learn to forgive and practice forgiveness, He rewards us with an incredible peace and the witness of the Spirit in our hearts.

Excerpted from *Total Forgiveness* (Charisma House, 2002).

Things to Be Thankful For

We show gratitude by respecting those God has put over us. Said Paul: "Hold them in the highest regard in love because of their work. Live in peace with each other" (1 Thess. 5:13). Moreover, "Remember your leaders, who spoke the word of God to you. Consider the outcome of their way of life and imitate their faith" (Heb. 13:7).

Thanking God is manifested by doing good works such as helping when it is needed. The King James Version refers to the gift of "helps" or, in the New International Version, "those who are able to help others" (1 Cor. 12:28). This can include such things as visiting the sick, the widow, those in prison, or the helpless (James 1:27). It includes feeding the poor (James 2:6, 14) or giving someone a ride to church. It may mean doing things in your church that nobody wants to do:

> *Let the peace of Christ rule in your hearts, since as members of one body you were called to peace. And be thankful.*
> —Colossians 3:15

cleaning up, helping with flowers, whatever needs to be done, or whatever makes your pastor's job easier and so that 20 percent of the people won't be doing nearly all the work.

For what are you grateful? If you cannot think of things to show how thankful you are, take the time to make a "praise" list!

Here are some suggestions to begin with: (1) for salvation: God sending His Son to die on a cross; (2) that He gave you faith; (3) your church—that person who had a hand in leading you to Christ; (4) your minister whose preaching and pastoring feeds your soul; (5) your job—your income; (6) your health; (7) the Bible; (8) what God is doing for you today and what He did for you yesterday. When you begin to count your blessings, you will see that the list is endless! For there is no end to the list by which we can demonstrate our gratitude to God.

Excerpted from *Just Say Thanks!* (Charisma House, 2005).

God's View of Marriage

Here we meet one of the most important things God has said in relation to the family: "I hate divorce." Why is this so relevant? We are living in a time when some newscasters, politicians, and many people who make headlines laugh at the family. The nuclear family, a husband, wife, and children, is God's institution. God loves the family, and His Word teaches the sanctity and permanence of marriage. This is something Dad drummed into me, and it is something that we should be drumming into our children. I thank God for a father who used to say to me, "Son, marriage is for life." Sometimes it made me afraid to go out with a girl, for I would find myself wondering if I wanted to marry her and be with her all my life. The idea of divorce was out of the question.

> *Has not the Lord made them one? In flesh and spirit they are his.... "I hate divorce," says the LORD God of Israel.*
> —MALACHI 2:15–16

And that is what Malachi is saying here. Jesus allows divorce in the case of infidelity, and the apostle Paul adds the case of desertion. What God is saying here through Malachi is what pleases Him best.

In Malachi's day this divine institution was being threatened just as it is today. It is my belief that the only hope for Britain, America, and the West at the present time, when marriage breakdown is bringing about a disintegration of the family and children grow up lacking sexual identity, is for fathers to be as strong as mine was. They would make a big difference, both as role models and through teaching. I believe that the lack of strong parenting, especially strong fathering, is one of the reasons for the ever-increasing homosexuality in the West, where it is even being taught in schools as a valid option. How that must grieve the heart of God. There is no hope for the family if this continues, and the only thing that will stop it is a massive turning to Christ. God's way is right. It is integrity.

Excerpted from *Between the Times* (Christian Focus Publications Ltd., 2003).

Let the Past be Past . . . at Last

When we say, "I'm sorry," and mean it, that's enough for God. He doesn't beat us black and blue and require us to go on a thirty-day fast to supplement Christ's atonement. He convicts us of sin to get our attention, but having done that, He wants us to move forward.

All accusations regarding confessed sin come from the devil. When you know you have applied 1 John 1:9, and you still sense

> *As far as the east is from the west, so far has he removed our transgressions from us.*
>
> —PSALM 103:12

an accusing voice over the past failure, mark it down: That voice did not come from your heavenly Father. It did not come from Jesus. It did not come from the Holy Spirit. It came from your enemy, the devil, who works either as a roaring lion to scare or as an angel to deceive—or both (1 Pet. 5:8; 2 Cor. 11:14). Never forget, perfect love drives out fear (1 John 4:18).

The sweet consequence of not keeping a record of all wrongs is that we let go of the past and its effect on the present. We cast our care on God and rely on Him to restore the wasted years and to cause everything to turn out for good. We find ourselves, almost miraculously, accepting ourselves as we are (just as God does) with all our failures (just as God does), knowing all the while our potential to make more mistakes. God never becomes disillusioned with us; He loves us and knows us inside out.

Having forgiven others, it is time to forgive yourself. That is exactly what God wants of you and me. It is long overdue: let the past be past . . . at last.

Excerpted from *Total Forgiveness* (Charisma House, 2002).

Why Do I Have Enemies?

When Jesus said, "Love your enemies," He assumed that we would have one or more, and most people do. Sadly, many, if not most of them, will be from within the community of faith. Certainly Jesus assumed this, and nothing has really changed. Much persecution comes from those who claim to believe in God as much as you do. And yet the issues between you may not be theological. You enemy may simply *not like you!*

> *God left him to test him and to know everything that was in his heart.*
> —2 Chronicles 32:31

The origin of such enmity may be explained almost entirely in terms of the flesh. For example, your enemy may just not be able to cope with your being the way you are or with your being on a particular side of a certain question or issue. It is usually no fault of your own.

They could be angry with God for blessing you or for putting you where you are. You have that prestigious job. It pays well. You are admired by your boss and the people in your office. God has blessed you with certain talents and gifts. There will always be someone who will be jealous and seek to bring you down. If you have been blessed with a good reputation, do not be surprised if someone resents it. Unfortunately, your enemy doesn't know that he or she is probably actually angry with God.

The ultimate reason you and I have an enemy is that it fits *God's purpose.* Why? It is what we need. It helps to humble us lest we take ourselves too seriously. An enemy shows us what we are like.

So don't be angry with your enemy! It is God who is at work on your heart!

Excerpted from *Total Forgiveness* (Charisma House, 2002).

Turn an Enemy Into a Friend

Have you a rival now? Is there somebody bugging you? Is there somebody needling you? Is there somebody trying to get your goat—or have they already got your goat? If you think long and hard about this, and you dwell on it, it could destroy you. There's no guarantee that the devil *will* overreach himself if we become full of self-pity and develop a judgmental spirit. It is then that the devil will be saying, "Oh, it's working! It's working!" Don't let that happen.

> *That is why, for Christ's sake, I delight in weaknesses, in insults, in hardships, in persecutions, in difficulties. For when I am weak, then I am strong.*
> —2 Corinthians 12:10

God trusts us in letting us have an enemy so that if we respond in the right way, we will be so much better off.

Satan works through our enemies to defeat us, but if we react without grieving the Holy Spirit, then the result will be that it will refine us, not defeat us.

Has it occurred to you that God would want reconciliation between you and your enemy? The heart of God is reconciliation. Here are three principles of reconciliation.

First, if reconciliation is delayed—that there is no chance of reconciliation at the moment—then be sure it's not your fault. Paul said, "If it is possible, as far as it depends on you, live at peace with everyone" (Rom. 12:18). Do everything that you can do to embrace that person.

Second, your enemy today might be your friend tomorrow. Be sure, therefore, that you show such love to that person now, for you may become friends later.

Third, pray for your enemy. How do you pray for them? You must not pray that God will deal with them or punish them, but you must pray for them to be blessed.

Excerpted from *The Thorn in the Flesh* (Charisma House, 2004).

Loving Your Enemies

Jesus instructs us to overcome our enemies, not by showing everybody how wrong they were, nor by matching their hatred with ours, but by loving them. This brings us back to the matter of choice. Love is not what you feel. Forgiving is not doing what comes naturally. It is often said, "You can't help what you feel." We therefore ask, does the choice to love involve repressing or denying our feelings? No. Repression is almost never a good thing to do. But love is a conscious choice

But I tell you: Love your enemies....If you love those who love you, what reward will you get?

—MATTHEW 5:44, 46

to forgive—even if you don't feel like it! If you wait until you feel it, you probably never will forgive. You must do it because it is right, because of a choice you have made that is not based on your feelings.

The paradox in total forgiveness is that it simultaneously involves selfishness and unselfishness. It is selfish—in that you do not want to hurt yourself by holding on to bitterness. And it is unselfish in that you commit yourself to the well-being of your enemy! You could almost say that total forgiveness is both extreme selfishness and extreme unselfishness. You are looking out for your own interests when you totally forgive, but you are totally setting your offender free.

Even the non-Christian understands the benefits of forgiveness in a physical and emotional sense. This surely leaves all of us without excuse. If a non-Christian is able to forgive others, how much more should the Christian follow a lifestyle of forgiveness?

As Christians we have no choice. We forfeit our fellowship with God and blessings here below when we don't forgive. If we have been forgiven of all our sins—and this includes even the sins we have forgotten about—how dare we withhold this from others?

Excerpted from *Total Forgiveness* (Charisma House, 2002).

Praying for Those Who Hurt You

Praying for the one who has hurt you or let you down is the greatest challenge of all, for three reasons:

1. You take a route utterly against the flesh.

2. Nobody will ever know you are doing it.

3. Your heart could break when God answers that prayer and truly blesses them as if they'd never sinned.

And yet Jesus' word to pray for such people is not just a polite suggestion. It is a command—one that may seem so outrageous that you want to dismiss it out of hand. Some see it as a lofty but unrealistic goal.

But this is not what Jesus means. He is commanding you to pray that your enemy will be *blessed*. If, however, you should pray that he or she will be cursed or punished instead of being blessed, just remember that is how your enemy possibly feels about you. After all, have *you* ever been

> *…and pray for those who persecute you…*
>
> —MATTHEW 5:44

someone's enemy? Have *you* ever done something that brought a fellow Christian to tears and brokenness? If so, how would you like that person to pray for *you*? That God will deal with *you*? That God will cause *you* to have an accident? Yet how would it make you feel if they prayed that you would be blessed and let off the hook? That you would prosper as if you'd never sinned? Would you not like that? "Do to others as you would have them do to you" (Luke 6:31).

Jesus wants a sincere prayer from you. It is like signing your name to a document, having it witnessed, and never looking back. You are not allowed to tell the world, "Guess what I did? I have actually prayed for my unfaithful spouse to be blessed." No. It is quiet. Only the angels witness it, but it makes God very happy.

Excerpted from *Total Forgiveness* (Charisma House, 2002).

The Mind of Christ Is an Attitude of Expendability

To take on the mind of Christ is to adapt an attitude of expendability. By attitude I mean perspective. Paul said he took upon himself "the very nature of a servant." Jesus saw Himself as a servant the whole time He lived. In a word: meekness. Quiet obedience, making no protest. It was a lifestyle. It was His pursuit.

> *Your attitude should be the same as that of Christ Jesus.*
>
> —PHILIPPIANS 2:5

This brings us to a question: Do we want the mind of Christ to be in us? How much do we want it? For Jesus it was a perspective, a passion, a pursuit. He lived this way.

Now, some may say, "Well, I did that once; I know what that is." But with Jesus it was an ongoing lifestyle, and we too are called to this lifestyle from now on. It is one thing to have a week of living like this; it's another to make it a lifestyle. Some may say, "I don't have to live this way now; I have paid my dues." We will never have the mind of Christ in us until this becomes a perspective that is a lifestyle with which we are going to live twenty-four hours a day, every day of our lives. No change!

To get a little closer to the meaning, we must look at what this attitude involves. Essentially, it is a self-emptying attitude. Jesus relinquished what rightfully belonged to Him. Are we like that? Are we always so concerned about our reputation that what people think of us is so important? Yet there is one who made Himself of no reputation.

We think ourselves so important—"Well, I've got to be there," "I'm needed," "What will happen if I'm not there?"—and we become sensitive and easily offended. We wear our egos—and our feelings—on our sleeves. Anything can upset us. This is because we do not think of ourselves as being expendable. But Jesus, who was the greatest gift there ever was to the human race, made no such claims. He humbled Himself even to death on a cross. Greatness is having this conviction of self-expendability.

Excerpted from *Meekness and Majesty* (Christian Focus Publications Ltd., 1992, 2000).

True Motivation

What do you suppose motivated Jesus? First of all, it was *reverence*. It was reverence for His Father. If you want to know something about the mind of Christ, I challenge you just to make a study of the Gospel of John and look at the relationship Jesus had with His Father. He put it like this, for example, in John 5:30:

> By myself I can do nothing; I judge only as I hear, and my judgment is just, for I seek not to please myself but him who sent me.

And then later in that chapter He said this, a verse that many years ago gripped me and I hope will grip you:

> How can you believe if you accept praise from one another, yet make no effort to obtain the praise that comes from the only God?
>
> —JOHN 5:44

If that kind of thinking will grip you, then you are a candidate to think about the mind of Christ.

All this will only make sense once there is embedded in you a true fear of God. All that a preacher or writer may say or expound will only become relevant if this is so. And that has to happen between you and God. As long as you are looking at someone else and hoping that you will be noticed by this person and are thereby

> Then I said, "Here I am—it is written about me in the scroll—I have come to do your will, O God."
>
> —HEBREWS 10:7

getting your motivation, then your motivation is phony and will not last. Perhaps you want your church leaders to notice your endeavors, and this drives you to carry on. But this cannot work. Something, sooner or later, has to happen so that your honor comes from God. That is all that matters. Then you are not looking to see who else notices you: you are consumed with the passion of wanting God to notice you, taking your orders from above.

Excerpted from *Meekness and Majesty* (Christian Focus Publications Ltd., 1992, 2000).

True Perception

Perception relates to our opinion and how we see things. Are you having a running argument with somebody at the moment? Arguing with your spouse? Having a problem at the office? You are just sticking to your guns on something and everybody but you can see that you are being ridiculous, but you say that you know that you are right. You are making the situation miserable by being a difficult person to work with. Is that possible?

> *Righteous Father, though the world does not know you, I know you, and they know that you have sent me.*
>
> —JOHN 17:25

Are you afraid to admit to the possibility that you could be wrong? Are you afraid of what might happen if you lost the argument? Do you worry about what other people would think about you if you gave in or someone just showed that you had gotten it wrong?

Now Jesus had a perception about Himself, that He *was equal with God*. But He did not think it necessary to hold on to that. In becoming like us He was not even omniscient. This may shock you, but He did not know everything. He admitted He did not know the day or the hour of His own coming. He had to learn.

In addition, Jesus *was right*. His opinion was infallibly right, but He even let that go. You say, "Well, I know I've got it right. I can't let it go." Jesus did. The amazing thing is that God Almighty did not even take Himself seriously, in this sense. That is your example, and yet you cherish your opinion. Why do you not just be like Jesus? He was right, and He let it go. You could be wrong, and if you are wrong, how much better that you let it go. By the way, if you are right, the truth will come out. It will win in the end. You do not have to do a thing about it. Let Jesus be your example.

Excerpted from *Meekness and Majesty* (Christian Focus Publications Ltd., 1992, 2000).

Put Away Childish Things

We expect children to behave in certain ways—to talk, think, and reason like children. We all recognize the sound of a child. For example, we don't expect a teenager to talk and act like a small child. Similarly, we can listen to people who claim to have been Christians for years and yet talk like a baby Christian. Immature speech in people who have been Christians for many years is to their shame, and Paul is challenging the believers over this.

> *When I was a child, I talked like a child, I thought like a child, I reasoned like a child. When I became a man, I put childish ways behind me.*
> —1 CORINTHIANS 13:11

Childhood is marked by a particular way of talking and also a particular way of thinking: "I thought as a child," said Paul. A child is the most selfish person that ever was. As far as he is concerned, the whole world revolves around him. He thinks only of himself and wants immediate gratification. He wants to be loved, but it never crosses his mind to be loving. And some of us, who have been Christians for quite some time, have never moved beyond just wanting to be loved, pampered, and encouraged. When will we take the responsibility and begin to grow up? If we are still waiting for others to show if they care about us, we need to start caring instead.

A third characteristic of children is shallowness. A child is easily influenced, is gullible, and has no discernment. This is why Paul says we should no longer be infants who are tossed about by every wind of doctrine.

So immaturity in Christians is just like the painless pursuit of childhood, characterized by baby talk, selfishness, and shallowness.

Rather, let us demonstrate the love of God through mature speech, selflessness, and discernment. As Christians, let us love one another and put away childish things.

Excerpted from *Just Love* (Christian Focus Publications Ltd., 1997).

Disappointed With a Word From God

Perhaps you have gone to church or to a Bible study hoping for a word from the Lord, and you have sat there thinking, *Well, so far God hasn't spoken to me. I don't know why I even came.*

Second Kings 5 tells the story of Naaman, who suffered from leprosy. He hears of the famous prophet Elisha through his wife's little Israelite servant girl. He makes all kinds of arrangements and finally goes to where Elisha is. But Elisha won't even come out to meet him! Naaman feels insulted. Here he is—a commander and an officer—and Elisha won't even greet him. Instead, the prophet sends a message (which Naaman doesn't like at all): "Go, wash yourself seven times in the Jordan, and your flesh will be restored and you will be cleansed" (v. 10).

> *Naaman's servants went to him and said, "My father, if the prophet had told you to do some great thing, would you not have done it? How much more, then, when he tells you, 'Wash and be cleansed'!"*
> —2 KINGS 5:13

Naaman goes away angry: "I thought that he would surely come out to me and stand and call on the name of the LORD his God, wave his hand over the spot and cure me of my leprosy" (v. 11). "How dare he insult me? Go to the Jordan and wash seven times?!"

Naaman's servants persuade him to believe that this really is a word from the Lord. Naaman goes into the Jordan once and comes out just like he was. The second time—still no change. When he goes in a third time, he thinks, *Well, I'll start getting better now.* But no. Even after the sixth time, there's no difference. But on the seventh time, lo and behold, he is healed completely!

It may be that God has given you a word and you don't like it. You want something else, some other word. Jesus said, "Whoever can be trusted with very little can also be trusted with much" (Luke 16:10). Accept what God has given you, and who knows what will happen in the end?

Excerpted from *When God Shows Up* (Renew Books, 1998).

True Success

To quote my friend Joseph Ton, "Success in the eyes of the world is how many servants you have. Success in the eyes of Jesus is how many people you serve."

God is looking for people who are willing to become servants, and we can expect that, like Jesus, we will be tested in that role to the extreme. Yet it is a great faith-builder, for one who is willing to be subordinate, and all that that means, must rely increasingly on God's faithfulness. So we must ask ourselves how willing are we to go in pursuit of God's standards rather than the world's, which will always be the reverse.

> *Though I am free and belong to no man, I make myself a slave to everyone, to win as many as possible.*
> —1 CORINTHIANS 9:19

Too often when we first come to God we are under the impression that God owes us something. We think we have bargaining power with God to ask Him questions and make Him answer us. Yet suddenly we begin to realize that we are nothing and that God owes us nothing. He owes us, if anything, a place in hell. It is at this point that we begin to say, "I subordinate myself to you."

Everybody you meet thereafter will be your superior in some sense. And this is why Paul said in Philippians 2, "Each of you should look not only to your own interests, but also to the interests of others" (v. 4). How humbling it is to accept authority from and be subordinate to one whom you think is less capable or qualified than you! How humiliating!

Yet the beginning of greatness is accepting authority. When the disciples asked for preferment, Jesus did not rebuke them. He just reversed the roles: let the greatest among you be the servant of the rest. This is just what Jesus did in His own life: He "emptied himself" and became a servant.

What we must ask ourselves, therefore, is to what extent will the marks of the bond servant, which characterized Jesus' life, be ours?

Excerpted from *Meekness and Majesty* (Christian Focus Publications Ltd., 1992, 2000).

The Promise of Gratitude

If we wait for circumstances to change before we heed God's command to rejoice, we may wait a long time! If then we begin rejoicing only when circumstances change—but only then, what kind of gratitude is that? If we promise to show gratitude, we can only make good that promise if we maintain a positive sense of being thankful no matter how adverse the circumstances.

What, then, is the consequence of rejoicing and showing thanks when you don't feel like it? It glorifies God. It shows a highly developed faith. It is observed by the angels. It is the greatest threat to our enemy, the devil. It shows how deeply we believe what we claim to believe. "If you falter in times of trouble, how small is your strength!" (Prov. 24:10). Rejoicing in the Lord, the proof of our gratitude, regardless of circumstances shows that we are genuine and that our faith is real.

> *In this you greatly rejoice, though now for a little while you may have had to suffer grief in all kinds of trials.*
> —1 PETER 1:6

What is more, it has an extraordinary way of moving God to act. This is the promise of gratitude. I never tire of reading or repeating the account of Jehoshaphat, king of Judah, who was told that a vast army was coming against him. Alarmed, the king called a fast for all the people. A prophet of God stepped forward. "He said, 'Listen, King Jehoshaphat and all who live in Judah and Jerusalem! This is what the LORD says to you: 'Do not be afraid or discouraged because of this vast army. For the battle is not yours, but God's'" (2 Chron. 20:15). Jehoshaphat and all the people fell down and worshiped. The battle began. There had never been a battle quite like it.

After consulting the people, Jehoshaphat appointed men to sing to the Lord and to praise Him for the splendor of His holiness as they went out at the head of the army, saying: "Give thanks to the LORD, for his love endures forever" (v. 21).

The result: God stepped in. The enemy was suddenly overturned.

Gratitude thus contains an inherent promise. The promise is, show thankfulness and you get God's attention. Show gratitude, and God gets involved. He is moved by praise and can't keep from showing it!

Excerpted from *Just Say Thanks!* (Charisma House, 2005).

Chosen by God

Why did God make you *you* and not somebody else? Do you think God misfired? Do you think that there are accidents with God? Do you not know that God had you in mind from all eternity and He shaped you in your mother's womb, overruling every experience you knew? It is all part of God fashioning you. For He has a purpose for your life, and He has given you something that is yours.

> *Who have been chosen according to the foreknowledge of God the Father, through the sanctifying work of the Spirit, for obedience to Jesus Christ and sprinkling by his blood…*
>
> —1 PETER 1:2

Your calling is irrevocable. This is the promise of a gift from God. It will not be something that you will lose. Something may be wrong with you, but your gift will be intact.

It is too easy to claim a false modesty in this. All of us who are in the body have been given a gift: you may be the eye, you may be the hand, you may be the foot, but the question is, how do you use it (1 Cor. 12:14–26)? Will you make others recognize it? To put it another way, suppose that you are right about something and you know it. You could, if you wanted to, by one word spill the beans and just vindicate yourself.

But what would Jesus have done? As we have seen, Jesus was God, yet He never thrust this upon anyone. They always saw Him only as a man. He revealed His deity to Peter, James, and John on the mountain when He was transfigured before them, yet even then He told them to keep it quiet. But Jesus was vindicated by the Spirit. The Spirit's witness was enough for Him, and the Spirit's willingness to show others who Jesus was, was enough for Him. He did not need to broadcast who He was.

He was always found where and when God wanted Him. We need to be found in the same place. Just to know that we are pleasing the Father should be enough. It is upon that goal that we must set our minds.

Excerpted from *Meekness and Majesty* (Christian Focus Publications Ltd., 1992, 2000).

R.T KENDALL

Perfect Parenting

No parent is perfect; that is what is so ironic about this title. Perhaps you think back to your own childhood and how your parents raised you. You

> *Our fathers disciplined us for a little while as they thought best; but God disciplines us for our good, that we may share in his holiness.*
>
> —HEBREWS 12:10

may want to go to your mother or your father and say, "You really made a mess of bringing me up!" Yet that's the way parents are. They do as they think best, punish when they lose their tempers, and scold their children in front of other people.

But only God is the perfect Father. God disciplines us for our good, and He doesn't make mistakes. Many of you have had an imperfect parent. Some of you can't call God Father because your only frame of reference for a father is that the man who fathered you wasn't very nice. Let me tell you something: if we have to have a perfect father in order to address God as Father—then no one would be able to do it. We are not supposed to look to our natural parents for the perfect frame of reference of what a father is supposed to be like. Look to Jesus. He is your frame of reference.

Let me say this: you and I need to remember God has a plan for our children as well as for us. The time comes when we have to release them. Maybe, after they are too old to discipline, we still want to point the finger and straighten them out. But perhaps you who have children need to join me in releasing them to God. He is the perfect Parent.

Excerpted from *All's Well That Ends Well* (Authentic Media, 2005).

God's Call to Humility

Have you ever noticed that the Bible never requires anything of us that the Son of God did not do Himself? The greatest hypocrisy in the world is putting demands on others that one would not do oneself. Everything that God asks of us, Jesus did on earth, yet we sometimes think when we first hear the call that it is something that we cannot bear to do because of the cost. This shows that our concern is merely with what we are going to have to relinquish and what our lifestyle would be like as a result. Indeed, that is our impulsive reaction the first time we hear any command from God. We are told that His commands are not heavy (1 John 5:3), yet we still think they are going to be. What we are told to do is to follow God's way. Indeed, only a fool would turn his back on a request God makes.

> *Do nothing out of selfish ambition or vain conceit, but in humility consider others better than yourselves.*
> —PHILIPPIANS 2:3

It does not matter what the request is; that is part of God's call to humility. That is emancipation, and it is worth it all, for everything that God requires of us is followed with commensurate grace.

Just as we are called by God to humility, so Jesus was called. You may have thought that it was not necessary for Jesus to do that. You may have thought Jesus was by nature meek and mild; after all, He did say, "I am gentle and humble in heart" (Matt. 11:29). However, I think that some people have the idea that Jesus was what we would refer to in America as "square." This is completely wrong.

Jesus was a real man. He became like us, and this is why the writer of Hebrews keeps talking about His humanity. Jesus was no "square" but showed His strength and power through what He endured. Jesus, in fact, was the most humble person that ever lived. Yet it was not a received humility: it was an achieved humility.

Excerpted from *Meekness and Majesty* (Christian Focus Publications Ltd., 1992, 2000).

Humbling Ourselves

Thinking of your own temptations, what are you facing in your own life at this moment? Could it be that you need to humble yourself? It is not a question of having it done for you. You must humble yourself. So we need to look at ourselves. Are you a strong-willed person? Do you have a reputation for proving your masculinity, your authority? Letting that image be tarnished requires humility. Or perhaps you can be a little difficult to get along with.

> *Go and humble yourself; press your plea with your neighbor!*
>
> —PROVERBS 6:3

Conversely, the opposite may be true. You may say, "I'm not a strong-willed person; I'm a weak-willed person." Does that make you exempt? That is just another form of pride, and you too need to humble yourself. Maybe the hardest thing you ever did was to accept responsibility and assert your input. It will take humility to do it.

None of us are humble by nature. There is no such thing. Even Jesus was not: He humbled Himself. There is a crucial difference, however, between our Lord and us in this connection. We are told that Jesus humbled Himself. In contrast, any humility that seems to flow from us is due to one thing: we have been humbled. Our humility, therefore, if you can call it that, tends to be passive: we are humbled involuntarily.

God sometimes allows something that brings us to our knees. It may be when our foolishness catches up with us and we are humiliated. We may not recognize it at the time, yet what is happening to us may be nothing but God judging us. It is painful to admit to that, and yet, if it is God so working, we have the example of David to show us humility. When David saw that God was going to judge him, he just said, "Let us fall into the hands of the LORD, for his mercy is great" (2 Sam. 24:14).

Excerpted from *Meekness and Majesty* (Christian Focus Publications Ltd., 1992, 2000).

Coping With Sudden Change

Did you ever wake up one day only to discover nothing is like it was? Everything has changed. You have different surroundings, different people around you, and a different outlook—and it happened almost overnight. It is as if the bottom of your life dropped out without any notice. You are having to cope with sudden change. That happened to Jacob.

Now there's more than one kind of change. There can be an unforeseen change for the better, and you are glad that nothing is like it was—you couldn't be happier; there can also be voluntary change—you made it happen. Yet, even though the change for Jacob was caused by external factors and he didn't ask for it, no doubt

> *Have no fear of sudden disaster or of the ruin that overtakes the wicked, for the LORD will be your confidence.*
> —PROVERBS 3:25–26

it had the inevitable effect of changing him inwardly in certain ways, and that for the better.

When we are living within the purpose of God, the trauma of unwanted change will improve us, and the day will come, sooner or later, when we will thank God for all of it, although at the time we couldn't be convinced that was possible. But for the most part, we don't like change, especially if everything has been going along fairly well.

Four things happened to Jacob in a very short period of time. Three involved deaths, and the fourth was a family tragedy. Jacob moved twice during this time. Psychologists say that the second greatest trauma in life is moving; the first is the death of someone close to you. Here, Jacob was experiencing both; coinciding with the deaths of three people very close to him was a change of place.

Why did all these things happen to Jacob? God brings us to a place that we have to face life without any tie to the past, so that we will get our pleasure, not from knowing who finds out about this or that, but from knowing that God is pleased with us.

Excerpted from *All's Well That Ends Well* (Authentic Media, 2005).

The Ultimate Goal of Obedience

Some people think that humility is the end in itself. Is it? Is humility the ultimate grace? I think there are those who just think that it is. They think, *If I can just achieve humility*, as if people will then say, "Ah, isn't he a humble person."

Humility is, in fact, the means to the end. Humility itself is not the ultimate goal; the ultimate goal is obedience to the Father. This goal can never be achieved without humbling oneself, because any obedience has to be achieved by humility.

> *Jesus gave them this answer: "I tell you the truth, the Son can do nothing by himself; he can do only what he sees his Father doing, because whatever the Father does the Son also does."*
>
> —JOHN 5:19

At the core of Jesus' humility was surrender. The word *surrender* means to yield to another; it means to resign or to relinquish. Jesus' humility was evident in His relinquishment of the form of deity. Without ceasing to be God He came to the earth and relinquished that ingredient by which men would see that He was fully God. Jesus constantly surrendered it to the will of the Father, and He kept saying, "By myself I can do nothing" (John 5:30). He could only *do* what He saw the Father do. He constantly yielded Himself to the will of the Father, and in the end He yielded to the authorities. He *let* them take Him. He could have called ten thousand angels; He would not even have had to do that. He was God and could have struck them dead. He could have let them see who He was. But no, He yielded to the authorities. He let them take Him to crucify Him.

We must ask ourselves, "Am I willing to subordinate myself, daily, to my heavenly Father? Am I willing to go before Him daily, and say, 'Father, I subordinate myself to You'?" If Christ was willing, then we should be, too.

Excerpted from *Meekness and Majesty* (Christian Focus Publications Ltd., 1992, 2000).

Vindication

The only solid vindication is what God does, and He will give it at the judgment seat of Christ. Judge nothing before that time. Lower your voices; keep all vindication in suspension and suspicion. One day, everybody will see the truth. Expect to be surprised how God does it and what the truth turns out to be.

But Jesus' vindication is the supreme vindication; He was given the highest place, and our worship throughout eternity will be, "Worthy is the Lamb, who was slain."

> *At the name of Jesus every knee should bow, in heaven and on earth and under the earth, and every tongue confess that Jesus Christ is Lord, to the glory of God the Father.*
>
> —PHILIPPIANS 2:10–11

That is what will give us our joy then. Do you think that you are going to get your joy by getting your name cleared? I do not say that there is not going to be some joy there, for the Lord promised it, but that will seem as nothing compared to the joy we are all going to have in worshiping Him, who came to this earth, who lived among men. He died on the cross, and nobody understood it. He was raised from the dead and still to this moment awaits the vindication He will have in the last day when every knee shall bow before Him.

We shall also bow, and whatever vindication we may have, whatever reward, whatever crown, we shall cast our crowns before Him. If that will be what will give us joy, then may it give us joy now, for this is our Lord's day of vindication. What the world will eventually see, we see now. We must worship Him—worship Him with all our hearts and know that this is His day.

Excerpted from *Meekness and Majesty* (Christian Focus Publications Ltd., 1992, 2000).

The Pain of Being Misunderstood

Y ou have been misunderstood, and it hurts. You feel in your heart that you are right, but no one else thinks so. It is a very painful thing. In fact, I do not know that there is anything more painful, and if you want vindication, it is a very real desire. I suspect that there is no one who does not have something in their background, some area of his life where he has been misunderstood or hurt. He just wants to have his name cleared in the eyes of maybe one or two.

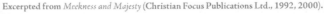

> *Jesus said to them, "Only in his hometown, among his relatives and in his own house is a prophet without honor."*
> —Mark 6:4

Here is the good news: God wants to vindicate us. Here is the bad news: it has to be done His way and in His time. A verse that confirms this is found in 1 Peter 5:6: "Humble yourselves, therefore, under God's mighty hand, that he may lift you up in due time."

There is no guarantee that vindication will come in this life. I personally have searched the Bible for an absolute promise that vindication will come earlier, and I think if there were one, I would have found it. God may do it: sometimes God will clear a man's name in advance of the judgment seat of Christ. That is His sovereign prerogative.

But He may want to continue using you while still letting some people question your service. You may have to live with that. Remember that Joseph was falsely accused of sexual advances to Potiphar's wife. Are you aware that Joseph's name never was cleared? The Bible does not say that his name was ever cleared, but God still went ahead and used him. No doubt Joseph would have wanted his name cleared. You may have a similar experience. But God might just want to use you and let this aspect be left as a sore spot in your life to keep you humble.

Our mind-set has to be that there is no promise of vindication in this life.

Excerpted from *Meekness and Majesty* (Christian Focus Publications Ltd., 1992, 2000).

Seeing With Eyes of the Spirit

I t is very easy for us to think that if only we could see Jesus we would believe and worship. Yet when we look at Jesus' resurrection appearances, this verse says that "some doubted." How could this have happened? How could anybody doubt when they are seeing? "Seeing is believing," it is often said, but here were some who saw but still doubted.

> *When they saw him, they worshiped him; but some doubted.*
> —MATTHEW 28:17

It is the Spirit of God who reveals Jesus and gives us the eyes to see as those first believers saw with their physical eyes. The more we have of the Spirit, the more we will see and feel what they felt.

C. H. Spurgeon used to say that the less we have of the Spirit, the more we will need to see physical things to inspire us. On the other hand, when we truly worship by the impulse of the Spirit, there is little need to have a lot of visual aids.

Even when Moses saw the burning bush, he was not allowed to get close or look for very long (Exod. 3:4–5). The Holy Spirit gave Peter the vision on the roof in Caesarea, but again, what was seen was upstaged by what was heard: "What God has cleansed, that call not thou common" (Acts 10:15, KJV). Therefore, even a vision, if one be so blessed by God, is not an end in itself, but the means by which the Word of God is magnified.

The ability to see with our spirit what God is doing and to hear with our inward ear what God is saying is God's gift to us. Some people can see more quickly than others what God is up to. It's not necessarily that the others are being rebellious or digging in their heels; they are just sincerely not sure. Does Jesus slap their wrist? No. He calls attention to what He is in Himself: "All power is given unto me in heaven and in earth." He just continues to speak. All we must do is continue to give all our attention to Jesus.

Excerpted from *Worshipping God* (Hodder & Stoughton, 2004).

Passing the Test

How you react to the trial you now have will determine whether you pass the test or not and hear God say, "Well done." Jesus passed many tests in His earthly life before He came to the final one, but along the way as He would pass tests, He would get the word from the Father, "You are my Son whom I love; with you I am well pleased."

Blessed is the man who perseveres under trial, because when he has stood the test, he will receive the crown of life.

—JAMES 1:12

That is what kept the Lord Jesus going. He actually had joy all along. Did you know that? It was not just the joy that was set before Him. He said in John 15:11, "I have told you this so that my joy might be in you and that your joy may be complete." All of us who have sat through exams of any sort know that sometimes you have to retake an exam or its equivalent. That is the way it is in this world. Only the very clever avoid this.

But in the kingdom of God it is not that way. Intellectual aptitude has nothing to do with it. Neither has social standing or class or any other worldly consideration. All Christians can go to the university of the Holy Spirit. The difficulty is that some have not even passed grammar school. They come up to a certain level and they blow it. Why?

They complained all the way through. They could not resist murmuring; they could not resist judging somebody, or gossiping, or holding a grudge. God gives them a trial on a silver platter, yet when it ends, they are still the same. But Jesus went straight through to the finals, because He never sinned along the way. He did it all in thirty-three years. God gives most of us more time than that. Three score and ten is the average: time enough for us to pass the tests that He sets before us.

Excerpted from *Meekness and Majesty* (Christian Focus Publications Ltd., 1992, 2000).

Seek First the Kingdom

There is nothing wrong with being middle class as long as the Christian who is middle class is not a snob and doesn't make somebody else feel second class. That was the danger in Corinth; there were middle-class people who treated the poor as second class, and that's why God dealt with them severely (1 Cor. 11:17–32). This warning came not because they were wealthy, but because they mistreated peo-

> *But seek first his kingdom and his righteousness, and all these things will be given to you as well.*
>
> —MATTHEW 6:33

ple. If a money problem is not your thorn in the flesh today, remember that it could be tomorrow. God can take it all away from you, just like that!

Are you greedy? Do you want to get rich? God in heaven may be folding His arms and saying, "Really?" Some Christians cannot get ahead financially. I am going to tell you why. God won't let them. He is doing them an enormous favor, because it could destroy them. They already have trouble handling money, and they think, *Well, if I had a little more.* Almost certainly, if they had a little more they would be deeper in debt. This is the way most of us are. We are, by nature, greedy. Very few people, truly, can handle money.

Matthew 6:33 was my father's favorite verse. He never became wealthy, but he was never really poor. Perhaps you reach out for those things that are to be added, but you have it all wrong. You may say, "If I had a little bit more, I will give more time to God. If I get this much money, then I am going to start going to church more and reading my Bible more." Wrong! You will never do it! Pursue righteousness and godliness *first.* Take time to be alone with Him, and *then* all these other things will just be there!

Excerpted from *The Thorn in the Flesh* (Charisma House, 2004).

"Jesus Is Lord"

Paul tells us that when the Father welcomed Jesus home, the same God who said that He would not give His glory to another has either changed His mind or has recognized Jesus to be very God of very God when He bestowed on Jesus the name that is above every name.

> No one can say, "Jesus is Lord," except by the Holy Spirit.
>
> —1 Corinthians 12:3

It is therefore a direct reference to the honor that Jesus deserved; it is a direct reference to the character of Jesus, as it was to the character of God. It is a direct reference to the reputation that Jesus deserved and to the worship that He deserved.

He, who stooped so low, now took upon Himself, from the Father, the honor above all others. He was given *the* name that was above every name. He who emptied Himself is now lifted up to the glorious ranks of equality with God and enjoyment of that dignity, which was ever His by right, but to which He never clung. Now it is given to Him as His personal possession. Meekness—majesty!

Paul puts it very carefully, showing that God gave the name for one reason only.

God has given this name to Jesus so that at the very name of Jesus, every knee should bow and every tongue confess that Jesus Christ is Lord.

The Holy Spirit confesses that Jesus is Lord. This is the very foundation of the Christian faith; it is the lowest common denominator. By this you may know whether or not you are a Christian. If you believe this, not in your head, but in your heart, you are a Christian, and if you do not, you are not. And if you do, it is not because you have done anything spectacular. As the psalmist put it in Psalm 115:1, "Not to us, O Lord, not to us but to your name be the glory." It is all because the Holy Spirit has enabled us to see the truth that Jesus is Lord.

Excerpted from *Meekness and Majesty* (Christian Focus Publications Ltd., 1992, 2000).

The Power of Love

The power of love is what it achieves. Stephen demonstrated the immense power of love when he prayed for the people stoning him: "Lord, do not hold this sin against them" (Acts 7:60). This is what God wanted—this display of love.

Stephen, who almost certainly was Paul's role model, is one of the most outstanding people in the Bible. I cannot express how much I admire him. And then I examine his mastery of the Old Testament (Acts 7) and observe how he put his opponents in the succession of the disobedient in ancient history: "You are just like your fathers: You always resist the Holy Spirit!" (v. 51). Although no one was immediately converted, never had one spoken with such power.

> *Love never fails.*
> —1 CORINTHIANS 13:8

The whole time he spoke, the pure love of God flowed through him and from him. The proof of this was his concern for them, not himself, when they were stoning him. He, therefore, fell on his knees and cried out, "Lord, do not hold this sin against them." It was a virtual reenactment of Jesus' prayer on the cross, "Father, forgive them, for they do not know what they are doing" (Luke 23:34).

The love of Christ that resided in Stephen got to Paul. Paul wasn't able to shake off the power of love that Stephen showed, which led to the conversion of the greatest of the apostles.

Again, when Paul and Silas were in prison, they sang praises to God, and love took over in extraordinary power. God affirmed them with such a violent earthquake that the foundations of the prison were shaken. Even the jailer was suddenly converted!

The one who is filled with love allows the omnipotent God to move in. It becomes vulnerable, that is, the one governed by love is losing the battle to win the war. That's power.

Excerpted from *Just Love* (Christian Focus Publications Ltd., 1997).

The Power of the Holy Spirit

This is a very interesting verse because it shows us that it was the Spirit that enabled Jesus to do all that He did. Similarly Luke 5:17 says, "One day as he was teaching, the Pharisees and teachers of the law...were sitting there. And the power of the Lord was present for him to heal them." It was the power of the Holy Spirit that enabled Him. This is a hint to all of us.

Jesus returned to Galilee in the power of the Spirit.

—Luke 4:14

Our difficulty is that we want to hold on to our own gift. I have observed time and again some very talented people not being used because they wanted the praise of men. I have noticed ministers who had a marvelous gift but who were so afraid that it would not be recognized that their pride destroyed them. It could happen to any of us.

But with Jesus, He actually said, "The Son can do nothing by Himself." That meant that the Holy Spirit vindicated Jesus. Do you want the Holy Spirit to use you? Then let the Spirit do it.

Jesus received His joy from the Holy Spirit. This is the reason He was able to handle rejection. This is why He could cope with the way people talked about Him. He did not take it personally; He knew it was their problem, because His joy was from the Spirit. Finally, on the Day of Pentecost, when the Spirit came down, Jesus was vindicated again.

This could happen because the essential function of the work of the Spirit is to point men to Christ. Therefore, after Peter said, "God has made this Jesus...both Lord and Christ," great conviction swept over the crowd and they began to cry, "What shall we do?" Three thousand were converted, and all because of the Spirit's power.

Excerpted from *Meekness and Majesty* (Christian Focus Publications Ltd., 1992, 2000).

Honoring God's Name

I do not make New Year's resolutions as such, but every year the first thing I write in my diary, on January 1, will be something with reference to my prayer for the coming year.

When I was preparing to write the book *Meekness and Majesty*, these were my words: "A jealousy for God's name." Jealousy is the sin nobody talks about, and it is most certainly the sin to which nobody admits. Yet how it crops up!

> *I am jealous for you with a godly jealousy.*
> —2 CORINTHIANS 11:2

Having a jealousy for God's name, however, will change our perspective. If I revere the name of Jesus, I will prefer the honor of the one whose gift is exalted. What I will not do is to say, "I've got a gift that is better than his. I don't know why they don't use me." If I honor His name, I will prefer the honor of the one whose gift is needed and whom God selects. God may select someone inferior to you, but if that is the way He chooses to honor His name, then you should honor it, because He must be doing it right; He has His reasons for it.

Maybe in your opinion that person does not deserve to be exalted, and maybe that is not whom you would have selected, but if that is what God has done, to show that you honor His name, you will make that subservient. You will make your name subservient to the honor of His name.

When we truly honor the name of Jesus, we will feel what God feels. We will hurt when He is hurt, and we will want only the honor of His name in the earth. We will say, "God, take me away, make me nothing, that Your name may be honored."

When we have this, we will begin to restore the honor of Jesus' name in the church and in the world.

Excerpted from *Meekness and Majesty* (Christian Focus Publications Ltd., 1992, 2000).

How to Handle Death

The first lesson the Bible teaches is that death is the punishment for sin. Death came into being only as the result of sin. If people had not sinned, they would have lived in their natural state forever. We have little idea what life would have been like, but what we do know is that when God created the world it was perfect:

> *For to me, to live is Christ and to die is gain.*
>
> —Philippians 1:21

He created Adam and Eve perfect beings in His own image and likeness (Gen. 1:27). But once they sinned, things were never the same again, and death came into the world. Paul put it this way: "...sin entered the world through one man, and death through sin, and in this way death came to all men, because all men sinned" (Rom. 5:12). Then, in Romans 6:23, he added, "The wages of sin is death."

The second important lesson is that death is not the end. Because God created us in His image, He gave us souls that are immortal.

The third lesson the Bible teaches about death is that God Himself became man to deliver you and me from its clutches. So not only did God become man, but also as man He died for us all!

Here we find what perhaps is one of the most stupendous claims about Jesus: He came to deliver us from the fear of death.

The fourth lesson we learn from Scripture is that Jesus, the God-man, rose from the dead so that we too may one day have a resurrection. Jesus offers eternal life to *everybody*. How, then, should you handle the prospect of your own death? My answer is, act now; do not wait until it is too late. It is so simple. Acknowledge before God that you are a sinner; thank Him for sending His Son into the world to taste death for you (Heb. 2:9), and receive Him as your Savior. You may then face death without fear, for you will have eternal life.

Excerpted from *A Vision of Jesus* (Christian Focus Publications Ltd., 1999).

God's Setup

Have you learned to recognize God's setup? This is what we find in John 6. When Jesus went so far as to say, "Unless you eat the flesh of the Son of Man and drink his blood, you have no life in you" (v. 53), that did it. "This is a hard teaching. Who can accept it?…From this time many of his disciples turned back and no longer followed him" (vv. 60, 66). They could not have felt more justified in their disgust. The offense in some people's anointing is camouflaged by God's setup.

> *"There is still the youngest," Jesse answered, "but he is tending the sheep." Samuel said, "Send for him; we will not sit down until he arrives." So he sent and had him brought in.*
>
> —1 Samuel 16:11–12

This way people can rationalize and dismiss the person and feel completely justified.

Eliab, Jesse's firstborn, was a setup. *This is surely the one*, even Samuel thought at first. But fortunately, Samuel kept listening to that voice he trusted.

If we are not truly tuned in to the voice of the Holy Spirit, we can let any prejudice of our own charm us to miss the authentic. On top of this, God may well test us by allowing our prejudice to overrule when someone's outward appearance is not up to what we think should befit an anointed servant of Christ.

Once Samuel saw David, despite his young age and utter lack of experience, the Lord said, "Rise and anoint him; he is the one" (1 Sam. 16:12). How did Samuel know? I only know that he knew. He knew he was not deceived. But he would not have been able to supply evidence to Jesse or anyone else that would be totally convincing. The pain of being today's man is that you can't convince another person of what you see unless the same Holy Spirit shows them as well.

Excerpted from *The Anointing: Yesterday, Today, Tomorrow* (Charisma House, 2003).

The Glory Assigned to Us

God has a glory in mind for each of His people, whoever they are. It does not mean that you will necessarily be famous or a great thinker, a great speaker, a singer, a politician, a doctor, an accountant, a theologian, or a philosopher. But God wants to make you great.

> *Do not be surprised at the painful trial you are suffering...but rejoice that you participate in the sufferings of Christ...for the Spirit of glory...rests on you.*
>
> —1 PETER 4:12–14

The point is that your glory is true spirituality, and it comes through tribulation: "We must go through many hardships to enter the kingdom of God" (Acts 14:22).

Although your gift under God could lead to greatness even in the eyes of men, it will never be apart from your receiving the glory that He has assigned for you. For God has a glory in mind for you, and that is that you become a truly spiritual person, an unpretentious person like Jesus.

When we are pretentious, people can see it, and yet we do not have any objectivity about ourselves. We go right on trying to pretend how clever, brilliant, sophisticated, or cultured we are, but that is not spirituality. Peter said, "Humble yourselves, therefore, under God's mighty hand, that he may lift you up in due time" (1 Pet. 5:6). Unless you become humble, unpretentious, and truly spiritual, all that you seek to do will not amount to a hill of beans.

When we speak of the glory of Christ, we are talking about the sum total or essence of all that He was; you could actually refer to Jesus, properly, as "His Glory." In fact, Paul called the very gospel that we preach, "the gospel of the glory of Christ" (2 Cor. 4:4).

Excerpted from *Meekness and Majesty* (Christian Focus Publications Ltd., 1992, 2000).

Universal and Unrivaled Glory

Having lived this life of humility and obedience, Jesus' glory is restored and enhanced in heaven. Yet God gave Him more: He gave Him universal glory, that every knee should bow and every tongue should confess that Jesus is Lord. There is coming a day in which all will be in perfect agreement, when everybody will be united.

At present we have places and people united in name only—the United

> *All kings will bow down to him and all nations will serve him.*
>
> —PSALM 72:11

Nations, the United States of America. But there is a day coming when every congressman...every United States senator...every Muslim...every Jew...every atheist...every journalist...every television commentator...is going to be in perfect agreement: every tongue will confess the same thing.

They are going to have to get down on their knees, all of them, because Philippians 2:10 says, "Every knee should bow." All men and women will be on their knees; every tongue shall confess that Jesus Christ is Lord. It is not a question of *if* we are going to do it; it is a question of *when*. But if we sacrifice our opinions for the opinion we will all have then, it brings Christ glory now.

There is coming a day when every angel will make way for the King; every human being will make way for Him, as will every demon. Then we will join the everlasting song and crown Him Lord of all. The same God who once said, "I am the LORD; that is my name! I will not give my glory to another" (Isa. 42:8), now says, "You bow to My Son and confess that He is Lord to My glory."

God calls you today to bow to Jesus and worship Him and, in so doing, give God the glory. In that day it will not be the preservation of your name or mine, but Jesus will have all the glory.

Excerpted from *Meekness and Majesty* (Christian Focus Publications Ltd., 1992, 2000).

"Call Me Your Father"

If we are serious about glorifying God, because it makes a difference, we can also glorify Him by perceiving Him as Father. The words that Paul uses point to this: "to the glory of God the *Father*" (Phil. 2:11).

Jesus called God "the Father." This is because they were of the same essence: there was therefore no alienation between Father and Son. However, He also told us to call Him Father. How can this be?

> *But you received the Spirit of sonship. And by him we cry, "Abba, Father." The Spirit himself testifies with our spirit that we are God's children. Now if we are children, then we are heirs—heirs of God and co-heirs with Christ.*
> —ROMANS 8:15–17

We can call God Father because Jesus' blood atoned for our sins. The blood that Jesus shed on the cross satisfied God's justice, and the consequence is that, because we are joint-heirs with Christ, we too can call Him Father.

Let me remind you of the most dazzling thought in the world: God loves you as much as He loves Jesus. Indeed, Jesus actually said it: "[You] have loved them even as you have loved me" (John 17:23). Now I do not have the vocabulary to convey how much God loves His Son. I only know that God spoke from heaven again and again saying, "This is my Son whom I love; with Him I am well pleased."

As a parent, I want my son and my daughter to know that they need never doubt my total and absolute love. Yet just as human parents want their children to know that they love them, so the Father in heaven wants you to know how much He loves you.

That is the kind of God we have. He does not tell us to stand in the cleft of a rock as He passes by; He just says, "Call Me your Father." By the merit of the blood of Jesus, all who love Him come before the God of the shekinah glory, the God and Father of our Lord Jesus Christ, the Father of glory, and He says, "This is what I am. Love Me for being what I am, because I love you as you are."

Excerpted from *Meekness and Majesty* (Christian Focus Publications Ltd., 1992, 2000).

He Gives Mercy to Those Who Ask

The only way to be saved is to ask God for mercy. Mercy, to be mercy, can be given or withheld and justice be done in either case. Jesus described two people in prayer: one a Pharisee and the other a tax collector. The Pharisee stood up and prayed about himself; the tax collector begged God for mercy. Jesus warned us, "For everyone who exalts himself will be humbled, and he who humbles himself will be exalted" (Luke 18:14).

> *I will have mercy on whom I will have mercy, and I will have compassion on whom I will have compassion.*
>
> —EXODUS 33:19

If you want to compare yourself with others, God says you are lost. You should climb down from your pride and say, "God be merciful to me a sinner. I'd be so grateful."

God sometimes chooses to withhold His mercy.

> Edom may say, "Though we have been crushed, we will rebuild the ruins." But this is what the LORD Almighty says: "They may build, but I will demolish. They will be called the Wicked Land, a people always under the wrath of the LORD. You will see it with your own eyes."
>
> —MALACHI 1:4–5

That is enough to bring us to our knees.

This word at the beginning of the Book of Malachi was an oracle to the people of Israel. You say, "Well that is fine. God loved Israel, but I am a Gentile." But in Romans 9:6, Paul says, "It is not as though God's word had failed. For not all who are descended from Israel are Israel." God has widened the family. His family was not to be continued along racial lines but through those who would hear the gospel and respond to it.

Because God decides to whom to show mercy, it makes all the difference in the world how we approach Him. He is sovereign. When you know that He has said, "I will have mercy on whom I will have mercy" (Exod. 33:19), you come to your knees and say, "Will You be gracious to me?"

Excerpted from *Between the Times* (Christian Focus Publications Ltd., 2003).

Thank God for Unanswered Prayer

I have lived long enough, as far as I can tell, to thank God for every unanswered prayer. That is, prayers prayed in the distant past. To be honest, I have offered prayers more recently that have gone unanswered (so far), which makes no sense to me at all. But I predict that, in the end, I will have no complaints. God is not only sovereign, but He is also loving and gracious. No good thing does He withhold from those who sincerely try to do His will in everything (Ps. 84:11).

You do not have, because you do not ask God. When you ask, you do not receive, because you ask with wrong motives...
—James 4:2–3

Unanswered prayer is still an enigma—that is, puzzling in the light of Jesus' words, "You may ask me for anything in my name, and I will do it" (John 14:14). God does not answer prayers that are not in His will. After all, John said, "This is the confidence we have in approaching God: that if we ask anything according to his will, he hears us" (1 John 5:14).

I can only conclude that asking in Jesus' name must in some direct sense relate to God's will. The enigma of unanswered prayer lies in the apparent incongruity between what seems good to us at the time and what God knows is good for us.

Sometimes our prayers, which seem so right, flow from a faulty theology. When we are in love with our theological assumptions—and can't imagine they could be wrong—we tend to presume God surely agrees with us! The disciples asked the resurrected Christ, "Lord, are you at this time going to restore the kingdom to Israel?" (Acts 1:6). It had not crossed their minds that Jesus never once planned to do anything of the kind.

Although unanswered prayer is a mystery, there is also an explanation. It is only a matter of time before we will be given an explanation. But it comes down to this: God has a better idea than that which we asked for.

Excerpted from *The Thorn in the Flesh* (Charisma House, 2004).

How Do We Weary God?

Y ou know the feeling of making another person tired, when you see that as you talk on and on they are looking bored and they want you to stop, but you are insensitive to it until the last minute and then you are so embarrassed. None of us want to do that to anyone. We don't want to tire people, and we don't want to tire God either. But how could we make God tired, especially as Scripture says, "The LORD is the everlasting God, the Creator of the ends of the earth. He will not grow tired or weary" (Isa. 40:28). According to that verse God cannot become weary, yet Malachi says that the Israelites have wearied the Lord with their words.

> *You have wearied the LORD with your words. "How have we wearied him?" you ask. By saying, "All who do evil are good in the eyes of the LORD, and he is pleased with them" or "Where is the God of justice?"*
>
> —MALACHI 2:17

If I made God tired by my words I would want to know about it. When Malachi told them that they made God tired, they wanted to know how they were doing it. So Malachi gives two reasons: one, by saying that all who do evil are good in the eyes of the Lord; two, by assuming that the Lord is pleased with them and by demanding to know where the God of justice is.

First, Malachi does not say that we weary God by our praying. The most encouraging passage in the Bible on prayer are the verses that follow where Jesus encourages us to ask for the same thing day after day until our prayer is answered (Luke 18:3–8).

Second, we do not weary the Lord by confessing our sins to Him. "If we confess our sins, he is faithful and just and will forgive us our sins and purify us from all unrighteousness" (1 John 1:9). Confessing does not just mean saying the right words in your head; it means being truly sorry.

Third, we don't weary God by pouring out our hearts even if we are complaining. "I cry aloud to the LORD; I lift up my voice to the LORD for mercy. I pour out my complaint before him; before him I tell my trouble" (Ps. 142:1–2). That does not weary the Lord.

Excerpted from *Between the Times* (Christian Focus Publications Ltd., 2003).

Fiery Trials Now Are Better Than Later

What are the differences between the fiery trial below and the one which is coming, when the Day will be revealed by fire?

> *If what he has built survives, he will receive his reward. If it is burned up, he will suffer loss; he himself will be saved, but only as one escaping through the flames.*
> —1 CORINTHIANS 3:14–15

First, the trial below may be hidden from others. You can be in a trial and nobody know it, but God's fire on that Day of days will bring us out into the open.

The second difference: the trial below is usually brought on by earthly pressures—people or perhaps our own stupidity. It may be persecution, it may be financial difficulty. But on that day the fire will be God's fire, without the need of earthly pressures to show where we are.

The third difference: the trial below sometimes comes by way of satanic attack. If you are in a fiery trial now, the devil is not far away. The fiery trial may be the devil attacking you, but on the Day of the Second Coming it will be entirely the intervention of God sending His Son with fire and glory. The devil will have no part in that trial.

The fourth difference, and perhaps the ultimate point that needs to be made, is that the trial below exposes where you are in our progress, but there's hope that when you fail, God will come a second time around and you will do better. But on that Day, it is final; there will be no repeats; that is it.

Do you see why James said, "Consider it pure joy, my brothers, whenever you face trials of many kinds" (James 1:2)? It lets us know how we are doing. It is preparation for the Day of days. It shows where we are spiritually, and it is showing that God is still working to get our attention. Our work will be tested.

Excerpted from *When God Says "Well Done!"* (Christian Focus Publications Ltd., 1993).

Marriage of the Word and the Spirit

If the Word and the Spirit come together in the church—both in emphasis and in experience—it will be the happiest event in many years. I believe this is God's heart. Yet it is my observation that most of today's church, speaking generally, emphasizes one or the other.

It can be argued that the two are always inseparable—for this is absolutely true. It is by the Spirit that we receive the Word; it is the Word that tells us about the Spirit. They cannot be separated.

> *Let the word of Christ dwell in you richly.*
> —Colossians 3:16
>
> *Be filled with the Spirit.*
> —Ephesians 5:18

But that is not the total picture. Jesus said to His disciples, "You are already clean because of the word I have spoken to you," yet He later breathed on them and said, "Receive the Holy Spirit" (John 15:3; 20:22). This shows that there was more that they needed, even though they had the Word.

Jesus said to the Father, "I gave them the words you gave me and they accepted them" (John 17:8), and yet He later told them to stay in Jerusalem until they had been "clothed with power from on high" (Luke 24:49). Jesus Himself was the Word made flesh, but He too received the Spirit (Luke 3:22; John 1:33ff).

When we say that the Word and the Spirit are inseparable, we need to state what we mean. It is possible that one may have the full and undiluted Word but have the Spirit in less measure. That was the disciples' experience prior to Pentecost.

Those who emphasize the Word are not without the Spirit, and those who emphasize the Spirit are not devoid of the Word. It is the degree to which one emphasizes the Word over the Spirit or the Spirit over the Word in one's own ministry that is the issue. What is wrong with either emphasis? Nothing. Each is exactly right. But neither is complete. It is not one or the other that is needed; it is both.

What is needed, in my opinion, is a remarriage of the Word and the Spirit—the simultaneous combination of both the Word and the Spirit in today's servant of Christ and the church. If the Word and the Spirit come together in your anointing and mine, then, as my dear friend Lyndon Bowring said, "Those who come to see [signs and wonders] will hear [the Word], and those who come to hear will see." That is tomorrow's anointing, my friend, and when it comes, the world will be awakened.

Excerpted from *The Anointing: Yesterday, Today, Tomorrow* (Charisma House, 2003).

Do We Want Revival?

Nearly all my life I have wanted to see revival. I am not sure when I first had an appetite for it, but I grew up in what was something of a revival atmosphere. In 1985, I introduced the first prayer covenant in Westminster Chapel. There were several petitions, and one of them was a prayer for true revival in the congregation. After five years we closed that covenant but revived the idea some years later. Then, instead of praying for true revival in Westminster Chapel, we prayed for the manifestation of God's glory in our midst along with an ever-increasing openness in us to the manner in which He chose to appear.

> *"Then suddenly the Lord you are seeking will come to his temple; the messenger of the covenant, whom you desire, will come," says the LORD Almighty. But who can endure the day of his coming?*
> —MALACHI 3:1–2

The people in Malachi's day prayed the equivalent of that prayer. Malachi tells them how their prayer will be answered, and I don't think it is exactly what they had in mind. What they wanted was for God to come in the way He had done in the great days of Solomon, when the temple was filled with His glory and all the nations stood in awe of Israel. They were looking not only for the honor of God's name to be restored, but also for the honor of Israel to be seen in the world. They sincerely believed that when God came that was how it would be. But things were to turn out very differently.

What is the difference? The difference is that praying for revival was, in a sense, setting a limit on God, and that is what these Israelites were doing. Praying for the manifestation of God's glory is not dictating to Him what He should do. Why did we use the word *glory*? The word *glory* is the nearest we can get to the essence of God. If we only had one word to describe the God of the Bible, that word would have to be the glory. He is a God of glory. We prayed that He would manifest His glory, and we did not tell Him how to do it. What is revival? Revival is certainly one manifestation of God's glory. Praying for such a revival is inviting God to be Himself. But we must not limit Him.

Excerpted from *Between the Times* (Christian Focus Publications Ltd., 2003).

Ingratitude Brings Spiritual Blindness

The failure of the nation of Israel to be grateful is the underlying explanation for their missing the promised Messiah when He came. You could never have convinced the ancient scholars in Israel that Messiah—a prophet like Moses (Deut. 18:15)—could turn up and not be recognized by them. The problem with both the Pharisees and Sadducees in Jesus' day was that they were arrogantly confident each would be the first to know it when that promised anointed One came.

But when He came—right under their noses—they missed Him entirely. They thought their judgment against Jesus was

> *But if anyone does not have them, he is nearsighted and blind, and has forgotten that he has been cleansed from his past sins.*
>
> —2 PETER 1:9

due to their brilliant minds, but that wasn't it. It was because they were blinded by the God to whom they had not given thanks.

Sadly, Israel had a long history of being ungrateful. And that ingratitude ultimately resulted in their being struck blind. Saul of Tarsus, a remarkable exception, said so:

> God gave them a spirit of stupor, eyes so that they could not see and ears so that they could not hear, to this very day.
>
> —ROMANS 11:8

The judgment of blindness upon Israel can be traced to their failure to be thankful.

If it is said that the people in ancient Israel dutifully maintained the sacrificial system, it has to be said also that they missed the point. In much the same way people can go to church in a self-righteous and dutiful manner and suppose they are worshiping God.

The final consequence of Israel's failure to remember was that they missed the greatest promise ever given. The penalty for ingratitude is incalculable. This is true for an individual, the church, and any nation.

Excerpted from *Just Say Thanks!* (Charisma House, 2005).

Keys for an Awakening

I believe that revival is coming—an unprecedented kind of outpouring such as was seen in Jonathan Edwards's day, unlike anything our generation has seen. This Awakening will come when the Scriptures and the power of God come together. Another way of putting it is that the Word and the name of God are rejoined—remarried. The two ways God unveiled Himself in the Old Testament were through His Word and His name.

> *Jesus answered and said unto them, Ye do err, not knowing the scriptures, nor the power of God.*
> —MATTHEW 22:29, KJV

What is the Word? It is what Abraham believed and so was saved. "Abraham believed the LORD, and he credited it to him as righteousness" (Gen. 15:6). It's the way people are saved still.

What about the name? It was first disclosed to Moses in Exodus 3:6, "I am the God of your father, the God of Abraham, the God of Isaac and the God of Jacob."

Like many of us, Moses wanted a rational explanation for what was happening. We all have our questions; however, some things are too deep to be revealed this side of eternity. God said simply, "Stop. Take off your shoes. You are on holy ground." (See Exodus 3:5.) And in that event, an event through which Moses would never again be the same, God unveiled His name—"I AM WHO I AM" (v. 14).

Unprecedented phenomena accompanied the unveiling of God's name. There were signs and wonders that defied a natural explanation. It began with the burning bush. It continued with Aaron's rod, which was turned into a serpent. It continued on with the ten plagues of Egypt, culminating with the night of Passover and the crossing of the Red Sea on dry ground.

How do we summarize the relationship of Word and name? The Word relates to God's integrity: His promise, His grace, His inability to tell a lie. It is the way we are saved. The name relates to His honor, His reputation, His power, and His influence.

In this coming awakening, God will use most those who have sought His face, not His hand, who have searched His Word and stood in awe of it.

Excerpted from *The Word and the Spirit* (Charisma House, 1998).

The Importance of Unity

We all have our opinions, and we are sure that we are right. And right beside our opinion is our pride.

If I hold to a particular point of view and you don't go along with me, then my pride is at stake. It is natural for me to want to be proved right, to have my opinion validated. So I want you to agree with me. If you do agree with me, I like it. But the fact that I want you to agree with my opinion doesn't make it right.

> Behold, how good and how pleasant it is for brethren to dwell together in unity!
> —Psalm 133:1, kjv

That's why the unity of the Spirit is a remarkable achievement. The unity of the Spirit is not natural, but it is supernatural; therefore, it cannot be explained naturally. What do I mean by that?

When we come across a person who is ambitious to achieve, we can understand this too, because this is natural. But unity of the Spirit is supernatural. It means that our natural ways, where we want to be heard and make our opinion felt, are not important, and we are willing to step down.

There are three observations that I suggest are important.

First, *blessing is given where there is unity*: "For there the LORD bestows his blessing" (Ps. 133:3).

Second, *unity is what Satan fears most*. He will come alongside like an angel of light to make you think something is of the Lord when it is not. The devil will remind you of every wrong in other people.

Third, *unity of the Spirit is not an optional matter*. Some of us have lost credibility with others because we have to have our way all the time, and people feel they are walking on eggshells because we are so difficult and so abrasive. What we need to do is to come to the place where the Holy Spirit is ungrieved, and we are willing to feel messy and not look so good; then the anointing will flow.

Excerpted from *Higher Ground* (Christian Focus Publications Ltd., 1995).

A Grateful Nation

God loves a grateful nation. Just as an individual cannot "out-thank" the Lord—for God pours out His blessing more than ever, so a nation cannot out-thank God either.

> *Save us, O LORD our God, and gather us from the nations, that we may give thanks to your holy name and glory in your praise.*
>
> —PSALM 106:47

Just as those individuals who praised God on Palm Sunday possibly did so selfishly, even ignorantly and for the wrong reasons—and God accepted their praise, so God accepts the praise of a nation that attempts to show gratitude to Him. It does not necessarily matter that every single person who participates in such thanksgiving is a faithful servant of God in his or her private life; God just notices a nation overall that makes any attempt to show gratitude to Him.

If this message were to get through to heads of state, even if they are not themselves born again, I believe most of them would still want to lead the nation to show thanks—if only for what it would do for that nation. God inhabits the praise of people. If any nation were to show thanks to the true God—the One who sent His only Son into the world, that nation would be so much better off.

We should be continually thankful to God (and remember to tell Him so) for laws in the land that outlaw theft, murder, and other crimes; for medical people, for the police, for firemen. God's common grace preserves a measure of order in the world. However chaotic things may seem from time to time—whether through terrorism or natural disasters, the truth is that if God utterly withdrew His hand from the world, all hell would break loose and civilization as we know it would end overnight.

It is in the interest of any nation to show reverence to the God of the Bible.

Excerpted from *The Word and the Spirit* (Charisma House, 1998).

This World Is Not My Home

Have you ever thought of your own thorn in the flesh as your having to live in a place that makes you unhappy? We all have to live somewhere until we die, and, for many, it is a case of very unhappy living conditions.

Unhappy living conditions might have been Paul's thorn, because he let us know that being an apostle was the opposite of living in luxury. I think of many big-name preachers today who live in luxury.

> *But in keeping with his promise we are looking forward to a new heaven and a new earth, the home of righteousness.*
> —2 PETER 3:13

Are you aware that there is a sense in which the main issue in both the Old Testament and the New Testament has to do with living conditions? The Old Testament stresses again and again the matter of living conditions. Moses and the people of Israel lived in a desert, and they were looking for a land flowing with milk and honey. The thrust of the Law was that if you obey, certain happy living conditions will follow. If you disobey, the opposite will follow. (See Deuteronomy 28:1–61.) In the New Testament, sadly, the Jews' expectation of the Messiah had to do entirely with living conditions. They thought that when Messiah came, He was going to change living conditions for them and set them free from Rome. This is why they couldn't cope with the thought that their Messiah would end up on a cross. Jesus warned them, for He knew exactly what they were thinking. He said in Luke 17:21, "The kingdom of God is within you." Jesus put it like that so they would understand that this present world is not all there is.

For some people, their only reward is in this present life. But Paul said, "For the kingdom of God is not a matter of eating and drinking, but of righteousness, peace and joy in the Holy Spirit" (Rom. 14:17).

Excerpted from *The Thorn in the Flesh* (Charisma House, 2004).

Boldness on That Day

How could anyone have boldness on the day of judgment? I myself would be reluctant to claim I will feel that way on the day of judgment. The thought of it, if I am honest, does not give me boldness, but soberness. Perhaps I will be given grace at that time. I certainly hope so, because the thought of that day is so terrifying that one cannot imagine having boldness. On the other hand, John said that the Lord's commands are not "burdensome" (1 John 5:3). I take that to mean that when we *think* God will throw the book at us, instead He will look down on us with tenderness and make us feel accepted because He knows our frame and remembers that we are dust (Ps. 103:14). Maybe more of us will have boldness on that day than we may think.

> *Herein is our love made perfect, that we may have boldness in the day of judgment: because as he is, so are we in this world.*
>
> —1 JOHN 4:17, KJV

John says boldness is possible because of perfect love that casts out fear. If we live in perfect love, or total forgiveness, there is no fear, and the result is that we do not need to be afraid when Jesus comes and is sitting on His throne.

I know one thing. If the Lord were to say to someone "Well done," that must be the ultimate in joy. It would be a joy greater than we can conceive. Unimaginable bliss. Relief. Wow! Whatever can be greater? I can tell you: nothing. It is the highest level of joy that ever was.

O Lord, may it happen to all my readers and to me—on that Day.

Excerpted from *Pure Joy* (Charisma House, 2006).

True Reward

Did you know that Jesus was motivated by *reward?* I hear people say, "Don't talk to me about reward. I don't want reward; I don't want recognition. I am just a humble servant of God. I am going to do it because it is right." By saying such things you are trying to upstage Jesus. And I marvel at this. Jesus as a man was motivated by reward.

He knew there was joy out there, and He was waiting for it. He knew too that He would get it then, not now.

> *Well done, good and faithful servant! You have been faithful with a few things; I will put you in charge of many things. Come and share your master's happiness!*
> —MATTHEW 25:23

For, you see, the reward is not here below. Sometimes God does reward us on earth. He can do it, but if that is your motive, then again it is not right. The reward that motivated Jesus was that which was beyond this life, and He was willing to wait until He got to heaven. And this mind of Christ, the motivation of Jesus, was waiting for the reward in heaven.

Do we know what kind of reward it will be? Well, I cannot be sure; this matter of reward is a great mystery to me.

I do not know whether it is a literal crown that Paul spoke of receiving (2 Tim. 4:8). I do not know, but I suspect the grandest moment of all would just be to hear Jesus say, as we find in the parable of the talents in Matthew 25, "Well done." I want that "Well done." I cannot imagine anything greater than that. I will do anything I know to get it.

Excerpted from *Meekness and Majesty* (Christian Focus Publications Ltd., 1992, 2000).

How Do We Turn Away From His Decrees?

God's accusation in this verse is that "you have turned away from my decrees." What does the word *decree* mean? A decree is a judgment or decision. In Psalm 119 there are seven words that can be used interchangeably: *law, statues, pre-*

cepts, decrees, commands, word, and *promises.* All these refer to the revealed will of God. When people come to me asking how they can know God's will, I tell them it is in the Bible. If you were stranded on a remote desert island with only five pages of

the Bible, there would be enough in those five pages, wherever they came from, to give you a glimpse of what God wants of you and how He wants you to live your life.

Two final points: how these people wandered and how they could come home. They wandered because they turned away from God's Word. How do you turn from God's Word? First, you stop praying. You can remember days when you took time to pray, but then you became busy, busy, busy. You think that God understands that you were too tired to pray, but eventually not praying doesn't seem to bother you any more. Next, you stop reading the Bible. The devil doesn't want you to read the Bible, and he will come up with every reason why you don't need to. He'll make you keep putting off regular Bible reading until you find yourself in a most precarious state.

Then you begin to yield to temptation. Now what is temptation for some may not be temptation for another. You begin to yield to temptation, and by this time you feel too ashamed to pray and read the Bible. The fourth thing that happens is that you return to a life not dissimilar to what you were converted from. At first that bothers you, but after a while you become anesthetized to it and you almost feel at home even though you are a long way from home. That is how you wander from God.

Excerpted from *Between the Times* (Christian Focus Publications Ltd., 2003).

How Do We Make Our Way Back Home?

How do we make our way back home? First, you have to recognize where home is. It is the center of God's will; it is those decrees, statutes, precepts, laws, word, promises, and statutes. The Bible tells you what God wants and how to live your life. That is how you begin to find your way back home. Second, admit how far from home you are. Don't play games with yourself. Admit you have become cold inside, that your attitude is not right. Third, know that God loves you. And even if you are a backslider, you are still loved. God, who made you so that you will only be happy when you are in His will and utterly miserable out of it, is asking you to come home. Fourth, you have to admit what is wrong. It is coming to terms with what you know is true. Sometimes it can be helpful to pour your heart out to another Christian, but the main thing is that you sort it out with God. Fifth, you need to ask for mercy. When you ask for mercy you know you have no bargaining power. You can't snap your finger and tell God that He has to do this for you.

> "Return to me, and I will return to you," says the LORD Almighty. But you ask, "How are we to return?"
>
> — MALACHI 3:7

Years ago, when Louise and I, with TR and Melissa, went back to Ashland, Kentucky, on vacation, I couldn't wait to go to the house in which I lived from the age of four until I was seventeen, the year my mother died. But when I found it, I discovered the owners had changed the house all around. I thought, *How dare they do that!* It wasn't home. You can't go back to things in this world, but you can come back into the will of God, and He will bring you home.

Excerpted from *Between the Times* (Christian Focus Publications Ltd., 2003).

Welcome Home!

During the era of President Theodore Roosevelt, who was famous for big game hunting in Africa, a Southern Baptist missionary completed forty years of Christian service in Africa. The missionary sailed from Africa to New York and heard a band playing as the ship was coming into the harbor. He was so excited! He couldn't believe it was happening, that his friends had brought a band to welcome him home. Tears filled his eyes as he quickly worked his way down the exit of the ship to walk down the gangplank. Suddenly a security man stopped him and spoke officiously, "Step back, sir." The old missionary waited while President Roosevelt, who had been on a big game hunting trip, was the first to disembark. As it happened, the old missionary was the last person to leave the ship.

> *But our citizenship is in heaven. And we eagerly await a Savior from there, the Lord Jesus Christ.*
> —PHILIPPIANS 3:20

He put his suitcase down as he stood on the dock. The band that had been welcoming the president of the United States had dispersed. Nobody was there to welcome the returning missionary home—not a soul. The old man made his way to a modest hotel in New York and fell to his knees as soon as he entered his room. "Lord," he cried, "I've served You for forty years in Africa, and no one welcomes me home. President Roosevelt spends three weeks hunting, and they have a band playing for him." The Lord then whispered to the old missionary, "But you're not home yet."

One day Jesus will welcome us home. There is coming a day when we will see for ourselves what John saw—the New Jerusalem "coming down out of heaven from God" (Rev. 21:2). That will be our eternal home, and one day we will be home never to move again.

Can you imagine how thankful we will be then? The bliss cannot be described now, and I wonder if we will ever be able to take it all in then. We will certainly thank Him then. Let's do it now more than ever before. In fact, all the time.

Excerpted from *Just Say Thanks!* (Charisma House, 2005).

The Eavesdropping God

I read the Bible over and over again without really seeing what was in verse 16 until a preacher said, "The Lord will eavesdrop on what you say," because the Bible says, "Those who feared the Lord talked with each other and the Lord listened and heard."

> *Then those who feared the Lord talked with each other, and the Lord listened and heard.*
>
> —Malachi 3:16

Why is this important? First, when you know that God is eavesdropping, it will affect what you say. Sometimes, when you are talking with a friend, someone else comes and you stop talking out of courtesy or change the subject. Keeping that in mind when you are talking with somebody and you suddenly are aware that God is eavesdropping, would you keep saying the same thing? Would you change the subject if you became aware that the Lord was eavesdropping? That is exactly what He is doing day and night.

Second, you should choose to spend your time with people who fear the Lord. On what basis do you make friendships? If you seek someone who fears God when looking for a friend, a partner, or when seeking advice, you will save yourself a lot of trouble. A person is known by the company that he or she keeps.

Third, you may be praying without knowing it. Wouldn't it be something if, when you get to heaven, you find out that the prayer that was answered was simply a desire you had expressed when you were speaking with somebody who feared the Lord? You may not realize it, but by talking to another person who fears the Lord and sharing your deepest thoughts and needs, God's heart is touched, and He hears the conversation as prayer. He listens and hears.

God, the Eavesdropper, is so faithful that He turns your conversations into petitions. When He hears the desire of your heart, He turns it into a prayer and answers it. That is how God is, and I just love Him for it.

Excerpted from *Between the Times* (Christian Focus Publications Ltd., 2003).

Being Accountable

Did you know that Jesus was always accountable? He was the Son of God, yet He was accountable to His Father the whole time. Paul used the little phrase in Romans 15:3, "even Christ did not please himself." Everything Jesus was doing, He was looking up to the Father, getting His approval and instructions. He said, "I seek…to please…him who sent me" (John 5:30).

> *He does not live the rest of his earthly life for evil human desires, but rather for the will of God.…But they will have to give account to him who is ready to judge the living and the dead.*
>
> —1 PETER 4:2–5

Now we know that we are accountable to God. We are not our own. There is also a sense in which we are accountable to each other. Both are evident when we consider some of these verses that we like to sweep under the carpet. Jesus said in Matthew 12:36:

> I tell you that men will have to give an account on the day of judgment for every careless word they have spoken.

Now when this matter of accountability grips you, I will guarantee you one thing—you will change. Knowledge of your accountability will change the way you live. You will watch your conduct, you will watch your attitude, you will watch your words.

If we really believed that, we would change, but we do not like to take verses like that. We would like to just cut them out and not have to worry about them, but this is part of humbling ourselves: that we take all of God's Word seriously.

That is the way our Lord got His joy, and it makes me wonder, have we learned the joy of just pleasing God and getting our approval from Him?

Excerpted from *Meekness and Majesty* (Christian Focus Publications Ltd., 1992, 2000).

Protection From Ourselves

Paul knew of the possibility that he could be an effective preacher, see people converted, and see people grow, and then he himself could be rejected in terms of a reward. He would be saved, yes, but as by fire (1 Cor. 3:15).

A thorn in the flesh protects you from yourself! That is why God does it. I therefore go this far: it is arguably the best thing that ever happened to us.

The thorn in the flesh is to make up for a deficiency. That is what compensation is.

> *Even if I should choose to boast, I would not be a fool, because I would be speaking the truth. But I refrain, so no one will think more of me than is warranted by what I do or say.*
>
> —2 CORINTHIANS 12:6

A typical deficiency is the Christlikeness that is lacking in us. God says, "I want you to be more like Jesus, and I have blessed you." If we are totally honest, we know God has been good to us. If He did not send a thorn in the flesh to compensate, who knows what we would be like!

I can think of many deficiencies that require the thorn in the flesh in my case. For example, I don't have enough faith. I don't have enough love. I don't have enough empathy, caring for others. These are things that the flesh by itself will never bring about. I need an increase in faith, love, and empathy.

How, though, does this thorn achieve its aim? Hoe does it actually keep us from being conceited? The answer is that it protects us from ourselves. If you are like me, you sometimes think, *If God hadn't stopped me, I don't know what I would have said or done.* I have lived long enough to say, when I see in any other person a weakness, malady, sin, or wickedness, "That's me—except God has kept me." It is what protects us from ourselves.

Excerpted from *The Thorn in the Flesh* (Charisma House, 2004).

A More Excellent Way

Paul's ultimate purpose was to show exactly what the New Testament means by love and to show if we are like Jesus, what Jesus meant by love. What is this most excellent way?

Love is first to be seen as a demonstration. Paul says, "I will show you the most excellent way."

> And now I will show you the most excellent way.
>
> —1 CORINTHIANS 12:31

It is a demonstration in words: Paul promises to demonstrate the most excellent way by language. By any account it is one of the most sublime pieces of writing on record; even many non-Christians stand in awe of it. These words are the Word of God, inspired by the Holy Spirit, and they should convict us. I know of a man who read 1 Corinthians 13 every day for a year—on his knees. He was never the same again!

It is also a demonstration of works. We are not saved by works; we are not saved by love; we are saved by faith. Paul is writing to those who are saved. If they will live this way, they will dazzle the world. Jesus said, "Let your light shine before men, that they may see your good deeds and praise your Father in heaven" (Matt. 5:16).

But it is also a demonstration of wisdom. What Paul calls love, James calls wisdom. Why? Possibly because James, a Hebrew, grew up in the wisdom tradition of Proverbs and Ecclesiastes. All of the wisdom in the Book of Proverbs can be demonstrated living by love.

It is a demonstration of the will. When I call love a demonstration of the will, I mean it is a choice. Every single one of us can live this way. It doesn't matter what our IQ is, our age, or our maturity. The Christians at Corinth had been saved for four years, and Paul calls them "childish." But this is the way to grow up. Love is a choice. We must never wait for a mood or feeling to overwhelm us. That may never come. Love is voluntary, an act of the will—what we deliberately and consciously choose to do.

Excerpted from *Just Love* (Christian Focus Publications Ltd., 1997).

Chastening That Leads to Joy

Chastening ain't fun (if I may be excused the bad grammar!). The writer of Hebrews acknowledges this. (Surprise, surprise!) Therefore what James calls falling into trials—which we are to consider pure joy—the writer of Hebrews calls being disciplined, which leads to pure joy.

> *No discipline seems pleasant at the time, but painful. Later on, however, it produces a harvest of righteousness and peace for those who have been trained by it.*
>
> —Hebrews 12:11

The way you know you are a true child of God is that you experience this unpleasant thing called chastening. It is an evidence that you are truly saved because the Lord *disciplines those He loves* and *punishes those He accepts as a son or daughter* (Heb. 12:6). So we could use this syllogism for those who may want to apply it:

1. All who are saved are disciplined, sooner or later (thesis).

2. But I am being disciplined (antithesis).

3. Therefore I am a true child of God (conclusion).

There is an important qualification to the above reasoning—namely, that it works to get your attention, and so you are led to a greater degree of holiness. Otherwise, any person who experiences something unpleasant may glibly conclude that he or she must be a genuine Christian. The syllogism applies only if such painful circumstances result in you seeking the Lord all the more.

The primary purpose of chastening is not to give assurance but to get our attention. God wants to bring us to holiness, Christlikeness, intimacy with God, peace, and joy. God disciplines us when there is a need for Him to have to resort to whatever it is that gets our attention.

Falling into trials or temptation is what God permits, but still by His sovereign design; being chastened is what God does—all because we are loved.

Excerpted from *Pure Joy* (Charisma House, 2006).

Called to Brokenness

Brokenness refers to the authentic person rather than to an awesome performance. Why is it that Paul says, "I am nothing"? What does he mean? He is showing what he is as a person.

> *If I have the gift of prophecy and can fathom all mysteries and all knowledge, and if I have a faith that can move mountains, but have not love, I am nothing. If I give all I possess to the poor and surrender my body to the flames, but have not love, I gain nothing.*
>
> —1 Corinthians 13:2–3

What Paul wants in 1 Corinthians 13 is to show what we are as Christians, as people who have been converted; we are going to heaven, and we are going to stand before the judgment seat of Christ and give an account of the things done in the body. Is God going to ask us to explain how our gift of prophecy functions or whether people thought we were great preachers? No! We will give an account of the things done in the body. So that the gifts, without brokenness, equal zero.

In these verses, Paul is referring to spiritual gain; without love there is no intimacy with God. John said that our fellowship is with the Father, but if we don't have love we won't be having fellowship with the Father; there will be no spiritual gain.

He could also be referring to spiritual progress. The only time we grow spiritually is when what we do is totally hidden from others and only God knows. Then we get the honor that comes only from Him: "How can you believe if you accept praise from one another, yet make no effort to obtain the praise that comes from the only God?" (John 5:44). Brokenness is when we are content with knowing that *He* knows. Are you suffering today? God knows. Are you going through a very difficult time? God knows.

What makes the giving of one's life, of one's possessions, of value…what makes the gifts effective is brokenness, the slain ego.

Excerpted from *Just Love* (Christian Focus Publications Ltd., 1997).

Understand How the Devil Works

I t is wonderful to know that the devil is subject to God's authority. So whenever I sense a satanic attack, I think, *Well, that's interesting.* But God knows I can take it. The devil can go so far, but *only* so far. I have discovered too that the devil always attacks me in an area of weakness. But this enables me to strengthen that area, so that the next time around he can't attack me in that place. I grow in grace because the devil attacks, even though satanic attacks are no fun.

> You, dear children, are from God and have overcome them, because the one who is in you is greater than the one who is in the world.
>
> —1 JOHN 4:4

Learn the secret that every satanic attack is with God's permission and has a purpose. Do you know what Job learned at the very end? It is so thrilling. Job said to the Lord, "*I know that…no plan of yours can be thwarted*" (Job 42:2, emphasis added). Indeed, no purpose of God can be threatened because God is more powerful than the devil.

There is never emancipation without conflict. But it is always within the scope of God's permission. Another thing about the devil is that he is the accuser. You see, the devil will come along and accuse you, and he does this because you did the right thing. The devil wants you to feel stupid. Furthermore, the devil is a liar.

He will always lie to you. The devil will always make you think that you have done the most foolish thing by following Jesus Christ. This is the way he works. He always makes you think you have done something stupid.

Do you want to know *how* the devil attacks? The devil will use a close relationship to get at you. You would not have thought that the particular person that the devil will use would ever be capable of what they say or do to you. He will play upon the weakness of somebody you trust.

The devil will use that to discourage you. I tell you something that we are all learning: we must put our trust in Jesus Christ alone, because even the best of God's people, and sometimes those closest to us, will disappoint us sooner or later.

Excerpted from *All's Well That Ends Well* (Authentic Media, 2005).

Limitations Bring Freedom

I have discerned by trial and error that the more conscious I am of God's presence, the more I feel like being myself. The less conscious I am of His presence, the more I feel the need to prove myself. But the more I am myself, the greater my liberty. This is because I am affirming God, who made me as I am. When I move outside my anointing, I am trespassing. When I try to mimic somebody else, I am stealing another's anointing, and it always backfires on me.

> *Now the Lord is the Spirit, and where the Spirit of the Lord is, there is freedom.*
> —2 CORINTHIANS 3:17

The funny thing is, when I try to imitate someone else I never capture their real genius but their eccentricity. It is a fact that what is most easily copied in any man or woman is their odd manner or even their weakness.

God made each of us as we are. He chose our parents before we were born, chose our environment, our childhood peers and shaped our interests—not to mention determining our IQ! When we come to terms with our limitations, we gain not only peace but also productivity in the end.

Accepting our limitations is essential to accepting our anointing. Perhaps God will not use us as long as we have unrealistic aspirations of ourselves. I was not being true to myself or the way God made me by entertaining such lofty notions. I was only wanting to make my peers envious by my accomplishments. It is best to accept our limitations and stop pretending. And God will begin to use us.

Excerpted from *The Anointing: Yesterday, Today, Tomorrow* (Charisma House, 2003).

The Result of a Slain Ego

The person whose ego has been slain will first of all be one who refuses to manipulate or control others. We all have a desire to control people and circumstances. If we have the gifts without brokenness, we use them to control others, to have a hold on them. If our ego has been slain, we won't want to be manipulative; rather, we will want to set people free.

If we are truly broken, we won't feel the need to teach others a lesson; we will refuse to send others on a guilt trip. We won't judge them; we will set them free.

> *Forgive, and you will be forgiven. Give, and it will be given to you. A good measure, pressed down, shaken together and running over, will be poured into your lap. For with the measure you use, it will be measured to you.*
>
> —Luke 6:37–38

I will never forget the time I came home after a Sunday evening service. I felt I preached poorly and was devastated. The response was disappointing, and so were the crowds. I pleaded with God for an answer. Before I knew it my eyes fell on Luke 6:37.

Those words hit me between my eyes. I am a very judgmental person. I do not suffer fools gladly. I knew God was telling me that my critical spirit must stop. I also felt that God was promising me an abundance of anointing (which I have so longed for) were my attitude to change. I began reading that passage literally every day; it is a life sentence. I am not what I want to be, but my life began to change.

The person whose ego has been slain will refuse to mention anything that will make himself or herself look good, anything that will bring credit. Brokenness leaves no footprints.

We are all afraid to be broken—I am. I am afraid of what it will cost me. It is scary. I am afraid of how I will appear if I am broken. I am afraid, but I want it. I am too old to live another day without it. May God let it happen to all of us!

Excerpted from *Just Love* (Christian Focus Publications Ltd., 1997).

How Do We Come to Brokenness?

Behind the slain ego, first, is the way of the cross. That is how Jesus did it. It seems that Jesus suffered more in the five days between Palm Sunday and Good Friday than in the rest of His thirty-three years on earth. His whole life was a life of suffering and self-denial, but what He endured in those five days was the greatest conceivable kind of suffering. He was helpless, nailed to the cross, refusing to defend Himself. He was willing to be misunderstood. And on top of that, God hid His face.

> *Then he said to them, "My soul is overwhelmed with sorrow to the point of death. Stay here and keep watch with me." Going a little farther, he fell with his face to the ground and prayed, "My Father, if it is possible, may this cup be taken from me. Yet not as I will, but as you will."*
>
> —MATTHEW 26:38–39

Behind the slain ego is a willingness to be broken. Salvation works in three stages: mind, heart, and will. I am grateful to Dr. Lloyd-Jones for this insight. It is the order in which we perceive, get gripped by things, and carry them out. It is true with salvation, and it is also true with suffering. For example, the mind perceives it as being the way forward. The heart is gripped by the opportunity to be more like Jesus.

But there is a third stage: the will. We make a deliberate choice. When the devil comes and hits us hard, and we are sorely tempted—that is when we make a choice for brokenness. Mind, heart, will—it becomes a choice.

Things may devastate us, and sometimes we cry to God, "Lord, how could You do this to me?" And God says, "You just blew it!" God would rather have us accept the hurt without the complaining, accept His timing in our lives, and be open to any further word from the Lord.

Excerpted from *Just Love* (Christian Focus Publications Ltd., 1997).

The Fruit of Brokenness, Part I

What is the point of being broken? Is brokenness an end in itself? No. The text shows that there is a fruit. Love is *patient*. Patience is a passive reaction, and it is the first fruit of brokenness. Patience, how we *react*. The Greek word for "patience" is *macrothoumei* and has a very complex meaning; it is impossible to translate it into one word. "Patience" is as good as any. There are three particular meanings of being slow (or patient) that I want us to look at here.

> *Love is patient...*
> —1 Corinthians 13:4

The first is *being slow to anger*. Does that make you think of God? F. F. Bruce has commented that the love of 1 Corinthians 13 really is nothing more than God. If we want to know what God is like, this is it. The more we have of God, the less angry we will be. When we are argumentative and judgmental, it is because we have forgotten God's patience with us.

The second example of slowness is *being slow to accuse*. Look at these words from Proverbs 19:11: "A man's wisdom gives him patience; it is to his glory to overlook an offense."

The third meaning is *being slow to assume*. A person who has not been broken is very quick to assume things and always assumes the worst, whereas 1 Corinthians 13 says, "Love always protects, always trusts, always hopes, always perseveres." The broken person is slow to assume anything, because he realizes that he doesn't know all the facts, and in the meantime he will give that person the benefit of the doubt.

Love demonstrates patience; love also demonstrates kindness. Is the fruit of brokenness displayed in your life today?

Excerpted from *Just Love* (Christian Focus Publications Ltd., 1997).

The Fruit of Brokenness, Part II

There is another demonstration of the fruit of brokenness—kindness. Most of us know what this word means. We certainly know when we are not treated with kindness.

Kindness is a positive action. Whereas patience shows how we *react*, kindness shows how we *act*. But how do we show this positive action of kindness? True kindness is the fruit of brokenness. It is more than being nice; we can be manipulative and still be nice. It is more than being courteous; we can be manipulative and courteous because we hope to achieve something. Niceness and courtesy are mere imitations, the fruit without the root. Kindness comes from the root, which is brokenness.

> ...*love is kind.*
>
> —1 CORINTHIANS 13:4

There are three words that demonstrate what Paul means by this word that is translated "shows kindness." It first of all means goodness. It is possessing that quality that could be called "unself-righteous-morality," that is, morality without being judgmental. That is what Paul means by love showing kindness. We can't manipulate that. It flows from within a person who has been broken.

Second, this word translated "shows kindness" also means graciousness. Graciousness accepts people just as they are, seeing the rough diamond that others want to dismiss out of hand, noticing the potential in someone that others are blind to. Graciousness puts the intimidated person completely at ease. God is gracious.

And so, when Paul says "show kindness" he means goodness, graciousness, and, third, gentleness. Gentleness is having the grace to use our words to diffuse tension as opposed to saying what is emotive. There is just something about this kind of person. I am not talking about syrupy, mushy emotionalism, but just a special quality in the person that makes us want to be around them.

There is one further description that transcends all the others: kind people are peacemakers. They are the mediators of the world; they get enemies together; they don't take sides; they are ruthless in their objectivity, but sweet in the way they talk to people. A person like that has been broken and has come to terms with suffering. There is a kindness that mirrors Jesus, expecting nothing but continuing to be good, gracious, and gentle.

Excerpted from *Just Love* (Christian Focus Publications Ltd., 1997).

Love Is Being Satisfied

A dictionary definition of envy would be something like "a feeling of discontent aroused by someone else's possessions." That is what I mean by being unsatisfied. However, love gives one a feeling of being satisfied. The person who is unsatisfied is still looking for his identity, wanting to know who he is.

Three things can be said about envy. First, it is of the flesh; it flows from nature.

> *Love...does not envy...*
> —1 Corinthians 13:4

We don't have to go to school to learn how to be envious; everybody grows up that way.

Envy is also a feeling. The feeling may or may not be verbalized, but it is there; you feel it. Envy comes from the Greek word that means "to boil," that is, with hatred. Often we won't admit that we feel this way. It flows from our dissatisfaction with ourselves and the feeling that other people are so much better off. Yet when this loves comes, we just don't feel that way!

Envy is based on fear. Fear because of what we don't have, being threatened by what others do have. But envy is misleading. Someone has put it like this: "If envy were not so tragic, it would be comical, because it is always based on a misconception of the other person's position." So, someone might say, "If only I had his money, what freedom I would have!" But when we are satisfied, we say: "The Lord is my shepherd; I shall not be in want" (Ps. 23:1). There comes a time when the love of God is poured into our hearts, and we don't feel any envy at all. We become happy with the way God made us and the way He has led us. That is what agape loves does for us: it doesn't envy, and it is not threatened by another person's position. Whenever we are tempted to envy someone, we need to remind ourselves that we don't know the other side. Perhaps if we knew the facts better we would realize there is not so much to be envious of.

Excerpted from *Just Love* (Christian Focus Publications Ltd., 1997).

Severe Mercy

St. Augustine said that God loves every person as though there were no one else to love. Likewise, He deals with each of us as though there were no one else to deal with. He knows all about us and therefore knows what it takes to get our attention. The way God gets our attention and brings us to a degree of humility is by manifesting His glory.

> Because the LORD disciplines those he loves, as a father the son he delights in.
> —PROVERBS 3:12

But are you ready for this: the thorn in the flesh is actually a manifestation of God's glory. If you pray for God to manifest Himself to you, you might say, "A thorn in the flesh is not exactly what I had in mind!" But there are many ways God shows up, both corporately and individually. Giving us a thorn is not the only way God manifests His glory, I am happy to say, but certainly this was one way in which He communicated with Paul and to each of us. See your own thorn as God's weighty stature in your life, the dignity of His will for you at this time.

As well as being a manifestation of God's glory, the thorn in the flesh is a severe form of chastening or disciplining. I will never forget my first introduction to the idea of being chastened. In that moment I felt an impulse to turn to Hebrews 12:6, which said, "For whom the Lord loveth he chasteneth, and scourgeth every son whom he receiveth" (KJV).

This verse gave me some comfort, but the pain did not go away. It was my introduction—not to the thorn in the flesh—but to the subject of chastening. I knew God Himself was behind everything that was happening. I could live with that. Can you? Just to know that the whole thing is of God.

The thorn in the flesh, then, is from God, and it is a way of making us learn. Nothing else will work for us at the time. So God, who knows this, sends the thorn. It is not unlike what C. S. Lewis calls "severe mercy."

Excerpted from *The Thorn in the Flesh* (Charisma House, 2004).

When God Tells Us Why

Not only will we be changed and able to look on the glorified Lord face-to-face, but something wonderful will also happen—God will tell us why. God wants to tell us why, far more than we even want to know. But the patience of God is extraordinary. He can wait. He wants us to know the answers to our questions, but He can wait.

> *Now we see but a poor reflection as in a mirror; then we shall see face to face. Now I know in part; then I shall know fully, even as I am fully known.*
>
> —1 Corinthians 13:12

Perhaps this appeals only to the person who is agonized with questions, who really longs for God to explain something. Perhaps the question is: Why is there a devil? Why didn't God just destroy the devil a long time ago? Why is there injustice? Why is there evil? But Paul says, "One day I shall know." F. F. Bruce has commented that the Greek word here, *epignosis*, should be translated as "understand." Some day God will make things plain.

Sometimes our questions are not on such a grand scale but are more personal: Did I make the right decision? Lord, have I been living out of Your will? Did I fail You? Paul is saying we see the Lord's glory only in a reflection, so we can't see things perfectly. The mirror that enables us to see ourselves has its limits: when we look at ourselves in a mirror, we do so with a little bit of bias.

God's Word is the spiritual mirror by which we see our hearts, but even here our self-understanding is limited; we will always be prone to self-righteousness and, therefore, be unable to see ourselves as we really are. Sometimes I will say, "Lord, show me." But if I saw my wickedness directly, I wouldn't be able to take it. If I saw the Lord's glory directly I would die. No one can see God and live.

And so God graciously reveals things to us a bit at a time, like peeling the layers off an onion. With each new bit of understanding we might ask why we had to wait so long to get it right.

Excerpted from *Just Love* (Christian Focus Publications Ltd., 1997).

"A Thorn Just for You"

A thorn in the flesh is not the same for every person. But if you are a Christian worth your salt, you probably have a thorn in the flesh. What may be your may not be mine. What may be mine may not be yours. For some it is a handicap or disability. For some it could be unhappy employment—or even lack of employment. It could be an enemy. It could be coping with unhappy living conditions. It could be a sexual misgiving. The list is endless.

> To keep me from becoming conceited because of these surpassingly great revelations, there was given me a thorn in my flesh, a messenger of Satan, to torment me.
>
> —2 Corinthians 12:7

The "thorn" may be recognizable to you but unseen by others. God may afflict you with some sort of impediment—by which you may feel He has stripped you of all self-esteem—but this could be utterly unrecognizable to anybody else. Why? Because this "thorn" is for you more than it is for them. Or it may be for them indirectly. It may be so embarrassing and humbling to you that it will make you a different person, such that others will not have an inflated opinion of you. But it is mainly for you—to keep you humble. Certainly it may end up being for others in the sense that they unwittingly do not extol you as they might otherwise have done. This is why Paul's thorn kept him from being conceited; it kept others from exalting him beyond that which was warranted. But Paul's thorn was mainly for him, and yours is mainly for you.

It is one that is not likely to go away very soon, if ever. You will ask, "Do I have to bear this forever?" Maybe not, but you could. You are probably, though, going to have it for a while. Paul said, "I prayed three times that it might go away." It's like a prison sentence. It may be a life sentence, or it may be a short period of time. Paul's thorn apparently remained. In other words, it will stay with you as long as you need it.

Excerpted from *The Thorn in the Flesh* (Charisma House, 2004).

Learn to Accept Yourself

Acceptance, therefore, means, you don't deny the handicap. Don't live in denial—pretending it is not there. God has allowed it, and it is there to stay. How do you get your nourishment, your strength? Accept your handicap or disability.

But there is more. Know that God loves you. Most important of all, know that you are saved. The greatest thing in the world is knowing that you will go to heaven when you die. There is only one reason you are saved: that God was good to you. He gave you the gospel; never forget that this life is not all there is.

> *O Lord Almighty, blessed is the man who trusts in you.*
>
> —Psalm 84:12

Know that you must be special, because you *are* special. There is a definite reason why God has given you this thorn in the flesh. It is to drive you closer to Him, not further from Him. It is to keep you from being smug, conceited, or taking yourself too seriously. God *could* step in and take it away. But if He doesn't, it will stay only because God's purpose in it all is still unfulfilled.

Although I wish with all my heart that God would remove my own "thorn in the flesh," I have to say also that I have become reconciled to its permanence. What I never thought I would say to God, I now find myself praying: "Lord, I believe now that it would be wrong if You took my thorn away." I have stopped praying that it will go away, because I think it is one of the best things that ever happened to me.

I would therefore urge you, if you are waking up each morning and saying, "It's still here," to admit that, though you want it removed, there is a greater purpose in it all that God alone understands.

Whatever your handicap or disability is, if you accept it as being from God, it is only a matter of time until you see a purpose for good in it. Take your handicap from God with both hands. Why? Because He loves you, and it was His inscrutable, sovereign way of getting you to develop intimacy with Him.

Excerpted from *The Thorn in the Flesh* (Charisma House, 2004).

The Sheer Grace of God

What are you most thankful for? What am I most thankful for? There is also a distinction between what we *feel* most thankful for and what we certainly *should* be most thankful for. Chances are, however, that what we should be most thankful for is what we feel most thankful for—once we think about it for very long.

> *For it is by grace you have been saved, through faith—and this not from your-selves, it is the gift of God—not by works, so that no one can boast.*
>
> —EPHESIANS 2:8–9

In one sense I am most thankful for my wife and for the children. But at the end of the day what ought we to be most thankful for? One word: *salvation.* The knowledge that we will go to heaven and not to hell when we die. Sublime knowledge doesn't get better than that.

The greatest reasons of all to be thankful are that (1) God sent His one and only Son to die for us on the cross, (2) that we heard this wonderful news, and (3) we were enabled to believe this message by the effectual power of the Holy Spirit. Not all have heard the message, but not all who have heard it receive it. Why do some receive it? Is it because they are nicer or better people—or more worthy? No. The only explanation is the sheer grace of God.

The greatest mystery of all is why God so loved the world that He gave His one and only Son to die on a cross for our sins. I don't understand it. Do you? All we can do is stand back and worship. And be so very, very thankful.

Excerpted from *Just Say Thanks!* (Charisma House, 2005).

The Perfection of Love

Paul is not talking about the perfection of a Christian, but about the love that enables the Christian not to fear. John wrote: "There is no fear in love. But perfect loves drives out fear, because fear has to do with punishment. The man who fears is not made perfect in love" (1 John 4:18).

If this glimpse of love we are given now is only in measure, how can it be called perfect? I answer: if you were to go to the

But when perfection comes, the imperfect disappears.

—1 CORINTHIANS 13:10

ocean and dip a glass into the water, you would then have a glass of water that is taken from the ocean, and what is in it is the pure ocean. In quantity, it is nothing compared to the vastness of the ocean, but everything that is true of the ocean is there. And so, the perfection that Paul and John are talking about is a taste of the pure love of God. It doesn't make us perfect, but it enables us to experience, that is, taste, perfect love.

When the pure love of God emerges in the heart, our world is turned upside down. There will be no grudging, no envy, no lust, no need to be seen or to be recognized. It is more wonderful than fulfilled ambition, more wonderful than the adulation of thousands. The pure love of God just wants the Father's glory.

But what happens when our experience of this love fades? When it fades, envy returns, fear returns, panic returns, the need to prove ourselves returns. So we may ask, what's the use of having it if it is going to fade? The answer: it is to let us know what to pray for, this most excellent way. Choose the route of perfect love, and do not be surprised if the charismata emerge stronger than ever!

Excerpted from *Just Love* (Christian Focus Publications Ltd., 1997).

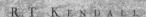

Loneliness Has a Purpose

Billy Graham said that London is one of the loneliest cities in the world. He also pointed out (and I didn't know this) that next to divorced people, university students are the loneliest people in the world. Paul said that loneliness may be a person's thorn in the flesh. As for Paul's actual thorn in the flesh, as we have seen, there is endless speculation. We do not know what Paul's thorn in the flesh was, but it is possible that it was loneliness. He said in 2 Timothy 4:16, "No one came to my support, but everyone deserted me."

> *But Jesus often withdrew to lonely places and prayed.*
>
> —LUKE 5:16

He said in 1 Corinthians 9:5, "Don't we have the right to take a believing wife along with us, as do the other apostles and the Lord's brothers and Cephas?" You can read between the lines. Whether Paul was single, married, or a widower, he said he had the right to have a wife.

He was no doubt lonely, and all you have to do to confirm this is to look at his description in 2 Corinthians 11:25–30. Whether or not this was Paul's actual thorn in the flesh, we don't know.

This may be your thorn in the flesh, ordained by God at least for the moment. The devil will use it to torment you, but remember this: there is a purpose in everything that happens, and God Himself takes the responsibility for it.

Everything is for a purpose, and if I am describing your own thorn in the flesh—loneliness—then God has allowed it. The devil will exploit it, but the loneliness has a greater purpose.

Excerpted from *The Thorn in the Flesh* (Charisma House, 2004).

The Greatest Fringe Benefit

Have you ever been in a situation where you have thought, *I wish somebody could see what is happening to me right now?* Or maybe something good has happened to you, but there is no one to share it with.

The greatest fringe benefit of being a Christian is found in Psalm 121:5: "The LORD watches over you—the LORD is your shade at your right hand." Do you know what that tells me? It assures me of God's very presence. It is the most wonderful thing to realize that our heavenly Father is there. And there will come a time, if you develop the relationship with Him that is available to you, when His attention will mean more to you than anything.

> *The LORD watches over you—the LORD is your shade at your right hand; the sun will not harm you by day, nor the moon by night. The LORD will keep you from all harm—he will watch over your life; the LORD will watch over your coming and going both now and forevermore.*
>
> —PSALM 121:5–8

The psalmist said in Psalm 16:8, "Because he is at my right hand, I will not be shaken." This means that God promises us *Himself.* Not only are we assured of going to heaven, but the greatest thing of all is that Jesus says to us, "You've got Me! I am with you always, even to the end. I will never leave you or forsake you." There is nothing more wonderful than knowing that we have Him.

True, you know that you will go to heaven when you die. But when you became a Christian God didn't just shake your hand and say, "Well done; see you in heaven!" No, He says, "I will be with you. I will see everything that is going on, your coming in and your going, both now and forever more."

Excerpted from *Higher Ground* (Christian Focus Publications Ltd., 1995).

The Lord Is Always Before You

I would like to discuss the circumstances of unhappy employment, for various circumstances can lie behind this. For some, a lack of education has meant that they will always be stuck in a certain kind of job.

> *I have set the LORD always before me. Because he is at my right hand, I will not be shaken.*
>
> —PSALM 16:8

Some travel considerable distances to get just what work they can find. Then, after they get there, it is really dull. They dread arriving, they look forward to leaving, and they look forward to Fridays and hate Mondays. On top of that they have to work hard and inconvenient hours. In other words, they experience a lack of fulfillment. Sometimes the way they are treated is degrading. And as for a bit of prestige? It is out of the question. No prestige. But that was how it was for Joseph, too.

But there is some compensation in unhappy employment. I don't refer to being paid a little extra or getting double pay for overtime. I am talking here about a different kind of compensation. The Bible says Potiphar bought Joseph from the Ishmaelites who had taken him to Egypt, but the Lord was with Joseph (Gen. 39:2). I call that a wonderful compensation! Now if I can get this point across, it could change everything and possibly give a person a different perspective. Unhappy employment is *not* unusual. What *is* unusual is the fact that the Lord is with you.

One of the greatest things you can ever learn as a Christian is to remember that you have the presence of God. Why does it say the psalmist "set the LORD" before himself? It means that he had to remind himself that the Lord was there. You see, setting the Lord before him didn't mean that by doing this the Lord managed to get there on time. No, the Lord was already there, because David went on to say, "Because he is on my right hand." The phrase "I have set the LORD" means that David put himself in a frame of mind to *remind* himself that the Lord was already there. "I have set the LORD always before me."

And if you can do this in the toughest moment and in the loneliest moment, then you know He is there. Remind yourself, He is there.

Excerpted from *The Thorn in the Flesh* (Charisma House, 2004).

The Blessing of an Unhappy Employment

Y ou may assume, because you have obeyed God, that He will fold His hands and say, "That's wonderful, and just for that, here is what I am going to do for you!" And you expect an immediate reward.

The challenge of unhappy employment is a test from God. So what's the challenge? Make the best of a bad situation. Don't always run away to look for another job. Don't promote yourself to the level of your

> *Whatever you do, work at it with all your heart, as working for the Lord, not for men....It is the Lord Christ you are serving.*
>
> —COLOSSIANS 3:23–24

incompetence. Don't jump out of the frying pan into the fire. Remember that God put you there for a purpose. God could change everything overnight. Remember that this life is not all there is. Many around you don't have heaven to look forward to, and God doesn't want any of us to be *too* happy here below.

Unhappy employment may also help you to appreciate even more the good things in your life. It may be helpful and self-edifying to thank God for things that are positive. Do you have good health? Do you have a home? Do you have loved ones? Do you have friends with whom you can share? Do you have a good relationship with God?

Your relationship with God is more important than your job. Get your joy from the inward anointing. There are some Christians who are happy with their jobs— so happy that they are not very spiritual. They don't pray; they don't have intimacy with God. With unhappy employment you may be enjoying a relationship with God that you might not otherwise have simply because you pray more than the person who is content. God loves you and wants your company. He knows what you would be like if you were too comfortable.

The greater the suffering, the greater the anointing and the greater your future. God will do this for you. It may not mean you will become prime minister, but you will reign one day, and, when it comes, it will be worth waiting for. You will treasure that worst situation.

Excerpted from *The Thorn in the Flesh* (Charisma House, 2004).

Humility of Attitude

Before it is ever obvious, humility has to begin in your heart. But how is that possible? It is because of a certain attitude. John put it in the practical terms of loving your brother. He said, "Whoever loves his brother lives in the light, and there is nothing in him to make him stumble" (1 John 2:10).

Looking further at the example of Jesus' humility, we can see that often Jesus approached people in different ways. He had to adjust to the person to whom He was talking, to the people He had to deal with, to the place where He was, and often the situation. His adaptability was obvious because He accepted people as they were. This was part of Jesus' humility.

> *For as he thinks within himself, so he is.*
> —PROVERBS 23:7, NAS

Humbling ourselves, therefore, does not mean making people adjust to you; it is making yourself adjust to them. Satan will throw people in your path and put people among you that annoy you and get your goat—people that are foolish, or not very clever, or not very attractive. Remember that you are praying to be more like Jesus. Then you have somebody in front of you that Jesus would adjust to because He humbled Himself. He had to do it all the time.

Just like sheep in a field, we always think the grass is greener on the other side of the fence. "I would be happy if I were living or working elsewhere," we say, or, "If only I were married to someone else." Let me tell you something: happiness in the external is fleeting. As long as you get your comfort and satisfaction because of the way the situation is, then it is only going to last until the situation changes. And it will change. Learn to find your peace internally. Then external changes will not alter it. You can be happy anywhere.

Excerpted from *Meekness and Majesty* (Christian Focus Publications Ltd., 1992, 2000).

God as an Enemy

I have never had an enemy in the non-Christian world. Yet that fact doesn't cheer me up. All my enemies have been Christians. Sadly, Christians are not exempt from jealousy and ambition. I sometimes wonder how many theological controversies—past and present—are, in reality, theological issues. The untold story in so many famous accounts is that there was often a spirit of rivalry that was masked as being a theological issue. The truth will come out in the courtroom of God.

Anyone who chooses to be a friend of the world becomes an enemy of God.

—JAMES 4:4

I know that God has enemies. His enemy is the devil; the enemy of Jesus Christ is Satan. The enemy of the Holy Spirit is the devil, the enemy of the truth is the devil, the enemy of the church is the devil, and God's enemies are those who are against the truth.

God may choose to get our attention and increase our anointing by the rival spirit of an enemy. Now a rivalry can be a friendly rivalry, but sometimes it can lead to hostility. A rival is a person who competes with you. And yet a friendly rivalry can be healthy: "As iron sharpens iron, so one man sharpens another" (Prov. 27:17). Every rival in our lives may be seen as a thorn in the flesh to get us to pray harder.

There can be a strategic rivalry. Saul became jealous of David, and David became the enemy of Saul for the rest of his life. David's hero became his enemy, but it was God's way of refining David's anointing—the best thing that could have happened to him. God uses an enemy to refine us. That is why it is strategic.

Be sure that you are in Christ. Be sure that you are covered by the blood of Jesus. Be sure that all your sins are under His blood, because you surely don't want God as an enemy. Be sure then, that you know that your sins are forgiven and that you are walking in the light (1 John 1:7).

Excerpted from *The Thorn in the Flesh* (Charisma House, 2004).

A Clear Path to Intimacy

Not only do we need daily forgiveness as much as we need daily bread, but we also need to pray daily that we have the grace to forgive others as a lifelong commitment. It is not easy. No one ever said it would be. It has been the hardest thing I have ever had to do, but following this phrase in the Lord's Prayer is the clearest path to fellowship with God.

> *For if you forgive men when they sin against you , your heavenly Father will also forgive you.*
>
> —MATTHEW 6:14

It is as though Jesus adds a "P.S." to the Lord's Prayer. It almost seems that that is why He gave us the prayer in the first place!

Why does Jesus add this further statement? He is demonstrating which of the petitions was the most important. The most natural tendency in the world is to want to get even when someone has offended you. It is as natural as eating or sleeping, and it is instinctual. Jesus is telling us to do something that is not natural but supernatural: totally forgiving people—sometimes those closest to us—for the wrongs they have done to us. I still struggle in this area myself. But when I truly and totally forgive, I have crossed over into the supernatural—and have achieved an accomplishment equal to any miracle.

The kingdom of heaven is the domain of the Holy Spirit. When the Holy Spirit is at home in us, it means He is not grieved. He can be Himself; He isn't adjusting to us, but we are adjusting to Him. When Jesus said, "If you forgive men when they sin against you, your heavenly Father will also forgive you," He was not talking about how to achieve salvation. He was referring to receiving the anointing of God and participating in an intimate relationship with the Father. Unless we are walking in a state of forgiveness toward others, we cannot be in an intimate relationship with God.

Excerpted from *Total Forgiveness* (Charisma House, 2002).

BY LOVE TRANSFORMED

God's Church Includes Everybody

I would think that a great sign of God's approval and anointing on any church is to see it filled with people with all kinds of handicaps, whether deaf, blind, or in wheelchairs. The reason is because such people obviously feel welcome. The word gets out that this church wants—and needs—the disabled. They know they will be treated with dignity and respect. People everywhere want to spend time with them; they will come and talk to them!

Do you do that at your church? Or do you hurry to be with the people you already know? God wants His church to include everybody.

> *When you give a luncheon or dinner, do not invite your friends, your brothers or relatives, or your rich neighbors....invite the poor, the crippled, the lame, the blind, and you will be blessed. Although they cannot repay you, you will be repaid at the resurrection of the righteous.*
>
> —LUKE 14:12–14

It's not just pain, difficulty, or the inconvenience; the real problem is the way disabled people are marginalized and cast aside.

There is more than one kind of handicap, and there are obviously various degrees of being disabled. There are generally two kinds of disabled people: those who are born disabled and those whose handicap affects them later in life.

Others become disabled through illness. This can happen to any of us. It can happen through an accident, or it may be the gradual loss of our hearing or sight. The loss of the use of limbs can be anyone's experience.

But there is another kind of handicap, mental impairment, those born with mental limitations. It may be a low IQ or those born with Down's syndrome. There are those who have a learning disability, such as dyslexia. Some lose the ability to think clearly. It may come from an accident, from an operation, or from senility—perhaps Alzheimer's disease.

Such people often love the Lord Jesus Christ with deepest devotion, but they wonder what's wrong with them. And yet God allows this because He has a purpose in it all. He loves us so much, and what is often seen as a negative in this life will be seen in the opposite way when we get to heaven.

Excerpted from *The Thorn in the Flesh* (Charisma House, 2004).

The Precedent for the Unprecedented

Discontinuity. That is what threatens us—when there is no precedent that we can put our finger on. The precedent for the unprecedented, however, is biblical. It is the theme running right through Hebrews 11, the faith chapter of the Bible. Not a single person mentioned there had the luxury of repeating yesterday's anointing. Enoch walked with God (Gen. 5:24). Noah walked with God (Gen. 6:9). There was the continuity.

By faith Noah, when warned about things not yet seen, in holy fear built an ark to save his family. By his faith he condemned the world and became heir of the righteousness that comes by faith.
—Hebrews 11:7

So, we are told, "By faith Enoch was taken from this life, so that he did not experience death" (Heb. 11:5). Noah therefore did what Enoch did—he walked with God. The continuity of a comfort zone may have made Noah feel that what happened with Enoch would happen to him. But no. It wasn't easy for Noah. But he set the precedent for God's glorious but painful discontinuity: "By faith Noah, when warned about things not yet seen, in holy fear built an ark to save his family." It had never happened before, and it never happened again.

Not knowing where we are going, yet knowing we are following God, can be most painful indeed. God has a way of giving us sufficient revelation for ourselves but not enough that it convinces others. The stigma is knowing you have heard from God but having to do what no one else may be required to do.

There is equally nothing so comforting as seeing that that is what happened in the Bible. And yet we have what the early church didn't have—the New Testament to keep us on the straight and narrow. If there is any word of knowledge or prophetic insight that *conflicts* with Scripture, we stay with *Scripture* and reject the word of knowledge—no matter who gave it. The Scripture does not replace the miraculous; Scripture corrects abuses when people hear "words" that *couldn't* have come from God because they don't cohere with biblical theology.

But the anointing will often offend. That is not surprising, for it stretches us. It brings together both the continuity and the discontinuity of God's dealings with us—the God of the past and the Lord who acts in the "now." Such majesty and mystery are rarely within our comfort zone.

Excerpted from *The Anointing: Yesterday, Today, Tomorrow* (Charisma House, 2003).

The Calling of God Is Paramount

Moses was a person who had the call of God upon him, and yet he voluntarily gave up the treasures of palace life. It was said of Moses, "By faith Moses, when he had grown up, refused to be known as the son of Pharaoh's daughter" (Heb. 11:24).

Here was a man brought up in a palace who "chose to be mistreated along with the people of God rather than enjoy the pleasures of sin for a short time" (v. 25). Can you imagine someone who lived in a palace

> *With this in mind, we constantly pray for you, that our God may count you worthy of his calling, and that by his power he may fulfill every good purpose of yours and every act prompted by your faith.*
> —2 Thessalonians 1:11

and who voluntarily gave it up in order to please God? Don't tell me this had nothing to do with Moses' anointing! I say it had everything to do with it.

The call of God on a person makes all the difference. Why did Moses do what he did? It was because the call of God was paramount.

Is the call of God upon you? Is your motivating sense of life the call of God? If you say, "Well, I am not sure if it is or not," you ought to fall on your face before God and ask, "What has gone wrong? What has happened?" Do you have no sense of destiny? No reason for living? Have you been derailed to such an extent that there is no sense of the call of God on you?

You may hope that living conditions will change and this will give you a little bit of happiness. But the most important thing is to know that God's call is on you. There is something for every one of us to do that is as important in our sphere as in any others in world history! Every Christian has a call from God, and when that grips you, and you know that God has a plan for your life, you will see everything else in a different light, including where you live.

Excerpted from *The Thorn in the Flesh* (Charisma House, 2004).

Making a Bad Choice

Abraham had a nephew by the name of Lot. The two of them reached a place where each of them had to make a choice, but it didn't matter that much to Abraham! Why? He had obeyed. A sense of destiny was upon him, which is what kept him going. He knew that everything was not to be understood in terms of material things. Sadly, do you know what it says about Lot? He made a bad choice.

> *So Lot chose for himself the whole plain of the Jordan and set out toward the east. The two men parted company: Abram lived in the land of Canaan, while Lot lived among the cities of the plain and pitched his tents near Sodom.*
> —GENESIS 13:11–12

Sometimes there is something you can do about this matter of living conditions. Your living conditions may be what they are because of a bad choice. As to how you know whether you should be doing something about changing your living conditions instead of just putting up with them, the answer is twofold. First, has God unmistakably put you where you are? If so, you should stay there for the time being. He has a purpose in it for you. Second, if your being where you are is because of a hasty decision—and you have had no peace since—I would suggest God has a better plan for you. Pray that God will move you without you "jumping out of the frying pan into the fire."

Could it be that God brought you to this place of crisis at this moment? Things can change. You may be living with the consequences of a bad choice, but it is a new day, and I would not write like this if there were no hope. Your life may not have to stay as it is. Something can happen in your heart before God, and you can say, "I am sorry!" and know that God loves you as much as He loved Lot and Abraham.

Excerpted from *The Thorn in the Flesh* (Charisma House, 2004).

Find Your Spiritual Gifts

Do you wish to discover your spiritual gift? Two passages in particular tell you how to do it.

In 1 Corinthians 12:31 Paul says, "Covet earnestly the best gifts: and yet shew I unto you a more excellent way" (KJV). In the Greek, this passage means: "The excellent *way by which you discover* your gifts is by love." It sounds almost too simple to be true: you can best discover your gift when you demonstrate agape love. Yet it is true. When we love people and long to serve them, when we totally forgive and keep no record of wrongs, then we spontaneously find ways of expressing that love, and the gifts of the Spirit emerge in us. There are no shortcuts to finding the gifts. We must have hearts devoid of bitterness.

> *For by the grace given me I say to every one of you: Do not think of yourself more highly than you ought, but rather think of yourself with sober judgment, in accordance with the measure of faith God has given you.*
>
> —ROMANS 12:3

The second principle is found in Romans 12:3. Basically, what Paul is saying is don't claim to have what you don't have.

Though we are to covet the gifts, we must not seek them for our own glory or impute to ourselves abilities that simply aren't there. We must live sacrificial lives, seeking at each moment only to love and serve God in holiness, humility, and prayer. Then, though we may not be the first violinist or the conductor, we will quite naturally and simply find our own gift, and our place in the orchestra, almost without realizing it. Sometimes the position may be quite prominent. But it will be under God's control and God's responsibility, and almost a matter of indifference to us, since all that matters is God's glory and not ours.

One further guideline here is that God does not encourage us to be incompetent, and if we feel that we are working incompetently, then it is a pretty strong hint that we are not where God intended us to be.

If you find that these are the marks of your life, ask God what He wants you to change in your life, and then offer yourself to Him again as a living and daily sacrifice.

Excerpted from *Worshipping God* (Hodder & Stoughton, 2004).

The Loneliness of Suffering and Service

There is the loneliness of suffering—in sickness, when you are ill and alone, with no one to take care of you. When you are in a deep valley or trial, no one to talk to, what must it be like? Perhaps you have a particular type of suffering or illness, weakness or trial that no one has had but you. You look high and low for some other person who will know exactly what you are going through. You feel so lonely.

Then Jesus went with his disciples to a place called Gethsemane, and he said to them, "Sit here while I go over there and pray."...and he began to be sorrowful and troubled. Then he said to them, "My soul is overwhelmed with sorrow to the point of death. Stay here and keep watch with me."

—MATTHEW 26:36–38

That is where Jesus comes in. There is not a single temptation that you can have that He doesn't understand. He sympathizes; He never lectures. You may go to another person, and he may say, "Oh, are you bothered about that?" And you just feel awful that you even went to him in the first place. You then look for one other person, and sometimes you won't find that other person or he just doesn't understand how you feel. But Jesus does. Is this your thorn in the flesh?

There is loneliness when you have to make decisions or a judgment that isn't going to be appreciated. And so you can be in ministry, doing the Lord's work, but nobody appreciates what you are doing. No one is going to do it but you, and they take you for granted.

Perhaps you have taken a courageous stand, but no one understands. Listen to Paul: "At my first defense, no one came to my support, but everyone deserted me. May it not be held against them" (2 Tim. 4:16). There are those missionaries who have left family and friends. They have gone to an alien country, away from familiar surroundings. The loneliness of service. There is the loneliness of doing things in your own church. Nobody knows you do it, but God knows.

Excerpted from *The Thorn in the Flesh* (Charisma House, 2004).

Seeing God's Purpose in Your Temporary Situation

Sometimes you may complain about where you are living and your conditions, and God lets you jump out of the frying pan into the fire. You think, *I'd love to be back where I was!* That's the way the Israelites were. They complained so much that they made God angry. God went to Moses and said, "I'm fed up with the people. I am going to destroy them and start a new nation with you!" Moses said, "Oh no! Don't do that!" Moses was free to leave at any time he wanted; he could have left them. For example, he could have gone to live with Jethro, his father-in-law, but he stayed right there. "So he said he would destroy them—had not Moses, his chosen one, stood in the breach before him to keep his wrath from destroying them" (Ps. 106:23). Moses accepted unhappy living conditions and stayed right there. Can you do that? Can you accept that God has put you where you are for a reason? It's not what you want to call home, but Moses made it home.

> *"What have you done to us by bringing us out of Egypt? Didn't we say to you in Egypt, 'Leave us alone; let us serve the Egyptians'? It would have been better for us to serve the Egyptians than to die in the desert!" Moses answered the people, "Do not be afraid. Stand firm and you will see the deliverance the Lord will bring you today."*
>
> —Exodus 14:11–13

Do you have to live with so-called Christians? Do you have to live with family, but you get on each other's nerves—perhaps you would like some space? It's one thing to have family to stay for a day or two, but it's quite another to have to live with them.

Could it be that God has sent that thorn in the flesh so that we would get our real joy not from the situation around us, but from the joy of the Lord (Neh. 8:10)? God could change our situation here below, and maybe He will. When? My answer: the moment His presence becomes more precious than the external circumstances that we thought were so important.

Excerpted from *The Thorn in the Flesh* (Charisma House, 2004).

Serving God Through Illness

I turn now to illness and the possibility of service. That means going to work and also doing something for God. After all, there are some people who are chronically ill and work forty hours a week. Others have problems far more serious; some are bedridden, and others are housebound but can still cope. Obviously Paul, who had an eye problem, kept going since it was because of that reason that he came to the Galatians. God can cause your illness to coalesce with an event, situation, or place wherein you would think, *I am actually glad I had that illness, otherwise this wouldn't have happened!*

As you know, it was because of an illness that I first preached the gospel to you.
—GALATIANS 4:13

Two of the greatest ministries—our deaf ministry and our prayer ministry—during our time at Westminster Chapel came into being as a result of Louise's physical problems. The deaf ministry would not have happened without Louise's ear problem. Our prayer ministry, through which we saw people healed and countless others blessed and refreshed, would not have happened but for Louise suffering severe depression for several years. It was because of chronic illness that she was open to letting others pray for her.

God may use you in His service because of an illness. He may turn you into one of the great intercessors of history. This, therefore, brings me to the subject of illness and spirituality. We are back to that word *intimacy*. God wants your company; He loves your company. "Me? I can't preach. I can't play a guitar. I can't compose hymns. He wants *me?*" *Yes.* The most insignificant person whom no one has time for, God wants. If this chronic illness is not going to go away, why don't you just say, "Lord, show me what You want"?

Excerpted from *The Thorn in the Flesh* (Charisma House, 2004).

Coming to Terms With Our Grudges

There's no doubt that Esau was angry with God, but that is not the end of the story, as we know from the remarkable events in Genesis 33.

The time came when Jacob had to meet Esau. But Esau, instead of taking revenge against Jacob, showed mercy.

Who would have thought that the very thing Jacob had dreaded was now reversed? What does this tell you? Something happened to Esau. What changed him? It may

> *"In your anger do not sin": Do not let the sun go down while you are still angry.*
> —Ephesians 4:26

have been time. As they say, time heals all wounds. And it could be that with time a person mellows, but if that's the way it happens, it is not a real victory. If you deal with your anger the same day, then that's spiritual victory.

Something did happen to Esau, and we too must learn how to come to terms with our grudge. When we learn to stand back and ask ourselves why we are as we are, we become objective.

It is so easy for us to be judgmental, but we don't know what process the mind of another is going through or what has happened to them. The truth is that we all do things that are not right.

God totally forgives because He sent His Son to die for your sins. And the reason Jacob could say, "To see your face is like seeing the face of God" (Gen. 33:10), was because the God whom you can turn to is a God whose justice has been satisfied by the blood of His Son. God can even take that unforgiving spirit, forgive you for your inability to forgive, give you a new heart, and bring you to the place where you can sincerely pray for those who have treated you unfairly. You can come to the place that you *want* them to be blessed, and eventually it even becomes a selfish prayer because when you pray that way, you get blessed more than anybody. And that's the truth.

Excerpted from *All's Well That Ends Well* (Authentic Media, 2005).

Called to Disciplined Prayer

Disciplined prayer arises from two things: first, a good general knowledge of God's Word; second, a strong desire to please Him. In other words, I am talking here about praying as an act of sheer obedience whether we feel like it or not. And it is the mature Christian who follows this way.

One day Peter and John were going up to the temple at the time of prayer—at three in the afternoon.

—ACTS 3:1

You may decide to spend more time in prayer, but then you find that everything seems to militate against it. So you think, *These things that are stopping me praying are providential.* So don't be surprised if, when you commit yourself to prayer, everything seems to be hindering you. There must be discipline.

One of the forgotten verses in the Book of Acts is the opening verse of chapter 3. The chapter goes on to describe how Peter and John healed the crippled man, but what is interesting is that it happened when they were on their way to the temple to pray. We see that even when the Spirit was present in great power, these early disciples were not afraid to go by a schedule. At this high peak in the history of the church it would seem that the first Christians still observed set times of prayer.

The principle is that if you live by the disciplined impulse, you will get the spontaneous impulse as well, and this is why I urge each Christian to pray for thirty minutes a day and to attend the weekly church prayer meetings. Here were Peter and John on their way to the temple, when the lame beggar held out his hand to them, expecting to receive some money. But Peter just turned to him and said, "Silver and gold have I none; but such as I have give I thee: In the name of Jesus Christ of Nazareth rise up and walk" (v. 6, KJV). And the man was healed.

You never outgrow the need to pray. It is my job, not only as a Christian minister but also as a child of God, never to excuse myself again for what I haven't done regarding time spent in prayer.

Excerpted from *Worshipping God* (Hodder & Stoughton, 2004).

What Is Worship?

I believe that every Christian has one fundamental calling and one primary duty—we are called, by the way we live and in all we do, to worship God. This is a full-time activity, not only here on earth, but in heaven, too.

But what exactly is worship? True worship is in the Spirit or by the Spirit of God.

> *God is spirit, and his worshipers must worship in spirit and in truth.*
>
> —John 4:24

Two Greek words in the New Testament are translated by our word "worship." One is *proskuneo*, which is used sixty times and means "to adore" or "to give reverence to." This refers to the condition of the heart. It is the word used by Jesus in John 4:24.

The other word is *latreuontes*, which appears as a noun or a verb twenty-six times and may be translated as "service." This is the word used to refer to public worship and comes in Philippians 3:3 (kjv): "...who worship [*serve*] God in the spirit." Both words are used in the context of Spirit-led and Spirit-controlled worship.

Here, then, is my own definition of worship: it is the response to, and/or preparation for, the preached Word. In worship, the Spirit prepares our minds and hearts to receive God's Word, and, as we see at Pentecost, it is the Spirit who brings about a change of heart and enables us to continue in the apostles' doctrine.

But if the first thing is the Spirit, what is the role of the truth? Truth—Christian doctrine as revealed in the Word of God—is the proof and guarantee that one is in the Spirit; it also serves as a yardstick for testing actions that are allegedly in the Spirit but that in fact are not. The truth keeps worship from detours. The Bible was not given to replace the Holy Spirit. The Bible is there to correct abuse and to help us make sure that our worship and our Christian walk are genuinely in the Spirit.

Excerpted from *Worshipping God* (Hodder & Stoughton, 2004).

Why Do We Worship?

Our aim should be to glorify God and edify the soul of every person present. It's easy to talk about glorifying God, but what does it mean? To glorify God means to please Him. We must continually ask ourselves this very searching question: when we meet together to worship God, is it our aim to please Him or to please ourselves?

> *So that with one heart and mouth you may glorify the God and Father of our Lord Jesus Christ.*
>
> —Romans 15:6

I know that the answer here can be "both," and in the end that is true. But we will never succeed in pleasing God until we forget about ourselves. With worship, we want to bring joy to God. However, it is not for us to try to decide what will please God. God has already decided what kind of worship He wants. Worship that pleases Him must be "by the Spirit of God."

"Well," someone may say, "if I'm going to worship God by His Spirit, then I'm not really doing anything. It's just God doing it for Himself. But I want to please Him by showing Him what I can do." But anyone who talks like this does not know God, because God doesn't want what we can do. He has already decided what He wants, and we must decide whether we are going to worship in His way.

Our aim in worship must be to please God, but the aim of worship is also to edify the soul of every person present. The key word here is *every* person. God is worshiped not just when we do certain things right, but when we are edified—that is, when our spirits are fed with His Word, so that we reach out to Him in repentance, gratitude, and trust. He is glorified when we worship Him with our understanding, not when we intone, parrot-fashion, words.

Excerpted from *Worshipping God* (Hodder & Stoughton, 2004).

Living Worship

What we long for is living worship. But how does this come about? Worship that is "by the Spirit of God" has three stages.

First, the *initiation of the Spirit*. Worship that is initiated by the Spirit is always of the Spirit, by the Spirit, and in the Spirit. *Of the Spirit* refers to those who have been brought to the new birth; *by the Spirit* describes what these reborn people are able to do—they serve God under the impulse of the Spirit.

> *For we are the circumcision, which worship God in the spirit, and rejoice in Christ Jesus, and have no confidence in the flesh.*
>
> —PHILIPPIANS 3:3, KJV

This leads me to my second point: *the impulse of the Spirit*. In true worship the people of the Spirit are enabled by the Spirit to participate in the worship that God feels for Himself. For God loves Himself—and if we don't like that fact, it is because a God of glory is offensive to our fleshly human nature. God does everything for His own glory and "worketh all things after the counsel of his own will" (Eph. 1:11, KJV). And everything in all creation was designed for the worship of God.

Third, *the inheritance of the Spirit* is when the Holy Spirit is utterly Himself in us. When someone comes into our house we say, "Do make yourself at home." If you really want the Spirit to be at home in you—to be Himself in you—you must open your heart directly to Him and say, "Lord, I do love You, and I will do what You say." Complete obedience to the Spirit at home within us is the key to true worship.

Excerpted from *Worshipping God* (Hodder & Stoughton, 2004).

Don't Take Yourself Too Seriously

One of my greatest fears is that God will pass me by because I might take myself too seriously if He gave me a greater anointing. Taking oneself too seriously is assuming one is more important than he or she really is. It results in our expecting more respect and attention than is warranted. We begin feeling that we, more than anyone else, should be notified the moment God has new plans for His church—and, of course, these plans should include us.

> He replied, "I have been very zealous for the Lord God Almighty. The Israelites have rejected your covenant, broken down your altars, and put your prophets to death with the sword. I am the only one left, and now they are trying to kill me too."
>
> —1 Kings 19:10

Even when we are seeking to walk in obedience to the Lord there is a danger of taking ourselves too seriously. We may fall prey to the "Elijah complex." Elijah's finest hour was followed by his taking himself very seriously. "I am the only one left," he said, having earlier lamented he was no better than his ancestors.

The twin sins of *self-righteousness* and *self-pity* so readily lift their ugly heads at us. For example, it is a rare person who can be an intercessor in prayer and not boast about it. It is a rare person who can pray for a leader and then refrain from giving advice. It is a rare person who can be greatly used of God today and tomorrow be quietly willing to watch God use another. It is a rare person who can see God answer prayer on one item and not question because He doesn't answer other prayers. It is a rare person who can enjoy sweet intimacy with Christ today and not feel sad when He doesn't manifest His presence tomorrow.

Few of us can handle much success, especially in the area of knowing God. God is the only one who can deal with us when we are like that. Sometimes the only way He can get our attention is by being ruthlessly silent. Don't fear His silence. Use it to examine your heart and motives. Listen expectantly for the silence to be broken by the glory of His manifested presence once again in your life.

Excerpted from *The Sensitivity of the Spirit* (Charisma House, 2002).

Release the Spirit

We honor the Spirit by releasing Him. Many of us think only in terms of the Spirit coming down, but He can flow out from a well deep within us.

How do we release the Spirit, both in ourselves and in others? In ourselves it will happen when we keep peace in our hearts with everybody we know. Sometimes we play games with ourselves and pretend we are at peace and that all is fine. It is like

> *Whoever believes in me, as the Scripture has said, streams of living water will flow from within him.*
>
> —John 7:38

someone who loses his temper and then says, "I'm not mad." We can justify ourselves until we are a hundred, but the Spirit will never be Himself in us as long as we are unforgiving or judgmental, prejudiced, or speaking evil of anyone. It may mean apologizing to someone, or it may be a little thing like raising your hand in worship. But obeying His impulse is all part of honoring the Spirit and releasing Him in ourselves.

And we can release the Spirit in others when we relinquish our control over other people. We can refuse to let another person be afraid of us or admire us too much. (We never do anyone a favor by letting them admire us too much, for sooner or later we will disappoint them.)

The flesh, you see, always wants to control. But the Spirit gives liberty, and through Him we must release others to be themselves—to think for themselves. There may be people who are in bondage just because they are afraid of us, but we can help them. And when we do, the Spirit will be released to be Himself in all of us.

Excerpted from *Worshipping God* (Hodder & Stoughton, 2004).

Truly Listening to God

What can be more important than correct listening? We only worship God to the degree that we hear Him speak. This is why there are injunctions throughout Scripture about hearing and listening. Jesus would frequently end a parable with the words, "He that hath ears to hear, let him hear."

> *Speak, Lord, for your servant is listening.*
>
> —1 Samuel 3:9

What we are talking about is the ability to recognize and respond to the Spirit's impulse. I consider this to be the highest level of spirituality that exists.

There are two reasons why God has difficulty in getting us to listen to Him. The first is our inability to absorb or take in His counsel. We all overestimate our capacity to grasp and take in things, not realizing that if God were to tell us all there is to know, our minds would snap. God has to deal with us where we are.

The second reason why God has difficulty in getting us to listen to Him is that there is sin within us as a result of not walking in the light. We say, "Lord, speak to me."

God answers, "I did speak, but you wouldn't take it."

We say, "I didn't want that. Lord, speak to me."

"I am speaking."

"No, Lord, speak to me."

God is trying to reach us, and we hear Him to the degree that we are walking in the light. Is it possible that God is trying to speak to you along a certain line, but you are saying, "I know God wouldn't say that to me"?

When we get to the judgment, the Lord could look at us in much the same way and remind us of certain areas of our life, and we will be speechless. It's very important that we should be transparently honest with ourselves. The final tragic result of disobedience, of course, is that God stops speaking to us.

Excerpted from *Worshipping God* (Hodder & Stoughton, 2004).

Pain That Produces Humility

How does the thorn work? Through pain. The thorn is given that we may "share in his holiness" (Heb. 12:10). It is not pleasant; it is painful. A thorn hurts. It gets and keeps our attention.

Why would God inflict us with pain? Keep in mind that this thorn doesn't kill us; it only hurts us. The pain is necessary because God's glory is a no-joke thing. He is determined that no flesh will glory in His presence (1 Cor. 1:29, KJV). To a great extent, the thorn will keep us from glorying in His presence. If there were no pain, we would forget; we would lapse into our normal, fleshly routine.

In the same way, the thorn in the flesh keeps us from competing with His glory. It ensures that we will not take any personal credit, and it gives Him all the glory.

> *I know, O LORD, that your laws are righteous, and in faithfulness you have afflicted me.*
>
> —PSALM 119:75

In other words, the thorn hurts. It is a constant trial, and it is ever obtrusive. It is always there; it is a reminder. It is a nuisance. Paul even says, "…to torment me" (2 Cor. 12:7). You may say, "God, that's not very nice." It keeps one's feet on the ground. It keeps me from thinking that I have arrived, that I am good enough, that I am worthy. It hurts so that I might be driven to love more. It is obtrusive so that I might develop empathy and won't be judgmental. Are you, like me, one of those who can hardly keep from pointing the finger? God has a way of sending a thorn in the flesh. It's a nuisance that produces humility.

Excerpted from *The Thorn in the Flesh* (Charisma House, 2004).

Faith for Faithfulness

Maybe we prayed every day during the week and yet have not experienced God's blessing or seen Him answer prayer. What then? "It is required in stewards [that is, those who have been given a trust], that a man [or woman] be found faithful" (1 Cor. 4:2, KJV). Anybody can be faithful when prayer is being answered, when the wind is at one's back, and everything is going well. But what is one to do when God suddenly hides His face? Until you have experienced the hiding of His face and come out on the other side, you won't really come to know God as a friend.

> *The just shall live by his faith.*
> —HABAKKUK 2:4, KJV

This was Habakkuk's experience. Habakkuk 2:4 is a famous verse that is quoted three times in the New Testament.

There is an intentional ambiguity here. The faithfulness can be God's faithfulness to us or our faithfulness to God: the verse can be read either way, and it means both. But it can equally describe the faithfulness of the individual himself, who doesn't give up hope. The person who trusts God and lives by His promise to bless is declared righteous in the sight of God. It applies to the future—to the fact that God will accept us in heaven—but it also applies to the present. God is saying that we are declared righteous now.

If we could only see this day, it would set us afire. If, in the moment when we don't see answered prayer, we could just look up to heaven and say, "God, I love You anyway," God would declare us righteous just because our faith pleases Him. That kind of faith has a cleansing result. We feel clean. We don't understand why God lets things happen, but we trust Him anyway.

Excerpted from *Worshipping God* (Hodder & Stoughton, 2004).

Overcoming Self-Pity

Self-pity doesn't receive as much attention as some sins receive, and it doesn't cause the scandal that some sins cause. For instance, everyone is interested in a sexual sin because it causes such a scandal. But you can be overcome with self-pity, and it won't be as scandalous. You may think that the devil only wants you to fall into sexual sin. Listen. The devil doesn't care how he gets hold of you, so if he can get hold of you by causing you to wallow in self-pity, he will do it.

> *Those I love have turned against me....I have escaped with only the skin of my teeth. Have pity on me, my friends, have pity, for the hand of God has struck me.*
> —Job 19:19–21

How can we define self-pity? It is feeling sorry for oneself, and it is a self-justifying condition. It always seems right. The frightening thing about it is that sometimes we fail to recognize we *are* in this condition. Self-pity is acquired without any training or discipline. It is as natural to us as a pig wallowing in mire.

The devil loves your self-pity, because once you start feeling sorry for yourself you will be no threat to him. He may leave you alone. He won't bring any other temptation into your life. He will say, "I've won with that person." He can now toy with you. If you stay in that condition, you are perilously close to self-destruction, and that's not just sin—that is gross, heinous sin. You are letting the archenemy of Jesus Christ have you where he wants you.

I will tell you where to begin to find your cure. You begin where Jesus ended His life on earth, at the cross. Until His last breath, He was being tempted to succumb to self-pity greater than any you will ever know. Jesus couldn't even allow Himself a single instant of self-pity, because it is sin.

Jesus never sinned despite being tempted at all points as we are. He knows what you are feeling, and He understands. But you need to recognize what self-pity is and come to terms with the problem. You have to stop blaming others and admit that you have sinned before God.

Excerpted from *All's Well That Ends Well* (Authentic Media, 2005).

Consolation When Things Don't Go Well

The very things Habakkuk had complained about—the fig tree wasn't blossoming, no fruit, no herd in the stalls—were still not there, and yet he was rejoicing. He wasn't complaining now. What changed his mind?

> Though the fig tree does not bud and there are no grapes on the vines…yet I will rejoice in the LORD, I will be joyful in God my Savior.
>
> —HABAKKUK 3:17–18

There were three things that consoled him. The first was that he could see that God was what he saw: "The LORD answered me, and said, Write the vision, and make it plain upon tables, that he may run that readeth it" (Hab. 2:2, KJV). What a relief to know that God sees!

The second thing that consoled Habakkuk was the knowledge that though full intervention might not come as soon as he wanted—"Though it tarry, wait for it" (v. 3, KJV)—it would nevertheless definitely come. There was a plan; there was a time schedule. Maybe it's a little longer that you want it to be, but wait for it; it will come.

The third thing that consoled Habakkuk was the understanding that God imputes righteousness to the man or woman who lives by God's faithfulness. When we say, "God, I don't understand it. I don't know why You have let me wait this long. I don't know why You haven't stepped in sooner. But I am trusting you," we are cleansed in that moment and given rest of soul. He says, "I like it when you trust Me that way."

Are you looking for the vine to blossom before you can rejoice? Are you waiting for the raise in pay? Or for that answered prayer? Are you waiting for everything to fit in before you start praising the Lord? If that is so, then turn in your badge now and give up. As Proverbs 24:10 says, "If thou faint in the day of adversity, thy strength is small" (KJV).

Like Habakkuk, you will be given grace to trace the rainbow through the rain.

Excerpted from *Worshipping God* (Hodder & Stoughton, 2004).

Abandon Self-Preservation

Now what are we like when we are full of ourselves? We want to talk about ourselves rather than listen; we want to defend ourselves and do not even want to consider the possibility that we could be wrong, which makes us defensive and touchy. We feel sorry for ourselves rather than look on another person's need. We want to excuse ourselves rather than facing up to our real responsibility, which makes us critical and negative. What we have is self-preservation.

> *By myself I can do nothing; I judge only as I hear, and my judgment is just, for I seek not to please myself but him who sent me.*
>
> —JOHN 5:30

I wish to focus on what I will call the abandonment of the self-preservation.

It is an abandonment, first of all, of rights. We live in the "me" generation. "Human rights" is a phrase that we often hear. But the New Testament says, "You are not your own; you were bought at a price" (1 Cor. 6:19–20).

Jesus gave up the right to Himself (Rom. 15:3). He said in John 4:34, "My food…is to do the will of him who sent me." What does this mean for us? If He did not come to do His own will, and He gave up rights to Himself, how does this relate to us practically?

What will be the consequences if we do live like this? The other side of emptying yourself is really trusting God for the outcome. When we let go of ourselves, we affirm God's manner of working things out. As long as we hold on to ourselves, we may not be impoverished, but we lose the fruitful outcome. But when we abandon self-preservation, surprise, surprise, we get it back a hundredfold! It means, therefore, that we trust God for the outcome. It may not be the way we would have done it, but remember that, as Christians, we have a loving heavenly Father who is all powerful and able to give what is best.

Excerpted from *Meekness and Majesty* (Christian Focus Publications Ltd., 1992, 2000).

Lifestyle Worship

The way we guard against being a hypocrite six days a week and acting piously on Sundays is by applying the Word of God to our lives. Revival in a church may be quite extraordinary, but it is only a question of whether each member is following the conductor's score in his private life. In an orchestra, the sound is no greater than the sum of the different parts. As Paul says in Ephesians 4:16, "From whom the whole body fitly joined together and compacted by that which every joint supplieth, according to the effectual working in the measure of every part, maketh increase of the body unto the edifying of itself in love" (KJV). So our worship ought to be a glorious symphony to God—no one out of tune, no one playing too loudly, each person following his or her own score.

As a prisoner for the Lord, then, I urge you to live a life worthy of the calling you have received.

—EPHESIANS 4:1

Though our worship is not a performance designed to attract other people, or pander to our own love of display, there is a sense in which it is a performance—a performance for God. Our worship is for God, the King of kings; should that not affect us as we prepare for the Sunday worship since our Sunday worship is the culmination of what we are all the time?

How do we actually achieve this? How does the right performance come about? The first is practice at the individual level.

We can all practice living in the presence of God from minute to minute. And in order to do this, we must outlaw all bitterness from our lives. We must seek to be filled with love, with total forgiveness, and acceptance of each other.

Excerpted from *Worshipping God* (Hodder & Stoughton, 2004).

BY LOVE TRANSFORMED

The Greater the Affliction, the Greater the Reward

Some scholars have suggested that Paul's thorn in the flesh was that his eyesight was deteriorating. Whether it was partial blindness or not, we do not know. Perhaps it was a disability.

Whatever our thorn in the flesh is, and regardless of whether we have asked for it to be removed (as we surely have), I urge all of us to realize that it is there because God says it is still right for it to be there. It is true that God will use you all the more and all the better because that disability is still there.

> See what large letters I use as I write to you with my own hand!
> —GALATIANS 6:11

I once asked Joni Eareckson Tada, "Would you like to be healed?" I thought she would have a quick answer, because I thought everyone asked her that. But it was as though she had never even thought about it! Finally she said, "Yes, but," she continued, "the most precious time of my day is when they put me to bed, and I am alone with the Lord. I am so afraid that if I didn't have this paralysis, I wouldn't have that intimacy."

The reward for being patient and not complaining is worth the wait. It is what helps ensure a great reward when you get to heaven. In my opinion, because of this kind of affliction, when one doesn't complain, the reward will be far, far greater.

The greater the affliction, the greater the reward. The greater the suffering, the greater the anointing. All this is guaranteed if you and I don't give in to self-pity or complaining.

The thorn in the flesh gives us the possibility of a greater reward than we would have had. The greater the handicap, the greater the impairment, the greater the disability, the greater the reward if we don't murmur. Here below you may have felt it was a deprivation. In heaven you will say (if I dare use this word), "How *lucky* I was to have it." I guarantee that this is the case.

Excerpted from *The Thorn in the Flesh* (Charisma House, 2004).

God Comes in a New Way

If someone were to say to you today, "The Lord is going to appear in your life between now and sunset," you would probably say, "Well, if He really is going to appear, I'm sure I'll recognize Him."

When Elijah heard it, he pulled his cloak over his face and went out and stood at the mouth of the cave.

—1 KINGS 19:13

Elijah was to see a manifestation of the glory of God unlike anything he had ever seen before (1 Kings 19:9–18). It comes at a time in his life when he is depressed, tired, and on the run from his enemies. As he shelters in a cave in hiding, God tells Elijah to watch and see what He will do: "Go out and stand on the mountain in the presence of the LORD, for the LORD is about to pass by" (v. 11).

First, a great and powerful wind tears the mountain apart and shatters the rocks around him. This has to be the Lord! He has appeared in this way before. But we're told that "the LORD was not in the wind." After the wind there is an earthquake. Ah, this must be it! But no—"the LORD was not in the earthquake." After the earthquake comes a fire. Elijah is sure this is the way it should be, because God had previously manifested Himself through fire. But "the LORD was not in the fire." After the fire there is "a gentle whisper," what the King James Version calls "a still small voice."

I daresay that God wants to appear in my life and in yours. The difficulty is that we tell Him how He can do it. Some of us who have seen God work think, *I'll know Him when He comes because I've seen Him before.* The truth is, God may come again and ignore all the traditional ways. He *has* worked through earthquakes. He *has* worked through wind. He *has* worked through fire. But this time He may come in a different manner. Will we recognize Him if He does?

Excerpted from *When God Shows Up* (Renew Books, 1998).

Speaking Out of Fear

Speaking out of fear always leads to evil (Ps. 37:8). God has not given us a spirit of fear (2 Tim. 1:7). Perfect love casts out fear (1 John 4:18). When we fear—and speak at the same time—what we say will come out wrong and may get us into serious trouble.

Take, for example, Abraham telling people that his wife was his sister. Abraham journeyed to Egypt and, knowing how beautiful his wife, Sarah, was,

> *Do not be anxious about anything, but in everything, by prayer and petition, with thanksgiving, present your requests to God.*
>
> —PHILIPPIANS 4:6

ordered her to say that she was his sister—so both of them would be spared. Abraham feared that someone would kill him in order to have her. So she did what he commanded.

It worked for a while. She was taken into Pharaoh's palace, where she was safe, while Abraham prospered. But God stepped in. The Lord inflicted serious diseases on Pharaoh and his household because of Sarah. Pharaoh somehow knew that God had caused these diseases and knew that Sarah was Abraham's wife. "Why didn't you tell me she was your wife?" (Gen. 12:18). Abraham and Sarah mercifully were spared. They would never know what God Himself might have done had they trusted Him. Years later Isaac made the same mistake, repeating the error of his father (Gen. 26:7–22).

Speaking out of fear comes from assuming God is not going to look after us—so we speak in unbelief. It is the folly of self-protection. The truth is, God stepped in for both Abraham and Isaac. He will for us, too. But when we give into unbelief and speak—thinking we are justifiably protecting ourselves, our sin has a way of backfiring on us.

Excerpted from *Controlling the Tongue* (Charisma House, 2007).

Spiritual Warfare

Satan already knows his doom, and he is also aware that his time is limited.

Something else that is certain about Satan is that he will try to take everybody down with him. He tries to do this by keeping people from being saved. He is called "the god of this world" who blinds "the minds of them which believe not, lest the light of the glorious gospel of Christ, who is the image of God, should shine unto them" (2 Cor. 4:4, KJV).

> *For we wrestle not against flesh and blood, but against principalities, against powers…against spiritual wickedness in high places.*
>
> —EPHESIANS 6:12, KJV

When Satan fails and people are converted, he then does all that he can to keep them from holiness. He will try to get them to grieve and quench the Spirit.

New Christians need to be taught these things. They also need to know the devil will attempt to push us to extreme views about him. He will either try to get us to be overly preoccupied with him or to disregard him completely. If we become preoccupied with the occult, even if it's on the grounds that we just want to learn more about the dangers of Satan, we open ourselves up to oppression, if not possession, by evil spirits. So we need to be very careful. At the other extreme, if Satan can get us to discount anything to do with the occult as foolishness, he will be very pleased because then we will fail to be on our guard.

Here are nine more things about the devil: he is jealous, insecure, vengeful, and persistent. He is also unteachable (he never learns from his mistakes), a liar and a deceiver, and he is full of hate. But, most of all, he is resistible.

"Resist the devil, and he will flee from you" (James 4:7). That is a promise, and it works!

Excerpted from *Worshipping God* (Hodder & Stoughton, 2004).

BY LOVE TRANSFORMED

Know Satan's Tactics and Overcome

If we are going to do spiritual warfare, then we need to know Satan's tactics in order to overcome them. Satan is out to deceive. Revelation 12:9 describes him as "that old serpent, called the Devil, and Satan, which deceiveth the whole world" (KJV).

How does he set about his deception? In 2 Corinthians 11:14, Satan is called "an angel of light," which means that he uses apparently respectable means and people to deceive us. He tries to lure us away from the truth and towards the counterfeit. Paul says: "For if he that cometh preacheth another Jesus, whom we have not preached, or if ye receive another spirit, which ye have not received, or another gospel, which ye have not accepted, ye might well bear with him" (2 Cor. 11:4, KJV).

> *They overcame him by the blood of the Lamb and by the word of their testimony.*
> —REVELATION 12:11

Satan is out to demoralize: "Now is come salvation, and strength, and the kingdom of our God, and the power of his Christ: for the accuser of our brethren is cast down, which accused them before our God day and night" (Rev. 12:10, KJV).

How does Satan accuse? Sometimes he tells us that we are not saved. Or if he can't succeed with that, he tries to convince us that God has finished with us and that we are irreparably out of His will. Nothing is more demoralizing to a Christian than this. But let me give you a rule of thumb here: all oppression is of the devil.

Another method of accusing and demoralizing us is to tell us that we are not fit to worship God as we are. The devil reminds us of some weakness or failing in our life, and he says, "You must get that right before you can worship God. You're not in a fit state to do anything." He tries to get in during the week, and if he fails there, he tries on Sunday morning. If we lose our temper or give in to some other weakness, he says to us, "You see, you're not fit." But God never says that.

So what are we to do in the face of Satan's strategies? The answer is that we must refuse to give place to him. We must realize that Satan's strategy is aimed to produce one thing—a grieved Holy Spirit. That is all he wants. And if he achieves that, then he has won.

Excerpted from *Worshipping God* (Hodder & Stoughton, 2004).

God Is on Your Side

Do you know what it is like to have somebody physically attack you? The trauma is one that, humanly speaking, you don't overcome easily. Or perhaps you have been verbally attacked. You know the awful feeling when somebody points a finger of blame at you.

The Lord's people in this psalm were the objects of anger. It is very frightening to be near someone who is angry. Perhaps you live in constant fear of a co-worker's temper or the angry outbursts of a loved one. You know how it feels to live in a situation from which you wish you could be delivered.

> *If the LORD had not been on our side when men attacked us...they would have swallowed us alive....Praise be to the LORD, who has not let us be torn by their teeth.*
>
> —PSALM 124:2–3, 6

The truth is, your *real* enemy is the devil. The devil's work is to cloud your mind. He can come as an angel of light; that means that he will work through someone who has the appearance of being very righteous, a person of integrity, a person who is believable. Or he may come as a roaring lion.

But we learn from verse 6 that God *can* step into the situation: "Praise be to the LORD, who has not let us be torn by their teeth."

Maybe you're saying, "I don't think God *is* on my side." Remember this: God is on the side of anybody who will openly identify with His Son, Jesus Christ. God has promised that everything that happens in the lives of believers will work together for their good.

You will know what it is like for the Lord to rescue you. Maybe you don't see God in it at the time, but that is the only real explanation. God mercifully stepped in.

Excerpted from *Higher Ground* (Christian Focus Publications Ltd., 1995).

Fasting

Many of us may not find the subject of fasting pleasant because it comes down to the disciplined impulse of the Spirit, but its rewards may well exceed our greatest expectations.

Fasting is going without food to achieve a particular end. It is a means to an end. There are nonreligious reasons for fasting: we may fast for health reasons, for example, or people may fast as a protest to get the attention of the authorities and of world opinion. But I do not want to deal with that kind of public demonstration, and neither do I necessarily recommend it.

> *But thou, when thou fastest…fast…*
> *unto thy Father which is in secret…*
> —MATTHEW 6:17–18, KJV

The Bible gives numerous accounts of fasting for spiritual reasons. It is often a sign of grief and mourning—even of desperation—as in the Book of Esther (chapter 4).

Fasting is not something one does flippantly, with joy or gladness. Yet the New Testament assumption is that the disciples of Jesus should, and in fact do, fast. Jesus said, "Moreover when ye fast, be not, as the hypocrites, of a sad countenance" (Matt. 6:16, KJV).

Moses fasted for forty days. Jesus fasted for forty days. And it was not unusual for David to fast. In Psalm 35:13 he says, "But as for me, when they were sick, my clothing was sackcloth: I humbled my soul with fasting" (KJV).

The apostle Paul says in 2 Corinthians 11:27, "In weariness and painfulness, in watchings often, in hunger and thirst, in fastings often…" (KJV).

When we read that people like Moses or David, Paul, or our Lord Jesus Christ were given to fasting, we may see an answer to the question of why there is such a dearth of spiritual greatness at the present time. And if fasting is something new to us, we must ask ourselves whether God is leading us to engage in this particular spiritual enterprise.

Excerpted from *Worshipping God* (Hodder & Stoughton, 2004).

When Should We Fast?

You might be thinking, *I'm willing to fast, but when do I do it?* I would therefore like to suggest five occasions on which fasting is justifiable.

I think the first of those would be when the burden we are under is so great that we do not really have a desire for food—for this may be a hint from God that we should fast. David experienced a time of great mourning when God smote the son born to him as a result of his adultery with Bathsheba (2 Sam. 12:15–16).

> ...*and humbled myself with fasting.*
>
> —Psalm 35:13

The second occasion that justifies fasting is when we are about to embark on a very great task for God or have to make an important decision. At the beginning of His ministry, after His baptism, Jesus fasted (Matt. 4:2). Maybe you need to know God's will and don't know what to do. It is justifiable to fast because you need wisdom for something in the future.

A third reason is if we feel that God is hiding His face. Perhaps we are in a rut or have known better days spiritually. Perhaps God is not as real as we have known Him to be, and we are not sure whether we have grieved Him or whether He has just chosen to hide His face for reasons we can't understand. Perhaps God is hiding His face from us in order to drive us to our knees to seek Him.

The fourth occasion is when we have experienced delay in the answers to our prayers. In the Old Testament in particular we have accounts of situations where God did not step in as it had been hoped He would, and as a result the people fasted.

The fifth occasion that justifies fasting is when we feel the need of unusual power that we don't have, such as in the case of demon possession in Matthew 17, which was too big for the disciples to handle.

Fasting is a way of ensuring that we are completely dependent upon God and open to Him. It seeks spiritual emptiness and cleansing, and it enables us to hear God speaking.

Excerpted from *Worshipping God* (Hodder & Stoughton, 2004).

The Effective Approach to Fasting

First, fasting must be secret (Matt. 6:16–18). When we are fasting we must not let the slightest hint of it leak out. Only God needs to know.

The second thing is that fasting must be special. I question if it ought to be done regularly. I don't see fasting as something to be done whether you really need to or not, for example, making a commitment to fast every Friday. I think if it is used that way it will lose its significance.

Third, as we have seen, fasting must have a purpose. We must know what we want to achieve. It's not like taking vitamins in the general hope that they will do us good.

The fourth point is that fasting must be sensible. Some people cannot fast for medical reasons. For example, if you are a diabetic, then that ought to disqualify you. And we must never fast without drinking plenty of liquids. There are various degrees of fasting. You can cut out one meal or two meals, or fast for a whole day or a number of days. However, anyone seeking to fast for more than two or three days should first seek the advice from an experienced Christian minister or counselor.

> *Is not this the kind of fasting I have chosen: to loose the chains of injustice and untie the cords of the yoke, to set the oppressed free and break every yoke?…Then your light will break forth like the dawn, and your healing will quickly appear; then your righteousness will go before you, and the glory of the LORD will be your rear guard.*
>
> —ISAIAH 58:6, 8

A fifth thing is that fasting must be spontaneous: that is, voluntary and from the heart. In my opinion, there could be danger in corporate fasting, for some may be acting reluctantly and under pressure.

The next thing I need to say is that fasting must be sacrificial. Isaiah 58 describes people who fasted but who loved it.

Finally, we must be quite clear about our motives, and we must have no mixed motives.

Fasting by itself is no magic answer to our problems. It is only effective when it symbolizes a deep longing for spiritual reality, and it demands a life of holiness and obedience to God. "Then," says God in Isaiah 58:8, "shall thy light break forth as the morning, and thine health shall spring forth speedily" (KJV).

Excerpted from *Worshipping God* (Hodder & Stoughton, 2004).

The Anointing of the Holy Spirit

One of the most frightening comments I have heard since I entered the ministry was uttered by an Episcopalian priest in America: "If the Holy Spirit were taken completely from the church, 90 percent of the work of the church would go right on as if nothing had happened!"

What a travesty of what the church was meant to be! And can it be true also of our personal lives—that many of us are churning out "Christian" activity that has no touch of God upon it?

> *You have an anointing from the Holy One.*
>
> —1 John 2:20

There is only one antidote to such a situation. It is breathtaking in its possibility, it is awesome in its power, and it is liberating in its effect. It is quite simply—the anointing.

The anointing is the power of the Holy Spirit.

Several years ago someone came into my vestry and asked me, "What do you mean by the anointing?" I remember replying something like this: "It's a gift that functions easily when it's working."

It does not follow, of course, that all that functions easily is our anointing. Some things come easily that are not necessarily good—eating, talking too much, or watching more television than is good for us. Temptation comes easily, and we may find it "natural" to do things that are not productive.

The anointing, however, leads to what is good; it blesses and encourages others. And its function is carried out with ease and without strain or fatigue.

When the anointing is working, it is as natural and easy for our gift to function as eating or talking with friends. The gift is always there but doesn't always function easily. The anointing of that gift makes it function with ease.

Whether you are a secretary, professional person, homemaker, truck driver, or minister, the possibility of the anointing is there all the time; you never know when God will manifest Himself in an unusual way.

Excerpted from *The Anointing: Yesterday, Today, Tomorrow* (Charisma House, 2003).

The Goal of Trials

The goal of trials is to look to Jesus. This happens when you are shut off from all here below so that only God knows.

As long as you envisage external vindication below, it is your hint that you are not ready yet. Are you like that young man who just wanted to be vindicated before his father, and when his father died, he had nothing else to live for? God is a jealous God, and He wants you to enjoy Him, alone.

> *Let us fix our eyes on Jesus, the author and perfecter of our faith, who for the joy set before him endured the cross.*
> —Hebrews 12:2

Sometimes I say to my wife, "Let's go out for a meal. Let's go to a restaurant."

"Fine," she says.

Then I ask, "Whom shall we take with us?"

"Don't you just want to be with me?" she asks.

That is what God is saying, and Jesus responded in getting His joy from the Father alone.

If this is your pattern, I will tell you what it will mean. It will mean that your best and closest friends may not understand. It was a trial for Jesus that He could not explain to the disciples all that He was up to. Yet His joy was internal, and when you begin to react to criticism and praise in much the same way, you are beginning to get free. When you begin to react to criticism and praise without taking either seriously, that signifies that you are passing the tests as Jesus did. The goal of trials is contentment with the glory that comes from God only.

A friend, Jon Bush, asked me once in connection with this, "Is it that ambition takes us so far and the glory of the Lord the rest of the way?" I agreed with him.

The goal is reached when our ambition dissolves and all we want is for Him to say, "Good. Well done."

Excerpted from *Meekness and Majesty* (Christian Focus Publications Ltd., 1992, 2000).

Worship in Quietness

There is a much deeper level of worship, one in which we are unable to express ourselves verbally or nonverbally—where we are utterly passive. The highest and most intense worship takes place when we can do nothing but be amazed, when we are rendered helpless and speechless with wonder and gratitude, when we just sit back and watch God work. This is what Isaiah is talking about in this verse.

> *In returning and rest shall ye be saved; in quietness and in confidence shall be your strength.*
>
> —ISAIAH 30:15, KJV

How many people are utterly frustrated? They have tried everything, and the result has only been fatigue. A minister once said to me, "I had to ask for a sabbatical. I'm burned out."

When we don't wait on God and are always trying to do things ourselves, the result is endless turmoil. But if we really want assurance of salvation, God will knock everything out from under us until we trust Him alone.

To rest in God means we leave everything to Him. We leave it to Him to put us in the right place at the right time and with the right people. In so doing, we will not experience fatigue, because we get our approval from the blood of Christ, not from our works, and because we live by the authority of the Spirit of Christ.

The result is that we live and worship in a state of amazement, awe, and admiration: which is the second principle I want us to see from Isaiah 30:15. We have quietness over the most difficult situations and over our deepest fears. For God says, "Leave it to Me." We lose the desire to get even with those who have hurt us, and we feel little need to prove ourselves.

Real worship is directed toward the One who doesn't want anything from us for what He has done for us. There are no strings attached. God only wants us to trust Him. He wants us to experience the joy of doing nothing but resting in the fact that He loves us. God wants us just to look to Him and say, "Lord, I don't know how much I love You. But I know how much You love me." Rest in that, and let God love you. Then you will stand in awe.

Excerpted from *Worshipping God* (Hodder & Stoughton, 2004).

God's View of Tithing

This verse teaches us five things regarding our money.

One, the Israelites of Malachi's day were backslidden because they were withholding from God what was His.

Two, the entire nation was under a curse because God's people were robbing Him.

Three, God wants all that is due to Him. It is not enough for you to give Him a part, even a large part. That is not what He says. God says He wants it all, and He wants it week by week.

Four, the tithe should go to the store-house. Now everybody knew then what

> "Bring the whole tithe into the storehouse, that there may be food in my house. Test me in this," says the LORD Almighty, "and see if I will not throw open the floodgates of heaven and pour out so much blessing that you will not have room enough for it."
>
> —MALACHI 3:10

that was; it was the synagogue or the temple. Today it means the church, your church. When a person begins to give to God, something is unlocked within him and he has a love for the Lord.

Five, God challenges us to discover for ourselves why this is true and that it is true. Think of this: God is angry with those who rob Him, yet He tenderly stoops to where we are to motivate us to give. That is why He tells us to test Him. God challenges us here.

While tithing is of huge importance, no one will be saved just by tithing. Tithing is not how you become a Christian. You are saved when you realize that God sent His Son into the world to die on a cross, to shed His blood, to do for you what you can't do—keep the law perfectly. You will go to heaven even though you have never tithed, and you will stay saved even if you don't become a tither, because tithing is not what guarantees salvation. The connection between spirituality and money is that when you don't give God what is His, you don't grow spiritually and you may also suffer financially. Your Christian life just won't be the same.

Excerpted from *Between the Times* (Christian Focus Publications Ltd., 2003).

Worship in Heaven

My worship and knowledge of God are not a means to an end, but an end in itself. For that is the way I will spend eternity: worshiping God for God's own sake and knowing that this brings Him pleasure. That is what will make heaven, heaven.

What will there be in heaven? First, *restoration*. Have you noticed that little phrase in Acts 3:21 (KJV): "until the times of restitution of all things"? This means the restoration of what was lost in the Fall. What was lost in Eden will be restored, never to be threatened again.

In heaven we will worship as Adam did before the Fall, with one big difference— we will worship with hearts overflowing with gratitude, for we will worship with the knowledge that we are redeemed by the precious blood of Jesus.

> *Behold, I make all things new.*
> —REVELATION 21:5, KJV

There will be *fellowship*— "a great multitude, which no man could number" (Rev. 7:9, KJV). So in heaven there will be restoration of friendships.

There will be *righteousness* in heaven. That means transparent holiness and perfect justice. There will be no miscarriage of justice in heaven. There will be no discrimination, no racial prejudice, no conspiracies, but total fairness. God looks forward to that. Do you think God doesn't care when somebody is kidnapped, mugged, or slandered? But He sees the end from the beginning. He never panics. He can wait for His name to be cleared.

What will heaven be like? It will be *revelation*. The truth will be equally clear to all then. And best of all, Jesus will be fully revealed. "Now we see through a glass, darkly; but then face to face" (1 Cor. 13:12). We are all going to see Him. My Lord and my God. The one I love.

There will be *rejoicing* in heaven. Rejoicing that will never end.

I don't know all we will be doing in heaven, but I do know we will worship spontaneously, by the Holy Spirit, without any limitation or hindrance whatever.

Excerpted from *Worshipping God* (Hodder & Stoughton, 2004).

God Wants Us to Pray

It began with Rebekah, the wife of Isaac, who had a barren womb. She had no children, and it looked as though she never would have. In ancient times this was considered as a kind of curse, but it turned out that God was signaling great blessing to come. Barrenness was sometimes a symbol of promise in disguise.

Maybe you feel that you are in a similar situation, and you want something to happen. Perhaps it is to have a baby, to know a particular success, or to have a prayer answered, but you have come to a dead end. You ask, "Why?" Yet, maybe that which looks so bleak is God's way of saying, "Just wait a little while longer, and you will see all that I have done. I do everything with a particular strategy in mind."

> *Isaac prayed to the LORD on behalf of his wife, because she was barren. The LORD answered his prayer, and his wife Rebekah became pregnant.*
>
> —GENESIS 25:21

Isaac prayed. One of the greatest mysteries that I know is the sovereignty of God in prayer. I know that God can do anything and doesn't have to answer to anybody, yet the same God tells us to pray. It amazes me. Perhaps you feel negative about the sovereignty of God, believing that there's no chance He'll give you mercy. Yet that's the point: *God doesn't owe us anything.* If we come to understand that, it might just put us in our place and lead us to pray.

Maybe the dead-end road you are on is God's way of trying to get your attention. When was the last time you prayed? How often do you pray? What is God doing to bring you to the place of prayer? Unanswered prayer is often God's way of getting our attention. You see, when we don't get what we want, we are more teachable; whereas when we are blessed, we can become more unteachable. God has a way of bringing you to such a place that you'll wait on Him.

Excerpted from *All's Well That Ends Well* (Authentic Media, 2005).

Worship That Pleases God

Worship that is pleasing to God has several characteristics, the first of which is *insight*: the awareness of God that precipitates and inspires the worship. Next there is *integrity*: the ability of the worshiper to come before God in truth, with his whole being and nothing held back. Then there is *indebtedness*: the sense of our debt to God. Fourth, there is a sense of *inadequacy*: our inability to express the depth of our feelings toward God. Charles Wesley could only say:

> O for a thousand tongues to sing
> My great Redeemer's praise.
>
> —CHARLES WESLEY, "O FOR A THOUSAND TONGUES TO SING,"
> PUBLIC DOMAIN

This quality of worship is possible only through the Holy Spirit. You cannot worship beyond the level of your insight. And you get that insight by the Holy Spirit. A feeling of indebtedness is proof that you realize that your insight is from God. A sense of inadequacy will also determine the quantity, or length of time, of your worship. You feel you must keep on trying to express your love and need of God. And this will continue throughout eternity. For we will always be unable to express our debt to God because we are in heaven and not hell.

> *Give unto the LORD the glory due unto his name; worship the LORD in the beauty of holiness.*
>
> —PSALM 29:2, KJV

True worship exposes our imperfection. It matters to God that we should see how imperfect we are. One of the most painful, as well as, usually, one of the last things we discover about ourselves is that we are self-righteous.

Our greatest joy and pleasure is to be found in God alone. So much of what is pleasurable in this life has to be shared with somebody else in order to be fully enjoyed. Even if we had tea with the queen, much of the joy would be in sharing what we had experienced. But the joy of being in the presence of God alone is the greatest joy there is, and it does not need to be shared.

Excerpted from *Worshipping God* (Hodder & Stoughton, 2004).

God Has a Purpose for You

Prophecy is where God speaks through a person that which He wants spoken at a particular moment. It could be something to do with the present, so you could say that a preacher who expounds God's Word and applies it directly to his congregation is prophesying. Sometimes we want a sensational word about the future, but what we *need* is knowing what to do now, and God speaks through the preaching of His Word. Yet there *is* such a thing as predictive prophecy, when we predict and God fulfills what is said. Isaac and Rebekah prayed, then a prophetic word came to Rebekah: "The LORD said to her, 'Two nations are in your womb, and two peoples from within you will be separated;

> *"For I know the plans I have for you,"* declares the LORD, *"plans to prosper you and not to harm you, plans to give you hope and a future."*
> —JEREMIAH 29:11

one people will be stronger than the other, and the older will serve the younger'" (Gen. 25:23). Prophecy is God's idea. He not only determines things in advance, but sometimes He also reveals things in advance.

It is no accident you were born when and where you were. There was a reason. You may say that your parents didn't want you, that you're an "accident," but you are wrong. God *wanted* you to be born, and He chose the womb from which you should enter this world. I understand if you have a low view of yourself because you feel you were never wanted. You've grown up with a feeling of rejection. But consider this: God *wanted you.* You are here on purpose. God determines where and when a person should be born. He alone gives life, and those who are born to us aren't ours, but His.

Equally important, God also determines our new birth. Jesus said to a man by the name of Nicodemus, "You must be born again" (John 3:7). The phrase *born again* has been abused, and people laugh at it. But the truth is, you can be born of the Spirit and come in touch with the true God. He put you here, and there is a plan for your life.

Excerpted from *All's Well That Ends Well* (Authentic Media, 2005).

Calling Precedes Greatness

We may refer to God's revealing Himself to Abraham as Abraham's "calling." Our verse says, "By faith Abraham, when he was called..." All greatness may be traced to one's calling, and so with Abraham.

> *By faith Abraham, when he was called, obeyed by going out to a place which he was to receive for an inheritance; and he went out, not knowing where he was going.*
>
> —HEBREWS 11:8, NAS

One interesting thing about the call to Abraham was the promise of greatness. God said to Abraham, "I'm going to make you a great name." (See Genesis 12:2.) And yet the very thing that made God angry with regard to the Tower of Babel was that people were going to make a name for themselves. Is there a contradiction?

God is not against greatness—as long as He is the architect of it. He resists the proud but gives grace to the humble (1 Pet. 5:5). But if we are thinking of making ourselves great and building a name for ourselves, we will be fighting against God. One of the most common temptations for a Christian, especially if he is involved in Christian service, is to think he must build up a certain image—or build up his name, as one would do in show business. The parallel between show business people and some Christians in the Lord's work is one of the most ominous signs of twenty-first-century Christianity.

God promised to make Abraham a great name, but not before Abraham was ready. Indeed, Abraham had much to go through before he was ready.

As you read these lines, God may be calling you to greatness. You may think you are the most insignificant person on earth. But God delights in making men great—provided that He is the One doing it. He created all things "out of nothing" and continues to make men great who hold no promise whatsoever.

Excerpted from *Believing God* (MorningStar Publications & Ministries, 1997).

Jesus Never Manipulates Anyone

We are told that Jacob manipulated Esau into surrendering his birthright. Esau was the elder, and that meant he would inherit double what Jacob would receive. We are all like Jacob. You say, "Not me." Yet, we are all manipulators. There are two kinds: there's the "top dog" or the passive manipulator, the person who's very quiet and achieves his aim by pouting or by just saying a word here and there to get their own way. If a person manipulates you into doing something, you really only have yourself to blame, because nobody can be manipulated unless they acquiesce. So if you manipulate me, it's because I have allowed you to do it.

> *Once when Jacob was cooking some stew, Esau came in from the open country, famished. He said to Jacob, "Quick, let me have some of that red stew! I'm famished!" … Jacob replied, "First sell me your birthright." "Look, I am about to die," Esau said. "What good is the birthright to me?" But Jacob said, "Swear to me first." So he swore an oath to him, selling his birthright to Jacob.*
> —GENESIS 25:29–33

There is an exception to the manipulating person: Jesus Christ never manipulates us to achieve His end or purpose. He never treats us as if we are mere objects. He always treats us with dignity, as people. Perhaps people have pushed you around and have taken advantage of you over the years to such an extent that it is impossible for you to conceive what it would be like to be treated with dignity.

The Holy Spirit, the Spirit of Jesus, is always a gentleman. The Holy Spirit will never manipulate; what He does is to apply the Word as it is in the Bible. When we hear His voice, suddenly it dawns on us, and we begin to see that God is making sense in our lives. We would be fools to reject Him.

When Jesus died on the cross, He died for all the manipulators of the world. Perhaps you are reading this as one who has given in to manipulation, and you are so ashamed. Maybe you have manipulated someone else. Jesus took the guilt of your sins on the cross and promises a new beginning. The blood of Jesus will wash away all your sins. God promises you a home in heaven; your past is forgotten. This God will treat you with dignity. He will not manipulate you.

Excerpted from *All's Well That Ends Well* (Authentic Media, 2005).

Coping With Stubbornness

Stubbornness means being unteachable, inflexible, holding firmly to your own opinion and not giving in. A stubborn person is incorrigible. They never improve, and they don't seem to learn. They will not admit to a fault, and nothing seems to change their mind. Have I described you? Do people who know you best think this about you? The chances are, if two or more people have thought it, there may well be something to it.

> *If someone is caught in sin, you who are spiritual should restore him gently. But watch yourself, or you also may be tempted.*
>
> —GALATIANS 6:1

However, there are two kinds of stubbornness: there's the stubbornness that can flow from the Holy Spirit, and there's the stubbornness that flows from the flesh. In other words, there's the good kind of stubbornness and the bad kind. The good kind is where you have been persuaded of something by the Holy Spirit and stick to your guns.

I am talking, however, about stubbornness in the flesh. What *are* we like when left to ourselves? We find we are proud; we have big egos that don't want to admit to a wrong. But pride has another side—insecurity. The person who has the biggest ego is equally the most insecure person there is.

What do you do if you have to cope with a person who is stubborn? First, you have to remember this verse. That means that you recognize that you also are vulnerable. Next, you have to get the person to face the facts. Then you must answer their questions honestly.

Yet, at the end of the day, only God can change a person. Sometimes the only way a stubborn person is dealt with is where God Himself brings them to the place where they are backed into a corner and there is only one way out. That is God's gracious way of dealing with them. I know what it is to have God box me into a corner, leaving me with no choice. It is painful at the time, and yet I know it is God's way of getting my attention.

Excerpted from *All's Well That Ends Well* (Authentic Media, 2005).

Passing the Point of No Return

When we are strongly tempted, we immediately start rationalizing to justify any decision we make. We all do this. Perhaps you've said, "I've been depressed, and this has helped me through my depression."

For some, immediate gratification is more important than the salvation of their souls. Jesus asked a question. It's one of those questions you can't answer: *"What good is it for a man to gain the whole world, yet forfeit his soul?"* (Mark 8:36, emphasis added). We are talking about where we spend eternity. Am I to believe that some, in order to satisfy a habit, are ready to give in to temptation and lose their souls? Some have been brought up in a Christian home and have turned their backs on the gospel. Some have heard the gospel preached and kept rationalizing, always thinking there would be another opportunity. But the Bible says that there will come a day when they will not hear the gospel that once stirred them.

> Then the LORD said, "My Spirit will not contend with man forever."
> —GENESIS 6:3

If the Holy Spirit is dealing with you, while there's a little tug in your heart, respond to Him!

You see, *this* is the way the devil works. Jacob had the stew *ready*. He didn't have to say to Esau, "Now that you've sworn the birthright is mine, I'll go and prepare it for you." It was ready. The devil will already have someone there to drink with you, to have sex with, or to give you easy money.

Esau wanted to do something to change everything, but he had passed the point of no return. The Bible tells us that he couldn't reverse it, though he tried with tears (Gen. 27:38).

Now is the time to weep. Weep for your sins. Be sorry, and thank God that He is coming to you again. Look to His Son and trust Him. If you hear His voice, are you willing to do that today? Jesus says, "Come to me" (Matt. 11:28).

Excerpted from *All's Well That Ends Well* (Authentic Media, 2005).

Walking With God Without Fanfare

That which set Enoch apart from the rest of his generation was his sudden disappearance, and yet there was something that lay behind that disappearance in which his real secret is to be found: Enoch "walked with God." Yet surely this man Enoch was not the man who would be voted by his contemporaries as the man "most likely to be remembered in history!"

> *By faith Enoch was taken up so that he should not see death; and he was not found because God took him up; for he obtained the witness that before his being taken up he was pleasing to God.*
> —Hebrews 11:5, NAS

Are you aware that the writer to the Hebrews passed by another Enoch as he referred to the Book of Genesis for source material? There was Enoch before our own Enoch in this chapter, and this other Enoch was a contemporary of our Enoch. The other Enoch was a son of Cain (Gen. 4:17), and without doubt Enoch the son of Cain was the more spectacular by contemporary standards. The first city mentioned in the Bible was named after Enoch the son of Cain. How many of us have had a city built in our name?

Consider the people you hear so much about at the present time, such as those you see on television. Consider the movie stars, the best-selling authors, the noisy politicians. The question is, will posterity even recall them? Even twenty years from now? It is quite likely that Enoch the city, not the Enoch who walked with God, was the talk of that generation.

Enoch was not a spectacular man, but he walked with God. The writer to the Hebrews adds that Enoch "pleased God." We are not told that Enoch pleased his friends or his family, for that is sometimes hard to do. We are told that he pleased God, and that is something any of us can do—by faith.

Excerpted from *Believing God* (MorningStar Publications & Ministries, 1997).

Every Christian Has an Anointing

The anointing stems partly from the natural—the way we were made. Our parents, our environment, and our background are all ingredients of no small consequence that figure into our anointing. These are the natural gifts that we operate as a result of the way we were raised, for the gifts we had before we became Christians don't disappear once we are saved.

But the anointing is also that which comes from above—the supernatural. The Holy Spirit comes on top of natural gifting; He is superimposed, and that is why we call the gifts *supernatural*. In fact, the word *anointing* is used in 1 John 2:20, when John says, "You have an anointing from the Holy One, and all of you know the truth."

This anointing will do something for you and will do something for others. If that anointing flows as it should, it will be almost impossible to tell who is blessed

> *As for you, the anointing you received from him remains in you, and you do not need anyone to teach you. But as his anointing teaches you about all things and as that anointing is real, not counterfeit—just as it has taught you, remain in him.*
>
> —1 JOHN 2:27

more, you or other people. There is no such thing as an anointing that is just for you, so that you can soak it in like a sponge. No. The anointing will bless you, *and* it will bless others.

Not everybody's anointing is the same, and no one person has every anointing that is possible. Only one person who ever lived had every conceivable anointing, and that person was Jesus. The Bible says that Jesus had the Holy Spirit without measure, that is, without limit (John 3:34). When you become a Christian, you receive the Holy Spirit. Don't you dare let anyone tell you that you can have the Holy Spirit and not be a Christian.

But the point is, I only have the Spirit in limited measure. I don't have all there is. Only Jesus had all there is. Not everybody's anointing is the same, and no one can do everything. That means we need each other.

Excerpted from *All's Well That Ends Well* (Authentic Media, 2005).

Tuning to the Impulse of the Spirit

When we speak of the impulse of the Spirit, we are in some sense talking about feelings. I admit this is dangerous, because feelings can lead people to do strange things. This impulse may take the form of an insight that is based upon accumulated knowledge. It may be a suspicion that is based upon knowledge experienced. But the impulse of the Spirit, when obeyed, always leads to a feeling of immense peace.

> *Let us therefore make every effort to do what leads to peace and to mutual edification.*
>
> —ROMANS 14:19

One of the most helpful verses in this connection is Romans 14:19. The proof that the impulse of the Spirit lies behind our feeling that we ought to do something is the peace that obedience brings. This verse applies not only to a situation where tensions among people need to be defused, but also to our own inmost feelings. God will never lead us to do what violates our conscience. When I am really following Him, I will have an inner peace that testifies to the fact that I have been true to myself. When heaviness or a feeling of oppression exists, I know that impulse was not from God.

God wants to communicate with us not just at an intellectual level. But God wants to communicate with our whole being—our emotions and senses as well as our minds.

We are to use our minds, yes, but we must also be careful not to quench the Spirit. We are to be harmonious, whole, and balanced people.

Excerpted from *Worshipping God* (Hodder & Stoughton, 2004).

A Problem of Forgiving?

Do you have a problem forgiving people? Perhaps you cannot forgive an unfaithful spouse. You cannot forgive your father because he wasn't a good parent, and when you think of praying to God and calling Him Father, something inside you just switches off. Perhaps you are angry with your mother because you were not her favorite. Perhaps that boss of yours wouldn't give you that recommendation. Maybe someone was unkind or unfair to your child, and you can't forgive them. Perhaps you have a son-in-law who has mistreated your daughter. You live with the feeling of being let down. Someone gave you a promise; you believed it, but he or she didn't keep it.

> *For if you forgive men when they sin against you, your heavenly Father will also forgive you. But if you do not forgive men their sins, your Father will not forgive your sins.*
>
> —MATTHEW 6:14–15

Do you know what it is to want to see another person hurt, smashed, humiliated, or put down? You'd like him to get sick, or you would love to hear of somebody falling into sin, all because he did something to you that wasn't very nice.

What a way to live! We can never come to terms with ourselves if we are unable to forgive others. When I can't forgive, I am the one who is hurting; I am the loser. And yet, because I have such a wicked, sinful heart, even though I know in my head I'm hurting myself, I still want to hurt someone else.

The truth is that the degree to which you hold a grudge will be the degree to which you damage your own health, and not just mentally. A person who holds a grudge and doesn't deal with it eventually gets out of touch with reality, not to mention the physical effects. The point is this: is there someone you need to forgive? Then do so; do it quickly, because the only one you are hurting is yourself.

Excerpted from *All's Well That Ends Well* (Authentic Media, 2005).

Experimental Faith

The vast possibilities of faith described in Hebrews 11, then, are derived from experimental faith. Why call it "experimental"? Because it is a word that not only implies our experience but also invites being tested at the empirical level. The marvel of faith is that it derives its strength from believing God without the evidence of things "seen" but produces works that are clearly visible to anybody who cares to observe.

The question of order is at stake in Hebrews 11:2. If we fail to see the nature of faith, as it is indicated in this profound verse, all that follows in Hebrews 11 will mean much less to us. The writer simply says that by faith these people "obtained witness" (v. 4, KJV). It is to be seen that faith produced the witness, not *vice versa*.

> *For by it the elders obtained a good report.*
>
> —HEBREWS 11:2, KJV

The things that they did, then, are not what produced faith; what they did came as a *result* of their faith. Thus by believing and not seeing, a great many things happened. But their doing these things did not earn them salvation. They were not trying to earn salvation—the opposite is true—it is because they were already assured of God's integrity and faithfulness that they accomplished what they did.

Yet, it was experimental faith, not saving faith, that produced the commendation. Saving faith is intangible; experimental faith is tangible. Hebrews 11 contains one graphic demonstration after another of what one can do experimentally if one already feels accepted by God. God motivates men by accepting them. Our wills are not set free to explore unlimited possibilities through faith until our hearts are first persuaded that God loves us. In short, saving faith must come before experimental faith.

So by saying that faith obtains a good report, our writer shows that what is at first saving faith should become an experimental faith. For the things that experimental faith demonstrates are not accomplished with a view to proving to ourselves that we are saved; we should already know that and be beyond the need for that assurance. Nevertheless, a good report gives proof that saving faith is there.

Excerpted from *Believing God* (MorningStar Publications & Ministries, 1997).

Discovering God for Yourself

Do you remember the time when you discovered God for yourself? I don't necessarily mean remembering the time and place where you were converted, but remembering the intense power of that experience. There's nothing like discovering God so powerfully for yourself that if every other person in the world renounces their faith, and you were the only believer left, you would still trust Him.

Jacob had been so dependent on his parents, especially upon his mother; he had never wandered far from home. He was not like Esau, who was a man of the fields. Jacob had never done anything like this before, so he must have been afraid.

Here was a man scared to death, having to leave home because his brother wanted to kill him. Perhaps you are away from home. You've been thrust out and are wondering what life is all about and what is happening to you. Yet, perhaps God has set this up so you may learn to know Him and to discover Him for yourself for the first time.

> *May God Almighty bless you and make you fruitful and increase your numbers until you become a community of peoples. May he give you and your descendants the blessing given to Abraham, so that you may take possession of the land…*
> —GENESIS 28:3–4

At this time in Jacob's life, if he had any relationship with God at all, it was secondhand. Are you like Jacob? Is your religion secondhand? Maybe you were spoon-fed something from your parents or from your grandparents and have a long Christian background.

Could it be that you are wrestling with the question, does God exist? "If He does," you may say, "He certainly wouldn't like me because of all the wicked things I have done."

Jesus died for those who have a guilty conscience, who know they don't deserve anything good. The only way you can come to know God is to recognize you are a sinner and repent and ask God for mercy. Perhaps you were never willing to hear the gospel before, but God has you in such a state you are hemmed in and willing to listen now. God may have brought events to such a situation where all you can do is just see His mercy.

Excerpted from *All's Well That Ends Well* (Authentic Media, 2005).

Being Broken

Jacob the manipulator had met his match. Let me introduce Laban. Jacob got what he deserved. Little did Jacob know that God was doing two things at the same time, and He will do it for every believer.

1. He gives you something to live for.

2. He will be in the process of breaking you.

Jacob needed to be broken. We all need to be broken. What does that mean? It means God has to break us of having a hard heart and walking over everybody.

> *Who is going to harm you if you are eager to do good? But even if you should suffer for what is right, you are blessed. "Do not fear what they fear; do not be frightened."*
>
> —1 PETER 3:13–14

Jacob did not realize it then, but for the next twenty years, after falling head over heels in love, he would see what it was like to be on the other end of manipulation, because Laban proved to be one of the most ruthless manipulators the Bible describes.

Do you know when we are broken? It is when we are treated unfairly and learn to keep quiet about it. God wants to bring us to the place where we can take pain and injustice without complaining, because that is what Jesus did. On the cross, He who knew no sin was made sin. Jesus did not deserve to be crucified and could only say, "Father, forgive them, for they do not know what they are doing" (Luke 23:34). He knew what it was like to take injustice, unfairness, and hate.

You see, it's one thing when you suffer because you deserve it—it's quite another thing when it's unfair. Perhaps you are wondering why you have been treated unfairly. It's so that you can accept what is unfair and keep quiet about it. This is the goal, and that is brokenness. If you are in a situation where what you are having to endure is very unfair indeed, then do I have news for you! That means that God has great plans for you, because the greater the injustice, and the quieter you are, the greater the blessing you are going to be to others.

Excerpted from *All's Well That Ends Well* (Authentic Media, 2005).

The Unloved Woman

Leah, Jacob's first wife, not his choice and not part of his plans, can be seen in the Bible as the unloved woman. Perhaps she was unloved by everybody. Jacob didn't love her. She was plain, and Jacob never pretended to notice Leah. So we see Leah was also unloved by her father, because no father would have treated his daughter like that if he cared about the way she felt. Leah was manipulated and controlled by an uncaring father. Can you identify with that?

So why is this story relevant? It is especially relevant to any woman who feels unloved. It could be because of an unhappy relationship with her father. You have felt unloved as long as you can remember because you haven't known a father's love. Perhaps you feel unloved because of an unhappy relationship with a brother or a sister. It could be you feel unloved because of a husband or because of another man who has hurt and rejected you. My word to you is this: God cares about that. Furthermore, this story is relevant not only to women, but also to any man, any husband, any father. If you have been insensitive to a woman's feelings and have underestimated the hurt she feels by her rejection, you may come to appreciate the depth of her pain.

> *When morning came, there was Leah! So Jacob said to Laban, "What is this you have done to me? I served you for Rachel, didn't I?"*
>
> —Genesis 29:25

We are all different, and because we do not share the same problems and weaknesses, we may feel it is hard to find someone else who will understand how we feel. The point is that God sees and understands, and to prove it, He sent His Son into the world, who lived on this earth, tempted at every point just as we are, yet He was without sin. And even if no one else understands, Jesus will understand completely. Do you know we can talk to Him and tell Him just what we're feeling? No one ever cared for us like Jesus.

Excerpted from *All's Well That Ends Well* (Authentic Media, 2005).

The Proof of Conversion

There are many women who are angry with God because they feel He did not give them good looks, and so men find them unattractive. Perhaps you feel this way. Let me ask you a question: Do you wish you looked different, that you were better-looking than you are? I suppose we all wish that. But maybe, one day, when we get to heaven, we'll see it was a particular kindness, which we couldn't see at the time, that God made us just as we are. Do you know what God wants to achieve in you and me? He wants us to come to terms with our looks, with our gifts, with our limitations, with our place in society, with our parents, with the way we've been treated, and to learn to like ourselves like that. One of the greatest evidences of grace is that we like ourselves just as we are.

> *In all this, Job did not sin by charging God with wrongdoing.*
>
> —JOB 1:22

The proof of conversion is that you see through to the true God and don't let circumstances divert you. I have often been amazed how black people in the Deep South ever became saved when I consider how badly their masters treated them. Yet they heard talk of heaven and knew one day they were going there, where they would be out of their misery. They could identify with that. That's why they were converted. God has a way of getting us past our circumstances. No matter how dreadful our experiences might have been, God has a way of reaching us, and the most unlikely person can be the most glorious convert. The experiences that may have caused us to feel the deepest bitterness can turn out to be our salvation. God has designed all things to get us to look to Him.

Excerpted from *All's Well That Ends Well* (Authentic Media, 2005).

God Loves Justice

The God of the Bible loves justice, and if you are being treated unfairly, God knows it. It is only a matter of time, and He is going to compensate. That's a promise. Let me tell you something about Jesus, God the Son: Jesus is full of compassion. Jesus sees your tears. He knows you're hurt.

Did the Lord notice how Leah was feeling? The Bible says, "When the LORD saw Leah was not loved, he opened her womb" (Gen. 29:31). What was Leah's compensation? Rachel, whom Jacob loved, was barren. Leah, the unloved woman, came through where it ultimately mattered. Nothing could stop Jacob being the father of many sons because God had foreordained it. Therefore, God's word was at stake (Gen. 22:17). You could call it His sense of humor, you could call it His sense of justice, but when God saw that Leah was not loved, He opened her womb. Rachel, the one who was loved, was contributing nothing to this oath that God swore to Abraham, Isaac, and Jacob.

> For I, the LORD, love justice.
> —ISAIAH 61:8

Leah gave birth to Judah, the one through whom the Messiah, God's Son, came. Her crown was that she graced the church with glory as no other wife of Jacob could have done. Leah's desire was to have a husband who loved her, but her crown was what she did for the future of Israel. Jacob never appreciated Leah, but God did. And so do we.

Are you an unloved woman? God knows that. He's going to do things for you, and if you start counting your blessings, He's going to make it up to you—it's only a matter of time.

Excerpted from *All's Well That Ends Well* (Authentic Media, 2005).

Loved by the Lord

Leah was unloved by her husband but was loved by the Lord, whereas Rachel was loved by her husband but was barren. The Lord did not honor Rachel in the thing that began to matter more than her beauty, her brains, and everything else she had going for her.

What is the difference between having love from someone here below and receiving love from the Lord? Earthly love is only of the here and now, but the love that is from above has the future in mind. I want to ask you this: Do you feel deprived because you haven't had a great education, you don't have a brilliant brain or good looks, you don't have a good job, and you feel unappreciated? But there's more to life than beauty or brains that make people excel.

> *When the LORD saw that Leah was not loved, he opened her womb, but Rachel was barren.*
>
> —GENESIS 29:31

I have this question: Are you loved by the Lord? That's what matters. You ask, "How can I know?" Well, to begin with, Hebrews 12:6 says, "The Lord disciplines those he loves." What does this mean? It means God begins to deal with you; He forces you to learn something in a way that is pretty tough. It may be the Lord who has kept you from getting that job or from getting married. It may be the Lord who has brought you to a place where everything happening around you is bad, and you wonder where God is. Are all the bad things that happen God's doing? Yes. God brings you so low that there's nowhere to look but up, and then, when you start looking at Him, He says, "Oh, good, you're coming to Me. That is what I wanted." And you begin to realize that the Lord loved you so much that He beckoned you in His direction. You see, those whom the Lord loves, He deals with, and those who are dealt with are truly His; they will go to heaven and no one else.

But one day you will find out that God loved you so much that, to get your attention, He brought you to the place where you just looked to Him.

Excerpted from *All's Well That Ends Well* (Authentic Media, 2005).

How to Face the Unexpected

Fear of what the future holds in store begins in childhood: we discover that our parents and friends may disappoint us or even reject us; we learn that illness or accidents may happen suddenly and that people we love die; we learn that we do not always succeed and begin to fear failure.

> *For everyone born of God overcomes the world. This is the victory that has overcome the world, even our faith.*
>
> — 1 JOHN 5:4

Yet wondering what the future holds in store does not end with our childhood. As adults, we know that life is filled with uncertainty and that even within the short span of twenty-four hours something can happen that will change our lives forever. Furthermore, none of us know when death will call us to stand before our Maker and account for the way we have lived.

I think we can define maturity as "learning to face the unexpected." Now if ever a person had to face the unexpected, it was John. So we will find it instructive to see how he faced his uncertain and uncompromising future on the island of Patmos.

How was he able to cope? John knew that faith was important. "Everyone born of God overcomes the world. This is the victory that has overcome the world, even our faith" (1 John 5:4). This gives you an idea of how John felt and how much he trusted in the Lord.

When you become a Christian, you may face the future without fear. John could face the unexpected because he was "in the Spirit." You may ask, "When will the Spirit of the Lord come on me?" The answer is simple: the Holy Spirit has *already* come, because Jesus said, "The words I have spoken to you are spirit and they are life" (John 6:63). He has come in God's Word with the best news you will ever hear: God has taken on your case and invites you to receive Jesus as your Savior.

Excerpted from *A Vision of Jesus* (Christian Focus Publications Ltd., 1999).

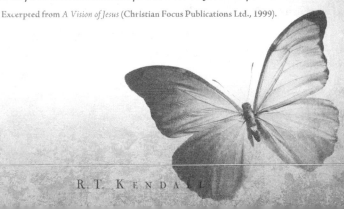

R. T. KENDALL

Coping With a Rival

Do you have a rival? Is there someone who is in competition with you? Is there someone who gets under your skin?

A rival is a competitor, someone who is a threat, a person who could upstage you. Sooner or later most of us know what it is to have a rival. It may be a close friend.

> *I saw that all labor and all achievement spring from man's envy of his neighbor.*
> —ECCLESIASTES 4:4

Perhaps you don't mention the rivalry between you, you rarely think about it, and yet it's just beneath the surface. Sometimes that rival is an enemy, and it would seem in this case it almost came to that. Leah and Rachel were so jealous of each other because although Rachel had the looks, Leah could produce children; that was her claim to fame. We don't know whether this caused rivalry between Leah and Rachel as they grew up, but it's possible.

Ambition will get things done, but achieving that ambition will make another person jealous. You know the feeling when you've achieved something and someone says, "I'm very happy for you," and somehow you don't really think they are. Sometimes it's the loneliest thing to have accomplished something and you don't have anyone you can tell who will be glad for you.

You see, an ambitious person may start out wanting people to admire them, but that won't be enough, ultimately, to bring glory to God. God wants to bring you to a place where you just want to please Him.

Perhaps a rival spirit has brought you to a place where you have lost all sense of pride, you've been put down, and you have lost all sense of self-esteem. Often a rival lives for one thing, and that is to make you look bad. It is very painful. What can you do if you have a rival? You can let a rival spirit throw you or destroy you, or you can let them be the best thing that has ever happened to you. The day will come when you are so thankful for that "thorn in the flesh."

Excerpted from *All's Well That Ends Well* (Authentic Media, 2005).

BY LOVE TRANSFORMED

Wait for Vindication

Isaiah could say that about one who longed for a special touch, a breakthrough, or vindication, and that's God's word for you. Do not be afraid. You will not suffer shame. Do not fear disgrace. You will not be humiliated.

In ancient times barrenness was regarded as a sign of God's disapproval. Rachel believed her inability to conceive and the withholding of vindication meant that God did not approve of her.

Perhaps you are blaming yourself for what you don't have. You keep thinking, *What have I done wrong? What can I do?* The truth is that God is sovereign. He can do what He pleases, with whom He pleases, when He pleases. This is His word for you. The day came when God remembered Rachel. He listened to her and opened her womb.

There is a possibility that God wants to do something for you in the future that will make it seem that what you have now is nothing in comparison.

Rachel's first son was the future prime minister of Egypt, although she wouldn't live to see it. She named him Joseph because she wanted another baby. Indeed, God gave her another son, Benjamin. She couldn't have known how strategic he would be. Paul said, "If anyone else thinks he has reasons to put confidence in the flesh, I have more: circumcised on the eighth day…of the tribe of Benjamin" (Phil. 3:4). What Rachel finally received was worth waiting for. To this very hour we all benefit from it, for it was Paul who took the gospel to the Gentiles.

> *Sing, O barren woman, you who never bore a child; burst into song, shout for joy, you who were never in labor.*
> —ISAIAH 54:1

We should see that her vindication was the result of prayer. The Bible says that God remembered Rachel. He listened to her. This means she had been praying. She needed and wanted something only God could do.

Have you settled for a premature, shallow vindication? God has your vindication scheduled, too. He has a plan for you, and it's far greater than the thing you thought would give you satisfaction.

Excerpted from *All's Well That Ends Well* (Authentic Media, 2005).

The Comfort Zone

I am a very nostalgic person. I love walking down memory lane. Years ago I was being driven to the airport in Cincinnati, Ohio. On the way I caught a glimpse of the old railway station in Cincinnati. I remembered as a boy how we always had to change trains at that station to visit my grandparents in Illinois. I asked the driver, "Would you mind if we drove over to the old Union Station (as we called it)?" He was happy to do so. I got out and walked inside. It did me a world of good. And yet it was sheer nostalgia—there was nothing spiritual about it at all. It was a precious memory being relived.

> *I am obligated both to Greeks and non-Greeks, both to the wise and the foolish.*
> —ROMANS 1:14

But it taught me a lesson. Not only can we not go back to yesterday, but also so much of what we think is valid today is whether we "connect" to it. Some call it our "comfort zone." If it reminds us of where we've been, we are more likely to accept it. If someone we trust says something new, we will take it on board every time, but if we don't like the person, we tend to be suspicious no matter how valid his or her point may be.

I once listened to a friend of mine read aloud a statement that gripped him. I replied, "I like that—read it again." He did. "Who said that?" I asked. When he told me, my stomach churned. It was by a person whose views on so many issues are those I reject categorically. I began to see what I could find that was *wrong* with it. Then I realized how childish I was behaving. Either I will recognize truth for its own sake, or I am going to embrace the thoughts only of those who adhere to my way of thinking. I felt convicted to my fingertips. I vowed then and there to be a seeker of truth, no matter who says it. Surely I can accept truth, even if it is stated by my enemy! We must be willing to follow truth no matter where it leads us. This is the only way you and I can recognize and experience today's anointing.

Excerpted from *The Anointing: Yesterday, Today, Tomorrow* (Charisma House, 2003).

How to Cope With Mistreatment

How do you cope with mistreatment? The story about Laban and the way he treated Jacob may have much to teach us.

Jacob worked for Laban fourteen years, keeping his agreement in exchange for Laban's two daughters. Then another six years elapsed before Jacob finally made the break, and it was after Joseph was born when Jacob turned his thoughts toward going home.

Maybe you can identify with the kind of mistreatment Jacob endured for so many years. I have known many people who have put up with so much from others, a controlling parent or a spouse, for instance,

> *Not with eyeservice, as menpleasers; but as the servants of Christ, doing the will of God from the heart; with good will doing service, as to the Lord, and not to men: Knowing that whatsoever good thing any man doeth, the same shall he receive of the Lord, whether he be bond or free.*
> —EPHESIANS 6:6–8, KJV

who makes life so unpleasant. It may be a boss. I dare say many reading this dread returning to work on Monday mornings.

I want you to see three ways in which Jacob coped with mistreatment.

1. Jacob was careful not to pick a quarrel with Laban. He knew that what was happening to him was God's way of breaking him. Jacob knew he had been a deceiver himself; now he had met his match. This is the way God may choose to break you: to let you meet your match.

2. Jacob preoccupied himself with what he did best. He gave himself to what God had called him to do. You may have been mistreated, but God has given you a gift. Use it well. One day your time will come and God will say, "Enough is enough."

3. Jacob didn't really break away until he had divine confirmation. "Then the LORD said to Jacob, 'Go back to the land of your fathers and to your relatives, and I will be with you'" (Gen. 31:3). Until then, it had been Jacob's idea, but God had been watching and He said, "Enough is enough. I am with you."

God knows how much you can bear, and He is coming to your rescue at this moment to remind you that the one who was mistreated the most was Jesus who died on the cross.

Excerpted from *All's Well That Ends Well* (Authentic Media, 2005).

The God of Bethel Sees and Speaks

There are things about you that only God knows. You have told nobody, but God has a way of getting inside your heart with a single word. This is the way He conquers the hardest heart and the greatest skeptic with his closed spirit.

Nobody but Jacob knew about Bethel. Bethel was a place so special to Jacob, and God knew exactly what to say. Jacob was so discouraged; he felt he had nothing to live for. And then God turned up with these words: "I am the God of Bethel." God could have introduced Himself by saying, "I am the God of your father, I am the God of Abraham, I am the God of Isaac." But He chose to introduce Himself in such a way that Jacob knew it was the true God.

> *I am the God of Bethel, where you anointed a pillar and where you made a vow to me. Now leave this land at once and go back to your native land.*
>
> —GENESIS 31:13

You may ask why Jacob waited twenty years to hear these words. I can't explain God's timing, but I know it is perfect. God sees the end from the beginning, but He knows we want answers now. It must hurt Him to see our pain, and He longs for the moment He can speak to us. But it will be at the time when it is best for us, and when He finally steps in, we will have no complaints.

It could be that you are struggling with a situation that is very painful, and you ask, "Lord, can You see what they are doing?" You may think you cannot go on because of the pressure you are under. But the God of Bethel is the God who sees. He knows what you are feeling. He sees what they are doing.

God said, "Never will I leave you; never will I forsake you" (Heb. 13:5). The God of Bethel will speak, and He will withhold nothing from you that is good.

Excerpted from *All's Well That Ends Well* (Authentic Media, 2005).

We Are Required to Bear Fruit

It is necessary to remember that as God's field, the true vine, we have the responsibility to be obedient. For if there is no obedience, there will be no fruit to grow on that field. We are told in John 15:8 what the gardener wants: "This is to my Father's glory, that you bear much fruit." What is required is abiding or remaining in Christ.

> Remain in me, and I will remain in you. No branch can bear fruit by itself; it must remain in the vine. Neither can you bear fruit unless you remain in me.
>
> —John 15:4

We cannot do things our way and still abide or remain in Him. Abiding in Him means obedience. So you can see why the mystery of God's sovereignty is not limited to His saving work. He alone *makes things happen* in the work of sanctification, but *without my obedience* there will be no sanctification. It is, as I say, a mystery.

> I am the true vine, and my Father is the gardener. He cuts off every branch in me that bears no fruit, while every branch that does bear fruit he prunes so that it will be even more fruitful.
>
> —John 15:1–2

The second aspect of the believer's responsibility is *observation* of what we are within ourselves. The crops in a field are observable, are they not? What is required, therefore, is that I examine myself. Is there fruit?

If I examine myself, it means I must have objectivity about myself. It is as though I stand back and look at myself; I observe myself. And if I see something that is not right, I deal with it. Paul calls this "judging" ourselves. He says, "But if we judged ourselves, we would not come under judgment" (1 Cor. 11:31). If by the Word of God or by external chastening I judge myself, I will not have further chastening. Yet Paul does say that when we are judged, it is chastening: "When we are judged by the Lord, we are being disciplined so that we will not be condemned with the world" (v. 32). Even when God steps in like that, it proves the person is a Christian.

Excerpted from *When God Says "Well Done!"* (Christian Focus Publications Ltd., 1993).

God Remembers Your Vows

Jacob made a vow to God: "If God will be with me…and will give me food to eat and clothes to wear…of all that you give me I will give you a tenth" (Gen. 28:20–22). Twenty years later, God turned up and said, "I am the God of Bethel. That was the spot where you made a vow to Me." The interesting thing is that when Jacob made a vow to tithe, he didn't have anything. But we read in Genesis 30:43 that he "grew exceedingly prosperous and came to own large flocks, and maidservants and menservants, and camels and donkeys." And now the Lord said, "I will remember your vow."

> *When you make a vow to God, do not delay in fulfilling it. He has no pleasure in fools; fulfill your vow.*
> —Ecclesiastes 5:4

Jacob could have said, "Oh, I didn't think You took notice of that!" But I think as soon as Jacob heard the words, "I am the God of Bethel," he knew exactly what that meant.

Maybe, at this moment, God is taking your mind back to a vow you made to Him. Maybe you took a vow to pray, and He took care of you. But God remembers your vision. He is saying to you, "Come back to Me! Renew that vow!"

That is something God shouldn't have to do, because when you break a vow, that is a serious thing, and in so doing, you effectively release God from having to do anything for you. But God is so gracious, and He is saying to you, "Here I am again. Life is not over yet. There's still time, and if you will turn your life over to Me, I will restore the years the locusts have eaten. I will forgive all that has happened, all the mistakes you have made and the sins you have committed. And not only that, if you will begin now, I will cause everything that you have done in the past, everything that haunts you, that leaves you terrified, to work together for good."

I guarantee that if you return to Him, you will find out that there was a purpose in everything that happened. God has not deserted you. There was a reason He let certain things happen. God meant it for good.

Excerpted from *All's Well That Ends Well* (Authentic Media, 2005).

The Value of Loneliness

Loneliness isn't for nothing. If you are in a situation of enforced solitude, there is a reason. God does not send the thorn in the flesh for nothing. Moreover, it is not punishment. Don't say, "Oh, I am getting my dues!" Wrong!

God got even at the cross. The thorn in the flesh is preparation. We all need preparation in some way. Part of my own preparation has been learning to cope with loneliness.

> *After he had dismissed them, he went up on a mountainside by himself to pray. When evening came, he was there alone.*
> —MATTHEW 14:23

There is loneliness in leadership. Every church leader knows the pain of having to make unpopular decisions, the pain of not getting very close to those you minister to, the pain of treating everybody the same. The loneliness of leadership is part of the job.

But there *are* advantages to loneliness. For example, you have time to pray; you may never have such time again. One reason for enforced solitude is that God wants you all to Himself. He loves your company, and you could be lamenting the very thing that He has designed in order to have your company.

This is your moment to develop two things: (1) to become an intercessor, where you can start praying for people, and (2) to get to know God with an intimacy beyond anything that you dreamed possible.

Another value of loneliness is to make you sympathetic toward others. That is one of the main purposes of any trial. As Paul put it, "And our hope for you is firm, because we know that just as you share in our sufferings, so also you share in our comfort" (2 Cor. 1:7). It produces in you patient endurance of the same sufferings. You will be able to sympathize, and you will be able to identify with another person. Pray you will never forget what it was like, should this thorn be withdrawn from your flesh.

Excerpted from *The Thorn in the Flesh* (Charisma House, 2004).

When God Lets You Down

Perhaps you know the feeling of God letting you down. Do you know when it usually happens? Not only will it be at the worst moment that it could possibly happen, but it will be at the very time when you are doing your very best to get things right—the moment you seek to do God's will.

> When Martha heard that Jesus was coming, she went out to meet him, but Mary stayed at home. "Lord," Martha said to Jesus, "if you had been here, my brother would not have died."
>
> —JOHN 11:20–21

Take the Christian who has strayed away or who has become lukewarm, who suddenly feels God talking to him and he answers, "Yes, Lord. I'll do what You say."

They fully expect God to say, "Wonderful! Let Me tell you what I am going to do to reward that act of obedience: I am just going to bless you; I am going to fill you with love, and you are going to feel My presence. I am going to cause all sorts of good things to happen to you because you are doing the right thing!"

That is the moment when God lets us down. Why? Well, it's always with a good reason. For example, when Lazarus was ill, Mary and Martha sent word to Jesus, "Lord, the one you love is sick," and Jesus did nothing (John 11:3). They were convinced that Jesus would stop everything and go heal their brother—just like that. Instead, Jesus turned up four days after the funeral. The Lord let them down. They felt betrayed, only to find out later that the Lord had a strategy in what He did. What He ended up doing was far greater than what they wanted to happen.

We are not promised that God will deal with those who have hurt us in *this* life.

If you have been mistreated and have been hurt, and you wonder if God sees it happening, I want you to know that God doesn't like it any more than you do, and one day He will correct the situation. It is only a matter of time.

Excerpted from *All's Well That Ends Well* (Authentic Media, 2005).

Forgiving God

Although we often do not see it at first—and for some it takes a longer time—all of our bitterness is ultimately traceable to a resentment of God. This may be an unconscious anger. Some "good" people would be horrified at the thought that they could be harboring bitterness toward God. But we often repress this, too; such knowledge is too painful to admit.

> *The LORD is good, a refuge in times of trouble. He cares for those who trust in him.*
>
> —NAHUM 1:7

The truth is, our bitterness is often aimed at God. Why do we feel this way? Because deep in our hearts we believe that He is the one who allowed bad things to happen in our lives. Since He is all powerful and all knowing, couldn't He have prevented tragedies and offenses from happening? What we ultimately believe is that God is to blame for our hurt.

God does turn evil into blessing. He causes things to work together for good. God did not send His Son into the world to explain evil, but rather to save us from it and to exemplify a life of suffering. Jesus, who was and is the God man, suffered as no one else has or ever will. One day God will clear His own name from the charge of being unjust, but in the meantime, we need to trust Him and take Him at His Word that He is just and merciful.

For all of us who struggle with God's right to allow evil to exist in the world, there still must be a genuine forgiveness on our part, for any bitterness toward God grieves the Holy Spirit. He was never guilty in the first place, but because He sometimes appears to us to have been unfair, we must relinquish our bitterness and wholly forgive Him before we can move on with our lives.

Excerpted from *Total Forgiveness* (Charisma House, 2002).

Never Give Up on Prayer

Did you ever let go when you had a struggle? Did you ever feel you were taking the right course of action, only to hear someone suggest otherwise, and so you gave up?

Then Jesus told his disciples a parable to show them that they should always pray and not give up.

—LUKE 18:1

There comes a time when we all need to be confronted with the fact that we don't know God as well as we may think. God has a way of putting us in our place lest our preconceived ideas and our small way of thinking keep us from seeing Him when He comes.

Reading church history reveals that God turns up in different ways. Take, for example, Hebrews 11. Not one of the people described there—Enoch, Noah, Abraham, Isaac, Jacob, David, and Elijah—could have the luxury of seeing God as He had appeared in previous times. They each had to accept that which was different to them and be regarded as a fool. That is what made faith, faith.

We have to come to the place where we see when God is at work for ourselves, and if no one else believes it, we do. That is how real God must become to us. The difficulty is that in knowing Him a little, we assume we know God better than we really do.

Perhaps you are seeking God, and someone, perhaps a person whom you greatly respect, has persuaded you to give up. Perhaps you have prayed about something, and because God didn't answer you within a short time you gave up. Have you ever wondered what would have happened if you had held on?

The point Jesus made in the parable of the importunate widow was to keep praying and not to give up. Wrestling in prayer isn't all that much fun, and I wonder how many of us have given up too hastily, feeling God was not going to answer.

God graciously comes again. Seek God again with all your heart, and you will find Him.

Excerpted from *All's Well That Ends Well* (Authentic Media, 2005).

Learning to Worship From Angels

The most perfect worshipers in all His creation inside or outside the universe are the angels. Angels are created, nonmaterial, spiritual beings who cannot be seen with the naked eye unless they choose to reveal themselves to us. There are various categories of angels. We know the names of two prominent angels, Michael and Gabriel, but it wouldn't surprise me to learn that every angel has his own name.

> *Holy, holy, holy is the LORD Almighty;*
> *the whole earth is full of his glory.*
> —ISAIAH 6:3

The first thing we can learn about angels with reference to worship is that angels adore God alone. The prophet Isaiah was given to see with his spiritual eyes what is going on in heaven all the time (Isa. 6:1–3).

Everything is done out of love for God. Whatever feeling angels may have for us, their priority is the glory of God. Angels exist to do God's will. As we have seen, they are God's messengers to us, and they reveal God's will to us. You can't argue with or bargain with an angel: they do what they are ordered to do. Angels never tire of worshiping God.

The focal point of the worship of angels is the triune God. They worship Him though they do not know the joy of redemption. They know nothing about the shed blood of the cross being applied to them. Another thing about angels is that they perceive the true essence of God's character. They know that God is holy. God will never cease to be God throughout eternity. Though they have been in His presence and have been worshiping Him for millions of years, the angels still show great reverence for God.

We can learn from angels. And the more we learn, the better we will worship God and the more they will rejoice.

Excerpted from *Worshipping God* (Hodder & Stoughton, 2004).

Letting God Love Us

Someone once told me that my main theme of my preaching could be summed up in one word—vindication. I didn't know what to think of that, but I think it could be summed up in the words "letting God do it." Then I realized something: I wished it could be said that my preaching was summed up in this phrase: "letting God love us."

There is a connection between the principle of vindication and the principle of letting God love us. "Vindication" means to have your name cleared. God alone wants to do that. The moment you and I start to clear our own names, God backs off and says, "OK! Now you do it!" Immediately we are in trouble, and we see the absurdity of trying to do it ourselves. So unless we let God do it, it won't really happen in the right way.

> *Because of the LORD's great love we are not consumed, for his compassions never fail. They are new every morning; great is your faithfulness. I say to myself, "The LORD is my portion; therefore I will wait for him."*
>
> —LAMENTATIONS 3:22–24

The same is true when it comes to this principle of letting God love us. In much the same way, we don't let God love us. Instead, we compete with Him by trying to perform for Him so that we feel worthy of that love. This message is intended for those who feel that God doesn't love them because they haven't matched His standards and feel, therefore, they don't have His approval.

You see, there is so much wrong with all of us, and if we knew just how much, we wouldn't hold our heads high. How is it that we manage to get through the day? How do we manage to come to the Lord's Table when we are all so unworthy? It's because Jesus shed His blood on the cross, and that means infinitely more to God than our getting it right. At the end of the day, despite all our obedience and our efforts to please God, nothing matches the blood that Jesus shed on the cross. Any one of us can hold our heads high in the presence of God, not because in ourselves we have come up to standard, but because of what God has done for us.

You see, that is what makes God, God. He's different. It's a wonderful thing when we come to the place where we just let God love us without our having to perform.

Excerpted from *All's Well That Ends Well* (Authentic Media, 2005).

Gaining Self-Respect

Have you ever heard someone say, "I hate myself"? People who hate themselves don't like other people, and they are miserable. But saying this also gives them a certain kind of self-righteous feeling, as if people will excuse them. But when you have real self-respect you like yourself. You may say, "Oh, I don't think God wants us to like ourselves." Wrong. The apostle Paul said that no man ever hated his own body. (See Ephesians 5:29.) Jesus told us to love our neighbors as ourselves, and that is part of being human. But when you don't appreciate yourself, something has gone wrong.

> *The second is this: "Love your neighbor as yourself." There is no commandment greater than these.*
>
> —MARK 12:31

The opposite of being confident is being fearful. Are you governed by a spirit of fear where you don't have confidence? Are you always looking over your shoulder thinking, *Look who's here! What are they saying? What will they think of me if I do that?* Have you ever wanted publicly to confess Christ but have been afraid of what someone would think if they heard about it? Confidence is lost when you lose self-respect.

The gospel of Jesus Christ was designed to give you self-respect. Jesus will never lead you to do anything that would prevent you being true to yourself. If you want to regain that feeling of self-respect, of liking yourself and feeling confident and unashamed, you need to come to the foot of the cross and get right with Him. Once you put your faith in Jesus, you are given the Holy Spirit. He will be with you and will guide you. The Bible will become the most precious book you have ever known, and you will know through the Spirit and the Word how to live your life. You will begin to like yourself and to have confidence, and you will not live with feelings of guilt and shame.

Excerpted from *All's Well That Ends Well* (Authentic Media, 2005).

We Need Mercy

Have you ever heard of David Brainerd? Had David Brainerd lived, he would have become Jonathan Edwards's son-in-law. He was an unusual man; he was a missionary to the Indians in the state of New York and became almost a model for missionaries. After Brainerd died, Edwards published his journal, and that journal is said to have been responsible for putting more people on the mission field than any other piece of literature.

> *The crowd rebuked them and told them to be quiet, but they shouted all the louder, "Lord, Son of David, have mercy on us!"*
>
> —Matthew 20:31

Once David Brainerd had a quarrel with God. The more he discovered about God, the angrier he got. Brainerd saw four things about God as he read the Bible, and they all made him mad at God. The first thing he saw was that God demanded a perfect righteousness, and he knew he didn't have it. It meant that he would have to have a substitute, and he kept thinking that he could do it alone, until he saw he couldn't produce the righteousness that God required.

The second thing David Brainerd saw was that God demanded perfect faith, and once again he knew he couldn't produce it. He would try to believe perfectly, but he'd find himself doubting. And he became frustrated and got angry with God. The third thing he found out was that God could give faith or withhold it and be just either way, and the fourth thing he discovered was that God could save him or damn him and be just either way. At last he saw that he needed God's mercy. Rather than being angry with God, thinking that he could snap his finger and God would jump, he began to cry out for mercy—and God saved him.

Seeing the God of the Bible makes us realize that we don't have bargaining power. We have no leverage. We have no claim that we could make. We come before God and ask for mercy.

Excerpted from *The God of the Bible* (Authentic Media, 2002).

How Does God Speak?

How does God speak? Primarily through His Word, the Bible. As far as I know how, I only preach what the Scriptures ask me to preach. I don't make up things or come up with ideas; I just follow the Bible and let it speak for itself. It means that when I speak the Holy Spirit can use my words, and thus they are not merely *my* words. At some stage, you become conscious that God Himself is speaking.

Sometimes God will speak in a particular context. You may be in a situation where you are suffering. Perhaps something traumatic has happened to you. Maybe you have gone through a particular kind of trial, and you happen to be in the service, and, lo and behold, the word that is spoken is so relevant and so intimate that it's almost embarrassing. You think that the preacher knows all about you, but it's only the Holy Spirit applying the Word.

> *And it is the Spirit who testifies, because the Spirit is the truth. For there are three that testify: the Spirit, the water and the blood; and the three are in agreement.*
> —1 JOHN 5:6–8

In other words, once we hear God speak, it's as if we suddenly understand it. The person who hears the same old gospel week after week may say, "I have heard it before, and I know all of that." Then suddenly the truth hits him, and he says, "Oh, I see it! I see that Jesus lived on this earth, kept the law for us, and because He did, He is our righteousness. I am actually saved by what someone else did. Jesus died on the cross as my substitute, and God punished Him instead of me. The blood He shed satisfied God's justice."

"You've got it. Well, you've heard it a thousand times."

"Yes, but tonight I heard it for the *first* time."

Someone has said that no one has the right to hear the gospel twice until all have heard it once, which is a fine statement. But a truer statement would be that nobody hears the gospel once until they have heard it twice, and suddenly they realize that God is speaking to them. You see, only the Holy Spirit can make you understand the gospel.

Excerpted from *All's Well That Ends Well* (Authentic Media, 2005).

God's Specific Word to You

God doesn't always pay a second visit to those to whom He has spoken before. He doesn't have to; He doesn't need to. What is it like when He does?

> *When Solomon had finished building the temple of the LORD…the LORD appeared to him a second time….the LORD said to him…*
>
> —1 KINGS 9:1–3

It will be very real, just as real as the first time. When God speaks a second time in the manner I refer— when He came to Jonah, to Abraham, to Solomon, and as when He came to Jacob, it would have been a very real experience.

It confirms what God said the first time. Sometimes a person needs to hear the same thing again. When God came to Abraham the second time, He said the same thing as before.

What does it mean then when you are one of those to whom God comes a second time and when He speaks powerfully again?

It means four things:

1. God cares a lot.

2. He wasn't speaking aimlessly the first time.

3. You are special. You are earmarked for something special.

4. He wants you to believe what He said the first time and never forget it.

So when God speaks a second time, it's because you especially need to hear Him speak to get you through what lies ahead. I can tell you this: if you want God to speak to you a second time—if that's what you need—that's what you will get.

Excerpted from *All's Well That Ends Well* (Authentic Media, 2005).

When the Spirit Leaves—Quenched or Grieved

The Spirit has feelings, and we can hurt His feelings when we grieve Him by the things we do. The Greek word translated "grieve" (*lupeo*) comes from *lupee*, which means "pain" or "sorrow." It is the opposite of joy.

We know from the apostle Paul that the Holy Spirit can also be quenched. Paul's words *put out* come from the Greek word *sbennumi*, which basically means "to quench." In the ancient Greek world it referred generally to extinguishing fire or burning objects. Paul's warning not to quench the Spirit can only mean that sometimes the Spirit's fire can be put out.

It is hard to know the difference between the Holy Spirit being grieved and being quenched. But there are nuances of understanding we can discover. *Grieving the Spirit* refers to actions of ours that hinder the Spirit from being Himself—from *being* what He could be *in us*. On the other hand, *quenching the Spirit* refers to actions of ours that hinder the Spirit from *doing* what He could do *through us*.

> *Do not put out the Spirit's fire.*
> —1 THESSALONIANS 5:19

When He is *ungrieved* in us we will manifest His personality—defined in Galatians 5:22–23 as the "fruit of the Spirit." If we have not grieved the Spirit *in us*, we will also demonstrate these characteristics—just as Jesus demonstrated them.

When He is *unquenched* in us we may well manifest His power, perhaps through the expressions of the gifts of the Spirit. (See 1 Corinthians 12:8–10.)

The anointing must be the totality of all that the Spirit is and is able to do. We must want to exemplify the personality of Jesus as much as to demonstrate His power. We must experience the Holy Spirit from within—*ungrieved* in our private lives—before we can anticipate an outward demonstration of His power. If we expect the Dove of the Spirit to *remain*, it is surely essential that all we *are* does nothing to cause the Dove to flutter away.

Excerpted from *The Sensitivity of the Spirit* (Charisma House, 2002).

The ABCs of Worship at the Lord's Table

From these verses we can discover what you might call the "ABCs" of worship at the Lord's Table. It is amazing how we can do something for years and years and think we know so much about it, only to find suddenly that we really know so little.

The first thing we can see is that worship at the Lord's Table was initiated by Jesus Christ Himself. It is the Lord's own design.

The second main thing we can see is that true worship at the Lord's Table only happens when certain conditions are in operation. Paul gives a series of sober exhortations, and whether or not we apply

The Lord Jesus, on the night he was betrayed, took bread, and when he had given thanks, he broke it and said, "This is my body, which is for you; do this in remembrance of me." In the same way, after supper he took the cup, saying, "This cup is the new covenant in my blood; do this, whenever you drink it, in remembrance of me."

—1 Corinthians 11:23–25

them will determine whether we will actually worship at the Lord's Table.

The first thing is that the eating and drinking be done in a worthy manner.

The second thing that must happen is that there must be self-examination. Let these three words help us, then, with our self-examination: self-importance, self-isolation, and insensitivity. We will have passed the test when we refuse to claim that we are in the right over another Christian, when we are at peace with all our Christian brothers and sisters, and when we feel abiding compassion for those who don't have as much as we have.

The third exhortation is that there should be a discerning of the Lord's body (v. 29). What is actually meant by "the Lord's body"? Simply, it is feeling Jesus near. It is *not* seeing physical bread and calling it Jesus. It is *not* seeing physical wine and calling it Jesus' blood.

When we partake of the bread and the wine, Jesus draws near. We know this because He said that He would be there. And the kingdom of Jesus is here, now. As Christians we are members of it. So when we come to the Lord's Supper, Jesus is there. The question to ask is, do we see Him?

Excerpted from *Worshipping God* (Hodder & Stoughton, 2004).

Suffering and Sovereignty

In a sense all Christians are chosen vessels, because a Christian is a person chosen by God from the foundation of the world. But there are those Christians raised for a *very* special work, and we call them "sovereign vessels." A sovereign vessel is someone chosen by God for special work, and the more special the work, the more specialized the suffering.

Jacob was a sovereign vessel, and we have already seen how he suffered—but he was undergoing the greatest trial yet. All that he went through in running from Esau, all that he endured after being with Laban, and all he suffered in losing Rachel, all of that was eclipsed when he saw the bloodstained coat of many colors. Not knowing that it had been dipped in the blood of a goat, he concluded his son Joseph was dead and he would never see him again. It was the trial of trials.

Perhaps you know great suffering, and just when you think you can't take any more, lo and behold, something happens that turns into the worst ordeal you have ever undergone. Listen. It is a hint from God—you are a sovereign vessel—He doesn't do that without a reason. Deep suffering is a strong hint that God has chosen you for a very special task. It's an honor to be a sovereign vessel. But if you want to volunteer to be a sovereign vessel, don't do it until you're ready for God to deal with the sore spots in your life, for you do have some. Some have sore spots, and it is as though they have them forever and nothing is ever done about them. But if you have been raised up for a special work, God is going to refine you by dealing with the sore spots in your life. You may volunteer to be a sovereign vessel—but don't do it until you are ready to pay the price. The connection between suffering and a sovereign vessel is inseparable. One day you will look back and see the hand of God in everything.

> *But if when you do what is right and suffer for it you patiently endure it, this finds favor with God. For you have been called for this purpose.*
>
> —1 Peter 2:20-21, nas

Excerpted from *All's Well That Ends Well* (Authentic Media, 2005).

The Providence of God

Providence means that God overrules. He sets aside something to take over. He works through evil and through our weaknesses. Do you know why He does it? It is so He receives all the glory and honor.

Are you presently in a situation where there seems to be no way out? God says, "Give that one to Me." Are you trying to make it easy for God? He says, "No, I want a difficult case. I want something that humans cannot possibly do. Leave it to Me! I'll do it!" Will you let God do it, or do you have to pull a string here and there and say, "Remember me? My name is…"

> *What is impossible with men is possible with God.*
> —LUKE 18:27

Humanly speaking, there was no way your situation could turn out for good, but God loves to work when everything looks absolutely bleak. God's providence sorts out the sore spots in our lives.

Do you have a sore spot? Of course you have. Could it be your pride that's getting you into trouble all the time? Are you hypersensitive? Is it your jealousy? Is it your negative spirit? Is it that you love gossip? Could it be sexual lust or some addiction? Have you stepped on people to get where you are? Do you have an inability to handle money? God has to deal with you. Do you want to be exalted? That's all right. There's nothing wrong with that. God wants to exalt you—in *His* due time—but the sore spot will have to be dealt with first.

Excerpted from *All's Well That Ends Well* (Authentic Media, 2005).

Living Between the Times

What do we mean by the phrase "living between the times"? To begin with, that is what life is—a series of events linking the past and the future. Most are mundane happenings, but others are so special in their nature.

Between the times is when you are waiting for it to actually happen. Could it be that is where you are? Perhaps you feel that you are living between the times. You may not realize that God has brought you to this place, but you will discover that God is up to something.

> *It will be good for that servant whom the master finds doing so when he returns.*
> —LUKE 12:43

Why is it that God makes us wait and for so long? There are three things I want us to see:

1. Some things take time—even for God.

How many of you have ever said in your prayers, "O Lord, how much longer?" But what about God? He has to wait, too. He has the power to end everything, but for reasons that we will not understand until we get to heaven, God subjected Himself to the conditions He created, whereby He too must wait.

2. Between the times there's something for us to learn.

Perhaps you have lost sight of God's promises and are still blaming everybody else. You may be a mature person, yet you still wallow in self-pity. If that is the case, you need to seek a fresh and wonderful outpouring of the Holy Spirit.

3. Between the times, God still looks after us.

Some people mistake God's care for their needs for being in right standing with Him. Now, God's provision *may* show that God is with you, but it doesn't mean that everything is right with you.

From our viewpoint it is sometimes difficult to understand why God doesn't act sooner. But when, eventually, He acts, we come to see that it couldn't have happened sooner, and it is a mercy that it didn't.

Excerpted from *All's Well That Ends Well* (Authentic Media, 2005).

Being Accepted

All of us can tell whether another person is going to accept us. We can almost feel it. You must have some inkling if you came to see me whether or not I would listen, whether I would care. What I wish is that I could radiate the love of Jesus, that you would feel that I want to be like Him.

> *A man with leprosy came and knelt before him and said, "Lord, if you are willing, you can make me clean." Jesus reached out his hand and touched the man. "I am willing," he said. "Be clean!" Immediately he was cured of his leprosy.*
> —MATTHEW 8:2–3

The leper knew that if he went to Jesus he would be accepted.

Some people teach that a precondition to becoming a Christian is that you have to do this or that, and only then will Jesus accept you. What we see here is that Jesus accepted the leper just as he was, and lo and behold, the leper believed Jesus could heal him, and Jesus did. Jesus is still the same today. He accepts you as you are.

In fact, we are told in John 8:3–11 that Pharisees, who were a self-righteous, legalistic group of people, brought a woman caught in adultery and said to Jesus, "In the Law Moses commanded us to stone such women. Now what do you say?" Jesus bent down and started to write in the ground with His finger. Then He said to these people, "If any one of you is without sin, let him be the first to throw a stone at her." Hearing that, they all left. Then Jesus said to the woman, "Where are they? Has no one condemned you?"

The woman said, "No one, sir."

Then Jesus declared, "Then neither do I condemn you. Go now and leave your life of sin."

What did He do? He accepted her. That is His way. Jesus displays such tenderness. I could give one example after another to assure you that whatever may be in your past, whatever it is that you've done, this Jesus will accept you.

Excerpted from *All's Well That Ends Well* (Authentic Media, 2005).

Follow Him—Even When It Causes You to Lose Credibility

Going outside the camp means to leave the traditional structures or establishment, the way of thinking that is common to you and your friends (or enemies), and even the people who may be hopelessly conservative. It is leaving them behind, and that is a painful thing to do. Those Hebrew Christians probably had it much tougher than anything you or I will have to endure. They broke from an ancient tradition that preceded them by over 1,300 years; they were also outnumbered by tens of thousands of Jews who stuck with the traditional way of worship. Talk about leaving your comfort zone! They really did this, and those who went outside the camp lost all credibility.

> *Let us, then, go to him outside the camp, bearing the disgrace he bore.*
> —HEBREWS 13:13

It hurts when people no longer believe in you: they do not trust you, and you have lost credibility with them. But Jesus has been there, too. In the early part of John 6, Jesus had to escape the crowds because they were determined to make Him king (vv. 14–15), but in the end they didn't believe in Him at all (v. 66)! Jesus lost credibility in their eyes.

What causes us to lose credibility will largely be what we believe and those with whom we associate. When what we believe is unfamiliar territory to our friends, they quietly tiptoe away, and we wake up one day with the realization that these people aren't behaving the same way toward us.

God has an amazing way of causing us to lose credibility in order to get our attention and make us want His opinion. When everyone believes in us and wants to "crown" us, it is not so easy to value God's approval of us. But when they back away and distance themselves from us, we are more likely to seek the praise that comes only from Him. He allows situations and circumstances to develop in such a way that drives us to our knees to seek His face.

Excerpted from *Pure Joy* (Charisma House, 2006).

Tough Love

D r. James Dobson has a phrase: "Love must be tough." Tenderness is central to Jesus' nature, but so is toughness. Jesus is God, yet Jesus is man. You can't reconcile the two, but they are both true. Jesus is tender, yet Jesus can be tough.

Jesus tests us to this very day because He wants to know how we feel about *His* Father. Let me tell you something: there is a lot of talk from people who say, "Jesus I can accept, but I don't like the God of the Bible." However, they need to understand that the God of the Old Testament is also the God of the New Testament. Not only that, but the God of the Bible is the Father of Jesus. You may think that you are endearing yourself to Jesus by saying, "Jesus, I can take You, but I don't like Your Father." But that will incur His anger. You could not have said anything worse.

> *Those whom I love I rebuke and discipline.*
>
> —REVELATION 3:19

Before you are saved, you have to be reconciled with God, the Father of Jesus. There is no way you can avoid the God of the Bible if you are going to go to heaven. Jesus makes it clear that His Father is the God with whom you must come to terms. He wants to test you. He wants to see how you are going to react, how you feel about His Father. Perhaps years ago you became disillusioned with God; you felt He let you down, that He hurt you in some way. You believed then that your feelings were justified. Jesus wants to know how you feel about God now.

How do we know about the toughness of Jesus? Take, for example, when Jesus saw His disciples on the Sea of Galilee in a storm; they were rowing but making no headway as the winds were so strong. Jesus saw them. He could have gone to their rescue immediately. He didn't. He waited. That meant He had to be tough, even though what He wanted to do was to go at once. So love is tough. And He will test you, too.

Excerpted from *All's Well That Ends Well* (Authentic Media, 2005).

Adversity Births Thanksgiving

When the *Mayflower* landed at Plymouth, Massachusetts, on November 11, 1620, the Pilgrim fathers were full of expectancy. Months before they were addressed by the pastor, John Robinson (c. 1575–1625), who said to them, "The Lord hath more light and truth to break forth his word." The future looked so bright once the Pilgrims landed, but they fell on unbelievably hard times their first year, when many actually starved to death.

Why did God allow such unexpected adversity to a group of people who sincerely thought they were glorifying God in their venture? I do not know, but I know this: once they had begun to experience God's bounty they *determined* to be grateful. The result was Thanksgiving Day.

The original Thanksgiving of the Pilgrims was ordered after the first harvest in Plymouth Colony (1621). Special days were often appointed in New England for thanksgiving or fasting. Beginning in Connecticut in 1649, the observance of an annual harvest festival spread throughout New England by the end of the eighteenth century.

> *From them will come songs of thanksgiving and the sound of rejoicing.*
> —JEREMIAH 30:19

George Washington proclaimed the first national Thanksgiving in 1789. With Abraham Lincoln's proclamation in 1863, it became an annual observance. By an act of Congress in 1941, Thanksgiving Day is the fourth Thursday of November. Sadly, few Americans know this history, and not many care. Although it is America's favorite holiday, it is sadly known largely now for eating turkey and watching football. Few go to church to thank God on that day.

I believe that the falling of the twin towers of the World Trade Center in New York City on September 11, 2001, was a wake-up call to all the nations of the world. Ungrateful nations will be judged—sooner or later. Ungrateful leaders, the rich and the poor, will be judged—sooner or later.

There's a great day coming! Are you ready? The best preparation for that day is to be found in repentance, thanking God.

Excerpted from *Just Say Thanks!* (Charisma House, 2005).

When It's Time to Move On

You will know it is time to move on when circumstances have coalesced in such a manner that you just say, "I can see there is only one thing to do." It is when God takes things out of your hands. Do you know what Christian conversion is? It is when God has caused things to happen in such a way that you really had no choice. God has sent one signal after another, and you know that the only way forward is to move on. That's what I am challenging you to do now—to make the step.

> Then the LORD said to Moses, "Why are you crying out to me? Tell the Israelites to move on."
>
> —EXODUS 14:15

Look at where you are and all that is there—famine—that which gives you no hope. Now look at what lies ahead: God promises life, and He will take care of you. Consider the possibility that one day you will go to heaven and you will see Jesus face-to-face. You will discover exactly what He looks like, what His voice sounds like, how tall He is. You will see Him. You will enjoy complete security: there will be no worries about employment, about where your next meal is coming from, about having to take exams, or having to prove yourself in some way. In heaven there will be eternal security, peace, and joy, no tears, no pain, no sorrow.

So I ask you, which do you prefer? Do you choose to go to heaven or live on this earth for another year or two of pleasure? How much time do you have left? Do you really want to cling to that habit, that lifestyle, that viewpoint, which have brought you near to ruin when the alternative is going to heaven?

I would challenge any Christian reading this to spend your time in prayer without seeking for a thing. Instead spend the whole time thanking the Lord. Sacrifice what you would like to ask Him. Sacrifice the time: just give it to Him, and be thankful. You have so much cause to be thankful.

Excerpted from *All's Well That Ends Well* (Authentic Media, 2005).

The Trap of Self-Pity

Self-pity is feeling sorry for yourself. You feel that you are the object of unfair treatment, that you have had to carry a load that few, if any, understand or appreciate. You perhaps feel you were unlucky with having the parents you had, the environment you grew up in, the education you received. You may have been abused by an authority figure, lied about, rejected, and discriminated against. Whenever you get a chance to excel, something happens to derail what had possibilities. The future looks bleak, life is passing you by, and there is little to live for.

Speaking to none other than God, Elijah said, "I have been very zealous for the Lord God Almighty....I am the only one left, and now they are tying to kill me too" (1 Kings 19:14). First of all, Elijah was not the only prophet left and should have known better. Obadiah had taken a hundred prophets and hid them in a cave—

> *Their father Jacob said to them, "You have deprived me of my children. Joseph is no more and Simeon is no more, and now you want to take Benjamin. Everything is against me!"*
> —Genesis 42:36

and Elijah knew that (1 Kings 18:1–15). There were a good number of prophets around. But owing to persecution he was feeling sorry for himself. He took himself too seriously.

Once before Elijah had stated publicly that he was the only prophet left and uttered thoughtless words before hundreds of the prophets of Baal. It shows he had completely dismissed those one hundred prophets that Obadiah preserved. He thought he was a cut above them, that he was the only true prophet.

God is so patient with us when we utter foolish comments like that. Had God required sinless perfection before Elijah could be used, God would have interrupted the proceedings at Mount Carmel at once—and called the whole thing off. God could have thundered, "No, you are quite wrong"—and stopped the whole thing. But He let Elijah continue.

It was some time later that God said, as it were, "Oh, by the way, Elijah, you might like to know that I have reserved *seven thousand* who have not bowed down to Baal." (See 1 Kings 19:18.) God patiently waited for the right time to deal with Elijah. So too with us.

Excerpted from *Controlling the Tongue* (Charisma House, 2007).

Be Prepared to Affirm God

Are you seeking God? How hard are you trying? Are you requiring that He meets your expectation? You say, "If God turned up, believe me, I would recognize Him." That is exactly the point I want to make: when we feel we know God so well, we are in danger of becoming too familiar with Him. The way we must love the glory of the Lord is not that we affirm Him because we see that which makes us feel comfortable, but that we know He is God and can manifest Himself in unusual ways.

And he made known to us the mystery of his will according to his good pleasure, which he purposed in Christ.
—Ephesians 1:9

Sometimes God puts us in a place where we can't give the reason we affirm Him. He continues to work in this way, so there are times when we have to take a stand, where we know the truth, but we are not allowed to explain ourselves. Are you prepared to be committed to Jesus Christ to the extent that you just affirm Him, even though you know you are not allowed to explain yourself except to say, "Jesus is my Savior; I am unashamed of Him"?

When we see God working in an unexpected way, we may fail to recognize Him. Sometimes theologians describe the "otherness" of God. He is different. He may turn up in a strange way. God may come with silence or by hiding His face and seeming not to answer. Sometimes the way in which He turns up seems silly. But God chooses the foolish things of this world to confound the wise.

Our reaction is, "How can God do this to me—if that's really God?" Then explain this: Jesus, dying on a cross, how can that be God? Why does God seem so detached from the way with which we are comfortable? The answer is lest we feel too familiar with Him and become presumptuous. The proof we love God is that we recognize He may appear in a way that feels strange, and we are prepared to affirm Him no matter how much it hurts and no matter how strange it seems.

Excerpted from *All's Well That Ends Well* (Authentic Media, 2005).

Trying to Prove Ourselves

My old friend Pete Cantrell often says, "The greatest freedom is having nothing to prove." I think this is one of the most profound statements I have ever heard. The person who needs to prove how right or how strong he or she is, is one who is not free. There is a struggle inside to make others think they are right and strong. The truth is, if we really are right and strong, we don't have to say anything! Freedom is being experienced, therefore, when one is having nothing to prove. He or she does not need to justify themselves, make themselves look good. It is enough that *God knows* for people like that. (See John 5:44.)

When you are justified before God, you are free. Seeking to be justified or vindicated before people is a crippling, endless, and counterproductive enterprise; you are never at peace. No freedom. But when you know that *God Himself* declares you righteous, you are free and have no need to get your satisfaction from comparing yourselves with others.

> *You are the ones who justify yourselves in the eyes of men, but God knows your hearts. What is highly valued among men is detestable in God's sight.*
> —Luke 16:15

The heart of the gospel is at stake here. What justifies us before God—our good works? Or is it our confession to God that we are sinners? Answer: we are justified when we do not try to prove ourselves before God but lean on His mercy. The way a person is converted is to ask God for mercy.

When we are trusting our works, there will always be a need to try to prove ourselves—by words. The greatest freedom is having nothing to prove. This freedom comes when we put all our "eggs into one basket," namely, the death of Jesus on the cross. That brings freedom because this alone is what justifies us before God.

Excerpted from *Controlling the Tongue* (Charisma House, 2007).

Presence of Mind of the Spirit

Something happens when we grieve the Holy Spirit: not the loss of salvation, but presence of mind. I like to call it the *presence of the mind of the Spirit*.

The Holy Spirit is depicted in the New Testament as a dove (Matt. 3:16; John 1:32). The dove is a very shy bird and extremely sensitive. When the Spirit is grieved He backs away, as it were, like a dove that quietly and unobtrusively flies away. The result of this is that we are not able to flow in the Spirit as long as the Spirit is grieved and the Dove is not around.

> *Rid yourselves of all the offenses you have committed, and get a new heart and a new spirit.*
>
> —Ezekiel 18:31

Bitterness and unforgiveness are the main ways in which we grieve the Spirit. We know this is true because the very next thing Paul says (after commanding us not to grieve the Spirit) is, "Get rid of all bitterness, rage and anger, brawling and slander, along with every form of malice. Be kind and compassionate to one another, forgiving each other, just as in Christ God forgave you" (Eph. 4:31–32). Bitterness is not the only way we grieve the Spirit, and Paul continues to show what else grieves the Spirit: sexual immorality, greed, obscenity, foolish talk, or coarse joking (Eph. 5:3–4). But bitterness is the chief way we grieve the Spirit, and that is why He puts it at the top of the list of things we can do to grieve the Spirit.

This means that all of us are accountable to God to forgive and to make sure the Holy Spirit is *ungrieved* in our hearts and lives. And when the Holy Spirit in us is ungrieved—like the dove coming down and remaining (see John 1:32–33)—we will show the fruit of the Spirit, be able to witness for Jesus with power, and flow in the Spirit.

Excerpted from *Pure Joy* (Charisma House, 2006).

How to Handle Guilt

Have you ever driven down the highway and heard the wail of a siren behind and seen that flashing blue light in the rearview mirror? What a relief when the patrol car overtook you and sped away! It was not you the police were after.

It is almost impossible *not* to feel guilty about some things. Moreover, sometimes guilt can motivate us to do strange things when it comes to our relationships with

> *And from Jesus Christ, who is the faithful witness.... To him who loves us and has freed us from our sins by his blood...*
> —REVELATION 1:5

others. For example, we may feel guilty because we dislike a person, and to compensate we try to be extra friendly.

But true guilt can be experienced beyond doubt through regeneration. We may *try* to make unconverted people feel true guilt, but we never quite succeed in making them aware they have sinned against God: it is the Holy Spirit who does that. When the Holy Spirit convicts people of sin, they see they have offended God, and they come to the place where David was when he prayed, "Against you, you only, have I sinned" (Ps. 51:4). Only a regenerate person can talk like that.

How, then, should we handle true guilt? I believe we have three options:

1. The "fatal" solution

Some people repress their guilt. God created us in His own image, and we ignore our conscience at our peril.

2. The temporary solution

I can change my life, and then I will have no reason to feel guilty. It's so easy to make a promise, but you will break it eventually. This solution will only work for a time.

3. The biblical solution

The Bible offers a permanent solution to the problem of guilt. We need to look at Revelation 1:5 for the answer. All our guilt was placed on Jesus when He took our place on the cross. And when we accept what He did for us and turn in repentance to Him, God looks at us, and His verdict is, "Not guilty!"

Excerpted from *A Vision of Jesus* (Christian Focus Publications Ltd., 1999).

Forgiving Ourselves

It is one thing to have this breakthrough regarding others—totally forgiving them and destroying the record of their wrongs; it is quite another to experience the greater breakthrough—total forgiveness of ourselves.

So many Christians say, "I can forgive others, but how can I ever forget what I have done? I know God forgives me, but I can't forgive myself."

We may wake up each day with the awareness of past mistakes and failures—and fervently wish that we could turn the clock back and start all over. We may have feelings of guilt—or *pseudo-guilt,* if our sins have been placed under the blood of Christ. But the enemy, the devil, loves to move in and take advantage of our thoughts. That is why forgiving ourselves is as important as forgiving an enemy.

> *If we confess our sins, he is faithful and just and will forgive us our sins and purify us from all unrighteousness.*
>
> —1 JOHN 1:9

Forgiving yourself may bring about the breakthrough you have been looking for. It could set you free in ways you have never before experienced. This is because we have been afraid to forgive ourselves. We cling to fear as if it were a thing of value. The truth is, this kind of fear is no friend, but rather a fierce enemy. The very breath of Satan is behind the fear of forgiving ourselves.

If we feel guilty, blame ourselves, and find that we cannot function normally—even though we have confessed our sins to God—it indicates that we haven't yet totally forgiven ourselves. It means that we are still hanging on to guilt that God has washed away; we are refusing to enjoy what God has freely given us. First John 1:9 either is true or it isn't. If we have confessed our sins, we must take this promise with both hands and forgive ourselves—which is precisely what God wants us to do.

Excerpted from *Total Forgiveness* (Charisma House, 2002).

Not Perfect, but Still Improving

Enjoying a measure of success in controlling the tongue on occasion does not mean you are perfect! I can assure you that you have not "arrived"—even if you go three days without an unguarded comment—or that the problem of controlling the tongue is now behind you. Tongue control is only a temporary grace—given one day at a time, and hour by hour when you are having a good day.

> *We all stumble in many ways. If anyone is never at fault in what he says, he is a perfect man, able to keep his whole body in check.*
>
> —James 3:2

Never being at fault in what one *says*, then, means perfection. James is obviously not expecting that of any Christian. So the tongue is something you must live with, work with, get victory over—little by little—every day. But one day at a time! It is terrific when you have a good day. It is very encouraging. But if you had a good day, I lovingly caution you: wait until tomorrow!

I know what it is sometimes to preach well, to come down from the pulpit with an inner confidence and say to myself, "Well, at last I have learned how to preach." But when I feel like that for very long, here is what happens—nearly every time: I do so poorly the next time I am in the pulpit that I leave saying, "If that is the best I can do, I should get out of the ministry." So if you have a good day with tongue control, thank God for it, but don't be deluded that you have mastered the art of tongue control; you just might be a miserable failure the next day.

The truth is, however, we can improve. We do get better at it. The reward is worth the effort, I promise you.

Excerpted from *Controlling the Tongue* (Charisma House, 2007).

How Does God Punish Sin?

Y ou thought that you were outwitting God. You thought that here He is trying to reach you, while you just say, "I'll show Him. I'll just enjoy living in sin."

> *Because of this, God gave them over to shameful lusts. Even their women exchanged natural relations for unnatural ones.*
>
> —ROMANS 1:26

What Paul is saying here is that God has already begun to punish you. It is a judgment of God that you remain in sin. When you think that you're getting away with it, that's the worst thing of all that can happen. The worst sign of God's judgment is that you're able to sin and get away with it.

Nor does God give us a bold sign, telling us, "Here's what I am going to do." He just gives up. He doesn't push us; He doesn't hammer us. In effect, Paul is saying this: Is it sin that you want? Sin you will get. That's the first way God punishes sin.

The second way is by exposure at the final judgment. Say you decide to live in sin; you're thinking, at first, that something's going to happen as a kind of warning from God, like thunder and lightening, but when it doesn't come you think, *I don't feel a thing; I'm able to go on and do this.* When a person does what is not right, he may say, "I don't feel any different; I feel fine." But how does God punish—by exposure at the final judgment. God "will give to each person according to what he has done" (Rom. 2:6).

A third way is that God's Son, Jesus, took our punishment on the cross. Eternally speaking, there are two ways whereby God punishes sin: the fires of hell and the blood of Jesus. He who knew no sin was made sin.

Let this be what lingers in your mind. It's not a question of whether your sin will be punished; it is the question of how. May God grant you to see why the Bible talks about "fleeing from the wrath to come." (See Matthew 3:7; Luke 3:7.)

Excerpted from *The God of the Bible* (Authentic Media, 2002).

His Faith and Our Faith

It is one thing for us to believe it once and be electrified and be thrilled, to have our world turned upside down, but quite another to keep believing it. The devil will come alongside and tell you that it can't be true, and he appeals to our natural reasoning. He appeals to what we know to be true about ourselves, that we are sinners. If he can, he will bring us right back to our bondage.

> *For in the gospel a righteousness from God is revealed, a righteousness that is by faith from first to last, just as it is written: "The righteous will live by faith."*
> —ROMANS 1:17

It was Martin Luther who rediscovered the Pauline doctrine of justification by faith. Luther was a very conscientious person. He had a sensitive conscience and was known to go to confession not only every day but sometimes two or three times a day, because after spending an hour confessing his sins, he would come back an hour or two later remembering there was a sin he didn't confess.

But during these days he was also reading Romans, as well as Galatians and certain of the Psalms. Here he had a breakthrough, largely from Romans 1:17. When Luther saw that what Paul was saying was that faith alone pleases God, and it satisfies, to use Luther's term, "the passive justice of God," his world was changed. He, in fact, woke up the world by his own world being turned upside down. He did not know that he would turn the world upside down by simply trying to save his own soul. The interesting thing is that Paul too rediscovered this teaching. Paul realized that Abraham saw it long before, and David saw it.

The principal thing that we are to see is that we are justified by the combination of two things: what Jesus did for us and our own faith in Him. Or, to put it another way: His faith and our faith. These two things must come together.

Excerpted from *The God of the Bible* (Authentic Media, 2002).

Knowing God Isn't Finished With You Yet

Is it possible for you to discover that God hasn't finished with you? Perhaps you feel you have no real future. Perhaps you can look back on that time when everybody said, "Oh, what a future!" But that's all over now; you feel there is nothing to live for, you've made real mistakes, and there is no way that God could use you now.

> *He who began a good work in you will carry it on to completion until the day of Christ Jesus.*
>
> —PHILIPPIANS 1:6

Jacob had come to the place where he anticipated nothing but sorrow. He was now an old man. He had made many mistakes, almost every mistake possible. He felt there was nothing to live for, and he anticipated the worst. The irony was that Jacob's best days were yet to come, because he had yet to do what God had raised him up to do: to give the patriarchal blessing to those twelve sons.

Are you like that? You feel you are finished. You know the greatest feeling in the world is to feel needed, to feel useful, and the greatest honor in the world is to be used by God. I can think of nothing more wonderful than knowing that God is using me. Perhaps you have known better days when God *did* use you in a particular situation, and you would give anything in the world just to know that it could happen again.

I can promise you on the authority of God's Word that if you come to the cross and get right with God, your happiest days, your greatest days, lie ahead. I guarantee it.

One has to be willing to live in grateful dependence from now on. If God is going to use you again, you have to make the break. You have no chance of going back. No way! You are going forward. Jacob's greatest days were now ahead. He had something to live for. God hadn't finished with him, and He hasn't finished with you.

Excerpted from *All's Well That Ends Well* (Authentic Media, 2005).

It Will All Work Out

This is one of those verses that you need more and more the older you get. It is the verse that, in fact, refers not to the future but to the past. If I may use a couple of big words here—it is not *a priori*; it is *a posteriori*. *A priori* is looking forward. *A posteriori* is looking backward. Romans 8:28 is the promise of *a posteriori*; it is after the fact. It is not *a priori* because if you could say, "Well, everything's going to work out all right, it doesn't matter what I do," then you would abuse this promise. But Paul knows that as members of the family, we all have a sense of shame over something in our past. We all have skeletons in our closets, and he can say because you're a family member and you're a joint-heir with Christ, anything that happens to you has to turn out for good. All things work together for good—all things.

> *And we know that in all things God works for the good of those who love him, who have been called according to his purpose.*
>
> —ROMANS 8:28

Having established your position in the family, Paul is saying that God knows the past; He knows what's bothering you. All things work together for good. You could almost call it the family scandal! How do you know that? Well, because it says it works together *for* good—it shows it wasn't good. If it had been good, he wouldn't need to say it, but it works together for good because it was bad. It doesn't mean that everything that happens is good. Things that can happen can be bad, but because you're in the family you have a promise: it will work together for good.

How do we know? We've found it out, for one thing. Look back; look across the years and remember the closed door that broke your heart and you lived long enough to thank God a thousand times it was closed. Learn the joy of God's providence, knowing that with every disappointment—give it time—you'll be thankful for it. He will sanctify to you your deepest distress. This is something that God does.

Excerpted from *The God of the Bible* (Authentic Media, 2002).

A Dove or a Pigeon?

The Bible does not say that the Spirit came down from heaven as a pigeon. There would probably have been nothing unusual about a pigeon descending on an individual—or even remaining. There are *some* differences (at least in temperament) between pigeons and doves. A pigeon—at least the pigeons of Trafalgar Square—would adjust to nearly any situation, but almost certainly a turtledove would not.

> *Then John gave this testimony: "I saw the Spirit come down from heaven as a dove and remain on him."*
> —JOHN 1:32

I often wonder how often many of us have confused a pigeon for a dove at a spiritual level. We may hastily assume that the Dove has come, but a more objective examination might just show that it was a pigeon! Such possibility has given me a new phrase—"pigeon religion."

I fear that so much today purports to be the presence of the Spirit—but in reality it is nothing more than pigeon religion.

It is my view that the genuine presence of the Holy Spirit is not as common as we may want to believe. It is also my fear that many of us have run slipshod over this matter and have forgotten that the Holy Spirit is a very, very sensitive person. I know that I have been very guilty in this area. I have done some things—and not done others—that I later realized have grieved the Spirit.

We all claim to want God's blessings on us—and even take strong public stands for the truth! But often there seems missing a real conscientiousness with regard to grieving the Spirit by attitudes and words. It is as if we think our official positions or titles exempt us from having to watch what we say. The sober truth is, God will not bend the rules for any of us, whatever our positions may be.

Excerpted from *The Sensitivity of the Spirit* (Charisma House, 2002).

Authentic Leadership Defined

Shadrach, Meshach, and Abednego were being trained for authentic leadership, although they may not have known it at the time. There are two kinds of leadership: authentic leadership and passive leadership. What is needed is authentic leadership, and this is determined by how we react to temptation and testing. Shadrach, Meshach, and Abednego were now to undergo a real trial. Here were three men that decided to stand up and be counted.

> Shadrach, Meshach, and Abednego, answered and said to the king, O Nebuchadnezzar, we are not careful to answer thee in this matter. If it be so, our God whom we serve is able to deliver us from the burning fiery furnace, and he will deliver us out of thine hand, O king.
>
> —DANIEL 3:16–17, KJV

These three men were characterized by a prior commitment—they had decided long before what they would do. Courage like this is planned in advance.

These three men didn't need to look at each other and wink or nudge; no, they looked straight at the king and said, "We don't have to answer you, and we don't have to defend ourselves; we can tell you right now."

Real strength is not in seeing how close you get to temptation without yielding; it is avoiding temptation altogether. When there is that kind of commitment, and temptation comes, you don't have to pray about it.

Shadrach, Meshach, and Abednego lived by what I can only call the impulse of the Spirit. Their peers listened for music and they fell down. Shadrach, Meshach, and Abednego listened to the impulse of the Spirit and they stood up. Unimpressed, the king had them bound and thrown into the burning fiery furnace.

Whenever you are in the fire, you know where to find Jesus. He is in the fire, and if you want to be changed from glory to glory, you may want the shortcut. I wouldn't blame you for that. Just remember this, though: if you are ever given a trial, what can only be called a fiery trial, see it as God issuing to you an invitation on a silver platter to be changed from glory to glory. In the fire you will find Jesus there; you will find Him to be real, and you will be amazed and say, "Look who's here."

Excerpted from *The God of the Bible* (Authentic Media, 2002).

God Has a Time for Your Success

Good had a message that He wanted to give to everybody just before the end, and He wanted to do it His way. So here was the handwriting on the wall.

> *Then commanded Belshazzar, and they clothed Daniel with scarlet, and put a chain of gold about his neck, and made a proclamation concerning him, that he should be the third ruler in the kingdom.*
> —DANIEL 5:29, KJV

What do the words mean? Everybody knew what they meant. They knew the words were, "*Mene, mene, tekel, upharsin.*" The word *mene* simply means numbered; it was in Aramaic, and everybody knew the word. *Tekel* means weighed. *Upharsin* means shared. They knew what the words meant, and yet they didn't know, because Belshazzar knew in his heart of hearts there had to be a hidden meaning.

Daniel was needed again, and yet they didn't send for him at first. I suppose the last person Belshazzar wanted to send for was Daniel. He wanted to defy his father's God, the God of Israel.

It may be that you are waiting to be noticed and to be used, and they are sending for everybody else but you. Don't worry about those who are sent for first.

Daniel had been refined over the years; he had been put to one side, and he wondered, "Will God ever need me again?" Daniel was waiting for this moment, and though there is no doubt he had been refined by the Holy Spirit as God chiseled away that which was unlike Jesus would be, Daniel was still in preparation.

You still need preparation. You never outgrow the need of preparation, but you may ask the question, "How will they know about me if I don't pull some strings?" Well, they came looking for Daniel, and they'll come looking for you. How will they know about you? It may be that the president will send for you, or an advisor to the president, but they will find you. God has a way of bringing right to the top those who are ready for it. The worst thing that can happen to you is to succeed before you are ready, and only God knows when you are ready.

Excerpted from *The God of the Bible* (Authentic Media, 2002).

God Loves to Surprise Us

The news to Jacob was unexpected. God loves to do things like that. Sometimes He plans and prepares for a long time. He waited thousands of years before He finally sent His Son into the world. Yet sometimes God likes to do something so suddenly that no one is quite prepared for it. For Jacob, the news that Joseph was alive was stunning. He fainted (according to the King James Version).

> They told him, "Joseph is still alive! In fact, he is ruler of all Egypt." Jacob was stunned; he did not believe them.
> —GENESIS 45:26

The news about Joseph surpassed anything Jacob had ever expected. If you were to ask Jacob what was his wildest dream, he would not have named what his sons told him. He had already concluded that Joseph was dead—that he was out of the picture. I wonder if you have already reached conclusions about which you are so certain that you are unable to conceive any alternative situation.

The wonderful thing was the news that Joseph was alive, but then to learn that he was the lord of all Egypt was almost inconceivable. God loves to do that. He loves to do that which surpasses anything that we ever thought of. When the queen of Sheba came to Solomon, she said, "I had heard of your fame, I had heard of your wisdom, I had heard of your riches. Having seen it, even the half had not been told to me." (See 1 Kings 10:7.)

The apostle Paul said that when we pray, God does that which goes beyond what we ask for or even think about. "No eye has seen, no ear has heard, no mind has conceived what God has prepared for those who love him" (1 Cor. 2:9). God has a plan for every single one of us. When we see what He has in mind, it will surpass anything we thought possible. He wants to give us the desires of our hearts beyond anything we thought possible.

Excerpted from *All's Well That Ends Well* (Authentic Media, 2005).

Are You Ready for God?

Zechariah wasn't ready. Are *you* ready for God? Are you waiting for God to answer prayer? Are there prayers that you have long since taken off your prayer-request list because you were sure God wasn't going to answer them? There are two important principles here.

> *Then an angel of the Lord appeared to him, standing at the right side of the altar of incense. When Zechariah saw him, he was startled and was gripped with fear. But the angel said to him: "Do not be afraid, Zechariah; your prayer has been heard."*
>
> —LUKE 1:11–13

Any prayer prayed in the will of God will be answered. How do we know this? Because the Bible says so: "This is the confidence we have in approaching God: that if we ask anything according to his will, he hears us" (1 John 5:14).

The trouble is that big "if" —*if* we know His will. You can pray in the will of God and not know it. Zechariah and Elizabeth prayed in the will of God. They didn't know it. Because God didn't jump to answer their prayer the first time, they just assumed it wasn't God's will. Think back on your own prayer requests, maybe for the last year, maybe going back before then. Think of one prayer that hasn't been heard, as far as you know, that you have long since given up praying. What's the principle to apply? That any prayer prayed in the will of God will be answered. So what's the problem?

It turns out—how sad it is—that Zechariah wasn't ready. He wanted to argue with the angel. Do you know why he wanted to argue? Because *he* wasn't right spiritually, which shows that a person can be involved in the work of ministry even if his heart isn't right. When our hearts aren't right, we want to argue with God.

Are we ready for answered prayer? Zechariah's story should give us encouragement to go back and start praying again. It's a wonderful, wonderful thing to be ready when God appears. When we're not ready, what should have been our finest hour will, instead, be under a cloud.

Excerpted from *When God Shows Up* (Renew Books, 1998).

Faith Pleases God Now

"Seeing is believing," says the world. But to God it is the other way around: believing is to see. But in heaven everybody will see everything clearly, and there will be no faith.

At the moment of the Second Coming nobody will need faith. "Look, he is coming with the clouds, and every eye will see him, even those who pierced him; and all the peoples of the earth will mourn

> *And without faith it is impossible to please God, because anyone who comes to him must believe...*
>
> —Hebrews 11:6

because of him. So shall it be! Amen" (Rev. 1:7). The reason for the weeping is that the possibility of true faith is removed; all will "believe," but such "believing" cannot be truly graced the title "faith."

Since there will be no faith in heaven, we have the opportunity now to do what we can't do there: to please God by faith. Faith pleases God. We might ask, will we not please God in heaven? The answer is yes, but it won't be pleasing Him by faith! This is something we can only do now. We can never get these days back.

I want to please God *now*—in a way I cannot please Him then. I want to be thankful now. I can bring a measure of glory and pleasure to God now that I will be unable to do then. How? By trusting Him more and more and by thanking Him more and more.

What ought we to do now? We can always pray for more faith. Trust God now and thank Him in a way you will be glad you did when you are in heaven. We won't be trusting God in heaven; we will be seeing Him. Therefore we won't need faith. We must trust Him now and thank Him now.

Excerpted from *Just Say Thanks!* (Charisma House, 2005).

When God Disrupts Your Life

Everything is going well. You're feeling on top of the world, sailing leisurely along with the wind at your back, comfortable, secure, and happy. Then everything changes. All of a sudden, without notice, something awful happens, and nothing is ever the same again.

> The LORD said to Satan, "Very well, then, everything he has is in your hands, but on the man himself do not lay a finger." Then Satan went out from the presence of the LORD.
>
> —JOB 1:12

Why do catastrophes like this happen? I would have to say, because God allows them to happen. It may not seem right, it may not seem fair, but when something goes wrong, it reminds us that this life is not all there is.

I can't be sure of all the reasons God allows a great disruption to change everything. However, it certainly means preparation for heaven above and preparation for usefulness here below. When you go through tribulation, it means that God is not finished with you yet. It could be that there's something wonderful around the corner.

God has a way of disrupting our lives. It could be through conversion. It could be by calling us to give up what we have. It could be through financial difficulties. It could be that someone very close to you will be ill and you will have to care for that person, or somebody around you will have a nervous breakdown and you will be affected by it.

Can I ask you this question? What kind of faith would you have if a great disruption came and your life was never the same again? Would you panic? Would you say, "God, how could You let this happen to me?" Or is it possible that you would be like Job, who refused to question God or to charge Him with foolishness, saying, "Though he slay me, yet will I hope in him" (Job 13:15)?

Excerpted from *When God Shows Up* (Renew Books, 1998).

Believe God Loves You

Are you ready for God to love you? It's easy to say, "I certainly am," but are you really ready to accept and affirm His love?

You cannot rely very long on your love for God, but you can rely on His love for you. He wants you to. Just think how much it would thrill Him if you really believed He loves you. If you could only grasp this

> *And so we know and rely on the love God has for us.*
>
> —1 John 4:16

life-changing truth—that God really does love you—what a wonderful feeling it would be.

Why are you so reluctant to believe that God loves you? Here are five possibilities:

1. You may have an overly scrupulous conscience, to use the Puritan phrase, and worry about every little thing that may be wrong in your life.
2. You may still be living under the Old Covenant, under the Law.
3. You may have a faulty theology.
4. There could be a psychological problem. I know people who can't call God "Father" because of the relationship they had with their own fathers.
5. When you are aware of how much you have failed God (and we have all sinned and let Him down), you can't believe that He still loves you. He wants to love you as you are, and you should not respond to His love by "performing" for Him. (See Isaiah 29:13.)

If you can identify with one or all of these criteria, at the end of the day you can still claim the promise that God loves you. But I sympathize. I find it difficult to believe God loves me. Yet I have come to see that it really is true: God loves me. God loves you. God really does love us.

Excerpted from *When God Shows Up* (Renew Books, 1998).

Accepting God's Call

Our God is a God who calls people. This fact is essential to His dealings with us. After they had sinned, Adam and Eve "heard the sound of the LORD God as he was walking in the garden in the cool of the day....the LORD God called to the man, 'Where are you?'" (Gen. 3:8–9). Could it be that God is seeking you? The sound of His voice is disquieting, and you may think, *Oh, no, it couldn't be that He's calling me.*

Brothers, think of what you were when you were called. Not many of you were wise by human standards; not many were influential; not many were of noble birth. But God chose the foolish things of the world to shame the wise; God chose the weak things of the world to shame the strong.

—1 CORINTHIANS 1:26–27

Let me define what I mean by God's call: I mean God getting our attention to make His own wish known. For example, He calls at conversion. Everyone who is a Christian is a Christian because he or she has been converted, and the reason of the conversion is that the person heard the call of God.

Allow me to ask you this question: When you get to the very center of God's will, is it perhaps at great cost? Could it be that there is a call to a spirituality at a deeper level than you have known? What if, in your midlife, when things are going well, God puts His finger on your lifestyle, the way you have been spending your time, your money—all the comfort you have taken for granted—and says, "I have something else in mind." The pain can be great, but the reward will be greater.

The "calling of God" is getting our attention to make His wish known. Are you ready for this? If not, get ready, for it is only a matter of time—God will call you.

Excerpted from *When God Shows Up* (Renew Books, 1998).

Are You Ready for Success?

The psalmist prays, "O LORD, grant us success" (Ps. 118:25), but have you ever explicitly prayed for this? Do you think you are ready for it? If your answer is a quick yes, then I would caution you to be careful.

Every Thursday I would spend two hours with Dr. Lloyd-Jones, sitting at his feet, discussing the sermon for the following Sunday. He once made this throw-away comment, and I immediately got my pen and wrote it down. It was the most powerful word I ever heard him say, yet it's in none of his books: "The worst thing that can happen to a man is to succeed before he is ready." It was a word of wisdom to me at the time.

If you do want success, do you think you are really ready for it?

What kind of success are we talking about? It may well be prosperity. God does indeed give financial prosperity to some, though Christians who have wealth tend to come in for a certain amount of criticism

> *Do not let this Book of the Law depart from your mouth; meditate on it day and night, so that you may be careful to do everything written in it. Then you will be prosperous and successful.*
>
> —JOSHUA 1:8

that may spoil their enjoyment of it. However, once in a while, God will raise up a Joseph of Arimathea or a Lydia. (See Matthew 27:57–60; Acts 16:14–15.)

God may want you to have influence with people, but how marvelous it would be if you could be trusted with a ministry of prayer. Some are more successful in prayer than others. Why? Because they want to be successful in prayer. I challenge you to make that your goal.

The worst thing that can happen to a person is to succeed before he's ready. But if you succeed because God says you're ready, there won't be that "after" of regret. If you succeed in prayer, you will have known success greater than any other. Maybe books won't be written about you, but when you stand before God and Jesus Himself looks at you and says, "Well done!" it will be the greatest feeling, and it will last forever.

Excerpted from *When God Shows Up* (Renew Books, 1998).

The Loneliness of Success

There is the loneliness of success. When you are successful, you will find that some people will desert you. They liked you when you weren't successful; they thought you were nice. You start succeeding, you get high marks, you obtain a good job, you have a higher income (it's envy, of course; that is all it is)—they can't cope with that. But *you* wouldn't be any different if it was reversed (you have to understand that), but you need to know that success means loneliness.

On the other hand, if you are successful, whereas some will desert you, others will cling to you. But what are their motives? It is not necessarily you they are interested in.

When you are successful or well known, you will find you can be very lonely. For when there is an anointing upon you, you will succeed in some sense. There may be those who are envious of you and believe that eventually you are going to fall. King Saul was so jealous of David that he would have done anything to get rid of him. King Saul had a great plan. He said, "I tell you what; how would you like to marry my daughter? But I think you should do something to earn it."

> *David led the troops in their campaigns. In everything he did he had great success, because the LORD was with him. When Saul saw how successful he was, he was afraid of him.*
>
> —1 SAMUEL 18:13–15

David said, "Oh, I am not worthy to be the king's son-in-law."

"Oh, well," said King Saul. "I'll tell you what I want you to do. All I would ask you to do is to bring back one hundred foreskins of the Philistines, that's all!"

The only reason King Saul suggested this was that he thought David would be killed in doing it; that was King Saul's sole motive. But David came back with two hundred foreskins.

When there is an anointing upon you, you will succeed at a certain level, but don't expect your enemies to clap their hands. They will hate you all the more.

Excerpted from *The Thorn in the Flesh* (Charisma House, 2004).

How to Handle an Enemy

Do you have an enemy? If your reply is, "No," then do you realize how much of the Bible is irrelevant to you? After all, when we pray the Lord's Prayer, we say, "Forgive us our trespasses, as we forgive those who trespass against us." Christians certainly know what it is to have enemies. When they accept Jesus as their Savior, they gain a new enemy: the devil. Not only that, but also they often find that the friends they had before become hostile toward them, and their loved ones often become their bitterest foes. Indeed, Paul said, "In fact, everyone who wants to live a godly life in Christ Jesus will be persecuted" (2 Tim. 3:12).

> *The fruit of the Spirit is love, joy, peace, patience, kindness, goodness, faithfulness, gentleness and self-control.*
> —GALATIANS 5:22–23

John knew what it was like to face persecution. He had many enemies, who, after failing in their attempt to boil him in oil, had banished him to Patmos and left him there to die. But John had expected oppression, and he told us not to be surprised if the world hates us, too (1 John 3:13).

One of the wonderful things about becoming a Christian is that, like John, you can see what is behind the persecution you meet, and you do not take it personally but understand that it is God with whom others are angry; it is Christ they hate. John realized this and knew that he needed to be in God's presence, so he did not indulge in self-pity; he was "in the Spirit." It is possible to be so filled with the Spirit that you do not regard others as enemies, but you have a love for them.

When we have the Holy Spirit, we grow the fruit of that Spirit, the fruit of love. When we become Christians, God shares Himself with us and we begin to radiate His beauty. This is not because we are better than others: we remain human and are often tempted to do wrong. The difference is that God has promised to be with us, so we can overcome these problems.

Excerpted from *A Vision of Jesus* (Christian Focus Publications Ltd., 1999).

R. T. KENDALL

Knowing God

The first three of the Ten Commandments are letting us see just a little bit of what God is like. These commands are deep teaching. In a sense they were spoon-feeding Israel, and yet the words are so profound, so deep. Israel was a redeemed community. As we have seen, the word *redeemed* means that they had been bought back. God loved the people of Israel. They knew God, but only just.

You shall have no other gods before me. You shall not make for yourself an idol.... You shall not bow down to them or worship them; for I, the LORD your God, am a jealous God, punishing the children for the sin of the fathers to the third and fourth generation of those who hate me, but showing love to a thousand generations of those who love me and keep my commandments.

—EXODUS 20:3–6

How well do you know God? How well would you like to know Him? How deeply is it burning in you that you would love to know Him better? If that deep desire is there, it means that there is a special anointing—the power of the Holy Spirit—on you. There could be no greater desire on earth. So you can mark it down; the flesh did not put that desire there. The devil did not put that there. This is one desire, if it is there, that only God could put there. And for giving you that kind of thirst and longing, be thankful for it. Take it with both hands and walk in every little bit of light God gives you. Walking in the light will show that you really mean business—that it is not just a passing yearning.

Whenever you discover something that you hadn't seen before, an awareness of sin or a higher level of obedience, take it. There may be that which offends you, but remember that God often tests us by letting us be offended.

God wants to see how much you want Him. So sometimes, if I may put it this way, He puts His "worst" foot forward; He lets you see the most "unattractive" aspect of His nature, or what He knows you may regard that way, to see whether you will still love Him just as He is.

Excerpted from *Grace* (Charisma House, 2006).

The Gift of Giving

Perhaps you feel you cannot tithe at the moment, but the ability to handle money (when you give God all of His) may be a gift you are given that you weren't expecting to have. It is just like Jesus multiplying the loaves and the fish; it doesn't have a natural explanation. It doesn't add up that 90 percent can go as far as 100 percent.

> *I will repay you for the years the locusts have eaten.*
>
> —Joel 2:25

I will never forget one day coming home shortly after Louise and I were married. God had hidden His face from me for days and weeks. I hadn't made any sales. I thought, *Will I ever get to be in ministry? Whatever happened to those visions that God was going to use me?* I walked over to a Bible my Grandmother Curley had given me, and, I promise you, my eyes fell right on these words: "Will a man rob God? Yet you rob me. But you ask, 'How do we rob you?' In tithes and offerings" (Mal. 3:8). I abruptly closed that Bible, walked over, and turned on the television that we still owed for, and I thought, *I certainly didn't want a word like that.*

Perhaps you feel this way at the moment.

But you know what happened? As a result of not tithing because I was paying my bills, *I owed more* a year later than I did when I made the decision not to tithe. And a year after that, I owed more. One day I said, "I will start tithing now!" In eighteen months, we were out of debt.

Tithing is a part of worshiping God. Abraham was the first tither. That's in the Old Testament. But look at what the New Testament says: "Remember this: Whoever sows sparingly will also reap sparingly, and whoever sows generously will also reap generously" (2 Cor. 9:6).

You should not give necessarily because a church needs it, although sometimes that is the case, but you should give because it is the right thing to do.

Excerpted from *The Thorn in the Flesh* (Charisma House, 2004).

Honor Your Parents

God could have added this word of promise to any of the commands, but He chose this one, thus giving an added incentive for keeping this command.

I find this sobering. In the light of this I ask, how long can I expect to live, based on this promise and my attitude toward my own parents? So if this command is true, and the promise is relevant, how long may you expect to live?

You could call this commandment a proposition. God makes a deal with His people. Honor your father and your mother so that you may live long in the land the Lord your God is giving you.

Parental respect must be taught in the home and in the church. It is the teaching of gratitude. We need to be taught gratitude, and that means to be thankful and respectful to our parents. And yet I must admit that this teaching will be easier for some than for others. Not all have good parents. My heart goes out to anybody

Children, obey your parents in the Lord, for this is right. "Honor your father and mother"—which is the first commandment with a promise—"that it may go well with you and that you may enjoy long life on the earth."
—Ephesians 6:1–3

who struggles here. I was once pastor of a church in which there was a lady who was abused by her father; her father had sexual intercourse with her as far back as she could remember. It messed up her life to no end.

Perhaps you have a father who was cruel and insensitive. Perhaps you had a mother who was not very loving. And now you are told to honor them, and you say, "I can't." I sympathize. I can echo the sentiments of David in Psalm 16:6: "The boundary lines have fallen for me in pleasant places; surely I have a delightful inheritance." That also means that I am without excuse. If you too have a father and mother who did not abuse you but who loved you, did their best for you, and loved the Lord, you ought to be very thankful.

Excerpted from *Grace* (Charisma House, 2006).

Don't Lie

Why did God give this commandment, "You shall not give false testimony against your neighbor"?

First, God wants His people to tell the truth when they speak. In ancient times two or three witnesses were required in a court of law. "One witness is not enough to convict a man accused of a crime or offense he may have committed. A matter must be established by the testimony of two or three witnesses" (Deut. 19:15). This was to protect an individual from being maligned by a personal enemy, from a vendetta, or from someone who just wanted to bring another down.

> *You shall not give false testimony against your neighbor.*
>
> —Exodus 20:16

The second reason God gave this command is that He wants to protect us from being falsely accused. He does not like it if anybody lies about you, for it hurts you. And if you feel that way, so does God. This is your comfort when you are lied about. Are you prepared to believe that God cares even more for you than you do? God cares about His children.

If you are a parent, how do you feel if somebody says something about your child that is not true? I myself can handle many things said against me, but when I hear of something said against either of my children, I have to work hard to contain myself.

You should know that God the Father feels that way about His children, too. Perhaps you have nobody who will defend you when people lie about you. But God heard it, and He does not like it. He said, "Vengeance is mine, I will repay." In other words, He will vindicate you. The word *vindicate* means "to have one's name cleared." It's what God does best. Anything God does, He does well. But if He has an "area of expertise," it is this.

Excerpted from *Grace* (Charisma House, 2006).

Having Two Sets of Ears

It is wonderful when we hear with both sets of ears. Every minister knows what it is like to preach and find that people only hear with their physical ears. So all they think about during the sermon are the preacher's mannerisms, his oratory, his eloquence, and his style. Sadly, that is all some ever take in.

> *Here I am! I stand at the door and knock. If anyone hears my voice and opens the door, I will come in and eat with him, and he with me.*
> —REVELATION 3:20

It was to the second set of ears—our spiritual ears—Jesus referred in the parable of the sower when He said, "He who has ears to hear, let him hear" (Mark 4:9). His promise of spiritual hearing in Revelation 3:20 is contingent upon the second set of ears being opened.

What happens, then, if your second set of ears are opened?

Well, first you find that instead of merely concluding that the minister was a good speaker, you suddenly think, *He is speaking to my soul.* Now you begin to view life from a new perspective and to think about issues you have never considered before: the question of whether there is life beyond the grave, for example.

However, there is another course of action you may take. Let us look at Revelation 1:3: "Blessed is the one who reads the words of this prophecy, and blessed are those who hear it and *take it to heart what is written in it*" (emphasis added). The Greek word for "take to heart" means "mark attentively" or "take heed." This means that the message of Revelation is not mere opinion or mythology; what is said is *true*, so you must consider this whole matter most soberly. In fact, you must heed its message.

The message of Revelation is the unveiling of the divine will concerning Jesus Christ. This book tells you all you need to know about Jesus and all you need to know about yourself.

Excerpted from *A Vision of Jesus* (Christian Focus Publications Ltd., 1999).

Enlarging the Soul's Capacity

Solid food is nourishment by which the capacity of the soul is enlarged. Sooner or later, a newborn baby must go from milk to something solid; if that does not happen, there will be a deformed child. It is the same with the analogy here.

What do I mean when I say solid food is nourishment by which the capacity of the soul is enlarged? The soul's enlargement

> *For every one that useth milk is unskilful in the word of righteousness: for he is a babe.*
>
> —HEBREWS 5:13, KJV

will mean simple trust in God, unfeigned love for one another, and the ability to understand what God is pleased to reveal. Now by simple trust in God, I would remind you of 1 John 4:16: "We know and rely on the love God has for us." That verse has gripped me for years. But it involves simple trust, simply taking seriously that God really does love us. When one really believes it, it changes everything. The ability to digest solid food is the enlargement of the soul, where you become able, simply in a childlike way, to trust in God. Jesus said, "Anyone who will not receive the kingdom of God like a little child will never enter it" (Mark 10:15). Christians need to rediscover this simple trust in God, which is the soul's enlargement.

I am referring to the ability to perceive God's will. That has to do with aptitude to receive what God wants to say. It is understanding His Word, and it is knowing His direction for today. It is His Word and His will.

Understanding His Word is simply being able to read the Bible and know what it means, that God speaks to you. Maturity includes seeing His will. By this I mean that you know God so well that you know what He is thinking. It's the same with my wife: I do not have to tell her or ask her what she thinks; I already know. When you know God, you know His will.

Excerpted from Are You Stone Deaf to the Spirit or Rediscovering God?
(Christian Focus Publications Ltd., 1994, 1999).

The Alpha and the Omega

I f we believe it is true that everybody is "destined to die once, and after that to face judgment" (Heb. 9:27), we will be eager to learn what will happen next. We find a clue in the words of Jesus in Revelation 1:8: "I am the Alpha and the Omega...who is, and who was, and who is to come, the Almighty." Alpha and Omega are the first and last letters of the Greek alphabet. These words describe who God is. Jesus was saying that He is the beginning and the end, the Lord of creation, the giver and withholder of knowledge.

> *"I am the Alpha and the Omega," says the Lord God, "who is, and who was, and who is to come, the Almighty."*
> —REVELATION 1:8

Did you know that all knowledge comes from God and that He gives or withholds knowledge as He wills? We enjoy the benefit of many scientific, technological, and medical developments, but we should remember we do so thanks to God's special grace and kindness to humanity. Yet science can only develop as far as God allows, and human knowledge will never be complete.

This is not so with spiritual knowledge, which we begin to grasp when we become Christians. In Colossians 2:3 Paul reveals that in Jesus "are hidden all the treasures of wisdom and knowledge." The knowledge of Jesus Christ is *saving* knowledge that comes through the revelation of the Holy Spirit, and it is He who enables us to grasp who Jesus is and what He did; this knowledge we call "faith." Imparting faith is the primary work of the Spirit.

It is the Spirit who imparts faith, but it is in obedience to the command of Jesus, for it is He who gives eternal life. In John 10:28 he said, *"I give them eternal life"* (emphasis added). Thus all knowledge, all revelation, stems from Jesus.

Excerpted from *A Vision of Jesus* (Christian Focus Publications Ltd., 1999).

We Will All Stand Before God

The most wonderful thing that ever happens is when Jesus reveals Himself to a person. If it happens to you, then remember that He is bestowing on you an honor and a dignity higher than anything the world affords, for none other than the Son of God has revealed Himself to you.

It is *He* who gives you life. You may think that you arrived in this world by some freak chance and life has no purpose or meaning: things happen at random, there is chaos, and you are a part of it and you conclude that when you die, you will be annihilated like any other animal. But God created you in His own image (Gen. 1:27), and He says, "I gave you life and I put you on earth for a purpose."

Yet not only is God the Creator, but also it is He who will bring all things to an end. Material things are not permanent. Life itself is transitory in nature: we meet friends for a while, and then we no longer see them. However, the ultimate thing to realize is that it will be God who will end all things and who will dissolve the whole of creation unto Himself (2 Pet. 3:10).

> *And I saw the dead, small and great, stand before God; and the books were opened: and another book was opened, which is the book of life: and the dead were judged out of those things which were written in the books, according to their works.*
>
> —REVELATION 20:12, KJV

However, *one* part of His creation will survive when the judgment is over: that part made in His likeness. The human race is the pinnacle of God's creation. We are not plants; we are not just animals; we are men and women! And someday God will summon us to give an account of the way we have lived.

What will happen then? We find the answer in Revelation 20. We discover there that some people will die *twice*. Nobody disputes that we die once, but have you heard of the second death? No matter how important we are or how insignificant, *everybody* will stand before God.

Excerpted from *A Vision of Jesus* (Christian Focus Publications Ltd., 1999).

Arrested Development

There comes a time when you must begin to help others. I know some Christians who after years are still needing the same old kind of help. It has not entered their minds to help anybody else. They figure if they once get sorted out, *then* they will be on their way to help somebody else. Yet years later they are still in much the same condition! Often the best way to solve your problem is to get your eyes completely off yourself and start helping somebody else.

> *For when for the time ye ought to be teachers, ye have need that one teach you again which be the first principles of the oracles of God; and are become such as have need of milk, and not of strong meat.*
>
> —Hebrews 5:12, KJV

What a pity, then, that these Hebrew Christians were right back to square one, needing milk, not solid food. It is a blatant rebuke. If milk is the only diet suited to a certain physical condition, it shows that one is in a serious state, but spiritually the writer means that one is in an immature but potentially dangerous state. It suggests an *arrested development*.

So if a person has an arrested development spiritually, then no matter how many more years he lives, he does not automatically get any better. Here is the person who has been converted and is going fine for six months, five years, or ten years, but then something happens. Maybe disappointment in their life. Maybe the loss of a job. And so the person is tried. But if he or she does not dignify the trial, if they do not learn to forgive, if they do not grow in grace and walk in the light, something backfires internally; they might continue going to church, but there is an arrested development, and they never move on.

I have thought about this in connection with myself, because I am absolutely sure that I have been like them, yet God is patient with me.

There was hope for these Hebrew Christians, and there is hope for each of us who hear God speaking in these lines.

Excerpted from *Are You Stone Deaf to the Spirit or Rediscovering God?* (Christian Focus Publications Ltd., 1999).

Who Is God?

Who is God? What is He like? These questions have intrigued people throughout the course of history. However, many have denied His exis-tence. In the nineteenth century the German philosopher Feuerbach said that God is nothing but man's projection on the backdrop of the universe. However, when I speak of God, I do not mean a God who exists only in one's imagination; I am talking about the *true* God. He is real; He exists; it is a question of getting to know Him.

> *Grace and peace to you from him who is, and who was, and who is to come, and from the seven spirits before his throne, and from Jesus Christ, who is the faithful witness, the firstborn from the dead, and the ruler of the kings of the earth.*
> —REVELATION 1:4–5

You may have many ideas about God and what He is like, but I want you to lay them aside and come with open minds to see what John says about Him. I believe he shows us four things.

1. *God is a triune being.* In his greeting in the Book of Revelation, John con-firms this.
2. *God is eternal.* The second thing John makes clear is that not only is God triune, but also He is eternal. He put it like this: "Grace and peace to you from him who is, and who was, and who is to come."
3. *God is spirit.* The third thing John saw was that God is spirit. He is not material; He is not a physical being. Jesus Himself said that God is spirit when He spoke to the woman at the well: "God is spirit, and His wor-shipers must worship in spirit and in truth" (John 4:24).
4. *God became a man.* The fourth thing John shows us about God is that God became human.

Grace and peace to you…from Jesus Christ, who is the faithful witness, the firstborn from the dead, and the ruler of the kings of the earth.

Jesus is Lord of lords and King of kings (Rev. 17:14). Someday He will come again, and on that day Paul tells us that everyone will worship Him.

Excerpted from *A Vision of Jesus* (Christian Focus Publications Ltd., 1999).

Revelation Reveals Jesus

Now the Book of Revelation is commonly referred to as "The Revelation of John," but it is not, in fact, about John, although it tells us a little about him. Nor is it a revelation of the church, although it gives us insight into the nature of the church. Nor is it to be understood exclusively as the unveiling of End-Time events. The Book of Revelation reveals Jesus. This makes it less interesting to some, but we cannot understand the book until we accept it as it is meant to be—an unveiling of Jesus Christ.

The second unique thing to note about Revelation is the claim it makes: it begins, "The revelation of Jesus Christ, which God gave him to show his servants." No other book in the Bible begins like this.

> *The revelation of Jesus Christ, which God gave him to show his servants what must soon take place. He made it known by sending his angel to his servant John, who testifies to everything he saw—that is, the word of God and the testimony of Jesus Christ.*
>
> —REVELATION 1:1–2

Moreover, this book came from Jesus in a way that is not claimed by any other book of the Bible. Now while we may deduce that other books came directly from Jesus Christ, they do not actually say this. But Revelation makes this unique claim.

Furthermore, in the last chapter we read: "I, Jesus, have sent my angel to give you this testimony for the churches" (Rev. 22:16). So if we need a direct word from Jesus, we have it here. This book, therefore, has an explicit claim to infallibility; even John's own theological view is absent.

John did not impose his own theology; he wrote what he saw and heard, a message from Jesus cohering perfectly with New Testament teaching: Jesus is the Lamb of God, sacrificed for us, the only one worthy to satisfy God's justice.

The wonderful thing about becoming a Christian is that not only are our sins forgiven but also that we have a home in heaven, a glorious hope, a glorious promise. Jesus, who takes all your sin upon Himself, offers you eternal life. God's Word is infallible and His promise is sure. One day I am going to that home Jesus is preparing for us (John 14:2). Will you meet me there?

Excerpted from *A Vision of Jesus* (Christian Focus Publications Ltd., 1999).

The Ministry of the Spirit

Now, the Christian faith is not merely head knowledge. This is why we have the Holy Spirit, who teaches us in such a way that we do not remain helpless and ignorant. What can be more basic than our need for the Holy Spirit to guide us? Many have let book learning, systematic theology, creed, and doctrine replace the Holy Spirit. And for this reason, many Christians today, I fear, have very little experience of the Spirit of God showing

> *The Spirit searches all things, even the deep things of God.*
>
> —1 Corinthians 2:10

them things, guiding them in the truth, seeing things are real and definite and right from God. So many of us are in a rut that it does not even enter our minds to break out of it, and the Spirit never shows us anything. The reason that the Spirit will not show us anything is that He is grieved. One way we grieve the Spirit is by *bitterness*.

My point is, when we do not forgive one another and we let any kind of bitterness creep in, the Spirit is grieved, and it causes a short circuit. Nothing happens, nothing connects, and we do not grow. I believe this with all my heart. So many have not taken seriously this matter of walking in love and, in consequence of that, have not been able to walk in the light. It does not seem to bother them a bit if they judge another person, if they hold a grudge, if they cannot speak to certain people in the same congregation. Look, this is wrong! The Spirit is grieved. Do you know what else that means? It means that they do not grow, although they come to church week after week, month after month, and year after year. This is what had happened to some of the Hebrew Christians.

We need to learn that the Christian faith is not like math or physics, because what we need is not intellectual acumen, but the Spirit shows us things.

Excerpted from *Are You Stone Deaf to the Spirit or Rediscovering God?* (Christian Focus Publications Ltd., 1999).

Who Is the Greatest?

Let me ask you a question: How would you feel if after worshiping your God for so many years, you discovered that there really is one who is greater? What would you do? Maybe you would say, "Well, I wouldn't want to give up God. I have come to know Him real well." Yet surely you want to worship the Most High God. Would you keep on worshiping Him? Never.

If I were to discover that there is one greater than who I thought was the greatest, I would stop praying, and I would reassess my ways, my worship, my allegiance, and my confession. Why? Because I want to locate not only the name than which no greater can be conceived, but also the one who is greater and worship Him. I only want to worship Him who is the First and the Last.

Whenever we make the claim that we worship the Most High, the one than which there is no greater, someone is bound to ask us, "How can you be sure?" The answer to that is the Holy Spirit. No man can say that Jesus is Lord but by the Holy Spirit (1 Cor. 12:3). It's easy to get a person to repeat a prayer, but to really believe that Jesus, who was born of a virgin, lived, died on a cross, arose from the dead, and who is the One who causes to be, cannot be done unless the Holy Spirit conveys it to you.

> *When the Counselor comes, whom I will send to you from the Father, the Spirit of truth who goes out from the Father, he will testify about me.*
>
> —JOHN 15:26

Indeed, the Holy Spirit authenticates not only the truth but also gives an assurance by which you know you have it right. In His strength you can face a thousand worlds and a thousand devils. This is why you can stand before men. That witness of the Spirit is given so that you know the truth beyond any doubt. This is how you know that Jesus of Nazareth is Lord, the One who causes to be, even from everlasting to everlasting.

Excerpted from *Meekness and Majesty* (Christian Focus Publications Ltd., 1992, 2000).

Coping With Temptation

It is said of Jesus that He "was led by the Spirit into the desert to be tempted by the devil" (Matt. 4:1). It seems that, although the devil can do the direct tempting, it is the Spirit who may lead us into a place where the devil can do his work.

Or take the example of Job.

The Lord said to Satan, "Have you considered my servant Job?" (Job 1:8).

God earmarked Job for greater blessing. He already was greatly blessed, but God

> *No temptation has seized you except what is common to man. And God is faithful; he will not let you be tempted beyond what you can bear.*
>
> —1 Corinthians 10:13

wanted to bless him more. You may think, *Well, why didn't God just go on and do it?* I don't know. For reasons I don't understand, God tests us. He tested Job and tested him to the hilt. Maybe He's doing that with you.

Now there are, in fact, two origins of temptation. One is the flesh; the other is the devil. Let's remember, when it comes to the flesh, these words of James: "When tempted, no one should say, 'God is tempting me'" (James 1:13). James said this because, when we are tempted, it often seems as if God is involved. Temptation comes so easily to us. It is so natural, so painless, that even the most mature people may think to themselves, *God is actually in this*, when in fact it is the flesh deceiving us every time.

What might help us to resist temptation? Three suggestions:

1. Remember that temptation is a test from God, and that any temptation is resistible. (See 1 Corinthians 10:13.)

2. Imagine how you're going to feel if you don't give in to it, and how you're going to feel if you do.

3. Remember that God is looking for those He can trust.

Excerpted from *When God Shows Up* (Renew Books, 1998).

Daniel's Secret

What do you suppose was Daniel's secret? It has to be said that Daniel, Shadrach, Meshach, and Abednego were exceedingly rare men. It is not every day that you meet someone who conveys the presence of greatness. I don't know about you, but I have a peculiarity, in that whenever I am in the presence of one I deem to be truly great, I instinctively ask, "What is their secret?" I want to absorb anything I can.

> Now when Daniel knew that the writing was signed, he went into his house; and his windows being open in his chamber toward Jerusalem, he kneeled upon his knees three times a day, and prayed, and gave thanks before his God, as he did aforetime.
>
> —DANIEL 6:10, KJV

What was Daniel's secret? He saw the overthrow of Babylon and a new king. Now Darius the Mede was none other than Cyrus the Persian, the man who would one day allow Israel to return. Despite the change of government, Daniel continued to enjoy royal favor.

Whatever the reason, we know that Daniel was not a threat to the new king and there was a real friendship. Real friendship is when there is no threat to each other. When you see one another as a threat, then there will always be tension.

The problem was that not everyone felt that way about Daniel. He had exceptional grace, and he so distinguished himself by his qualities that the king planned to set him over the whole kingdom; that was too much for his peers. Daniel knew, no matter what he did, they were out to get him.

It is at this point that we discover Daniel's secret. It had something to do with God, and the most encouraging thing of all is that it was not his ability at the natural level, which no doubt was an ordinary secret. Prayer takes discipline, and Daniel had regular times of prayer. Extraordinary man but an ordinary secret; it is something anybody can do. Daniel simply loved God so much that he gave time to Him. We tell how much we care about another by how much time we give them. The secret of Daniel was not his intellect; it wasn't his personality, his visions, or even his ability to debate—it was his prayer life.

Excerpted from *The God of the Bible* (Authentic Media, 2002).

The Name Above All Names

Although there are terms or words for God, there is only one word given in the Old Testament for God's Name: *Yahweh*, LORD. It is used 6,800 times in the Old Testament, set in small capitals: LORD. Now whenever we see the word *Lord* in the New Testament, even without small capitals, it is a reference to Jesus. The Greek word is *kyrios*, but it is the translation of *Yahweh*.

> *Let them praise the name of the LORD,*
> *for his name alone is exalted.*
> —PSALM 148:13

When Paul, a Jew, would use the word *kyrios* to describe Jesus, he ascribed to Him not only deity but also the very name of *Yahweh* Himself, for *kyrios* was the word most frequently used in the Septuagint to translate *Yahweh*. Any Jew knew that.

Now to call Jesus *kyrios*, *Lord*, was not only saying that He was God but was also ascribing to Him the name that is above every name.

After Jesus died on the cross, He was raised from the dead, ascended to heaven, and welcomed home by God the Father. The first thing the Father said to Him was, "Sit down at my right hand." That in itself meant equality with God.

Not only was Jesus exalted to the highest place, the position that can only be described as that which belonged to God alone, but Paul said Jesus was also given the "name that is above every name" (Phil. 2:9). In other words, there was no room for doubt or speculation: there was only one name known in heaven and in earth that was above every name. It was to demonstrate His sheer *majesty*.

It is the name of the One who is worthy of our worship; it is the name of the One who fights our battles—*Jehovah Sabaoth*. It is the name of the One who supplies our every need—*Jehovah Jireh*. It is the name of the One who made the sun in creation's morning and later took dust from the ground and made man after His own image. It is the name of the One who put His name in the temple and allowed His name to dwell there. It is the name of the One who has put His name in the midst of the church.

The name that is above every name is called the Everlasting One, the Most High God, the King of glory, the One who inhabits eternity, the One who controls the destiny of nations.

Excerpted from *Meekness and Majesty* (Christian Focus Publications Ltd., 1992, 2000).

The Need for Fresh Anointing

Our reward in heaven will not be determined by yesterday's anointing but by today's *fresh* anointing. I will not receive a reward for how well I preached, how many thousands I reached or blessed, or even how many people were con-

> *The LORD's anointing oil is on you.*
> —LEVITICUS 10:7

verted under my ministry. To be rewarded for my *gifts* is nonsense! "For who makes you different from anyone else? What do you have that you did not receive? And if you did receive it, why do you boast as though you did not?" (1 Cor. 4:7). God is not going to reward me for the ability He alone gave me. My reward in heaven (may God grant that there is such) will come *entirely* by whether I practiced what I preached: walking in the light, dignifying the trial, totally forgiving others, and placing utmost priority on my intimacy with Him.

And yet my *continued* effectiveness here below is also determined by my hearing God's voice today. If my anointing given me yesterday is replenished by a fresh anointing that comes by the way I live personally and privately, I will continue to hear God speak and will know His will daily. I will not miss what He wants of me or what He wants me to see around me. I can think of nothing worse than missing out on what God is doing. And yet my knowledge of the Bible will not in and of itself guarantee that I will recognize what He is up to today.

We must all learn to distinguish the difference between what is important and what is essential—and always do the latter. Whether with our use of time, money, our diaries, or social relationships, the issue is what is essential and being sure we do what is *essential*. Yesterday's anointing is important; today's *fresh* anointing is essential.

Excerpted from *The Anointing: Yesterday, Today, Tomorrow* (Charisma House, 2003).

Acknowledgments

This devotional has been compiled from several books by Dr. Kendall, which we have listed below. We gratefully acknowledge the publishers of the following titles and thank them for their permission to extract text from their books in order to compile this devotional:

A Vision of Jesus. Ross-shire, Scotland, UK: Christian Focus Publications Ltd., 1999. Used by permission of publisher.

All's Well That Ends Well. Bletchly, Milton Keynes, UK: Authentic Media, a division of Send the Light Ltd., 2005. Used by permission of publisher.

Are You Stone Deaf to the Spirit or Rediscovering God? Ross-shire, Scotland, UK: Christian Focus Publications Ltd., 1994, 1999. Used by permission of publisher.

Believing God. Charlotte, NC: MorningStar Publications & Ministries, 1997. Used by permission of author.

Between the Times. Ross-shire, Scotland, UK: Christian Focus Publications Ltd., 2003. Used by permission of publisher.

Controlling the Tongue. Lake Mary, FL: Charisma House, 2007.

Grace. Lake Mary, FL: Charisma House, 2006.

Higher Ground. Ross-shire, Scotland, UK: Christian Focus Publications Ltd., 1995. Used by permission of publisher.

Just Love. Ross-shire, Scotland, UK: Christian Focus Publications Ltd., 1997. Used by permission of publisher.

Just Say Thanks! Lake Mary, FL: Charisma House, 2005.

Meekness and Majesty. Ross-shire, Scotland, UK: Christian Focus Publications Ltd., 1992, 2000. Used by permission of publisher.

Pure Joy. Lake Mary, FL: Charisma House, 2006.

The Anointing: Yesterday, Today, Tomorrow. Lake Mary, FL: Charisma House, 2003.

The God of the Bible. Bletchly, Milton Keynes, UK: Authentic Media, a division of Send the Light Ltd., 2002. Used by permission of publisher.

The Sensitivity of the Spirit. Lake Mary, FL: Charisma House, 2002.

The Thorn in the Flesh. Lake Mary, FL: Charisma House, 2004.

The Word and the Spirit. Lake Mary, FL: Charisma House, 1998.

Total Forgiveness. Lake Mary, FL: Charisma House, 2002.

When God Says "Well Done!" Ross-shire, Scotland, UK: Christian Focus Publications Ltd., 1993. Used by permission of publisher.

When God Shows Up. Ventura, CA: Gospel Light/Renew Books, 1998. Used by permission of publisher.

Worshipping God. London, England, UK: Hodder & Stoughton, 2004. Used by permission of publisher.

16:41	123	84:11	212	**Proverbs**	
		84:12	243	3:6	144
2 Chronicles		95:10	137	3:12	240
20:15	190	103:2	121	3:25–26	195
20:21	190	103:3–5	121	6:3	194
31:2	123	103:12	65, 179	8:17	156
32:26	153	103:13–14	16	10:19	151
32:30	123	103:14	86, 222	15:1	175
32:31	66, 180	105:42	131	19:11	237
		106:1	123	22:1	59
Nehemiah		106:23	259	23:7	250
1:8	131	106:47	220	24:10	190, 272
8:10	259	115:1	202	24:17	120
		116:17	118	26:20	74
Esther		118:25	355	27:2	151
2:22	36	119:49	131	27:6	79
4	281	119:75	269	27:17	143, 251
		120:1–2	79		
Job		120:5–7	10	**Ecclesiastes**	
1:6–12	22	121:1–2	12	4:4	308
1:8	371	121:5	247	5:4	314
1:9	116	121:5–8	247		
1:12	352	123:2–4	125	**Song of Solomon**	
1:22	304	124:2–3, 6	280	2:15	151
13:15	27, 116, 352	125:2	12		
19:19–21	271	126:1	70	**Isaiah**	
23:10	20	126:4	169	6:1–3	319
42:2	233	126:5	169	6:3	319
		126:5–6	70	11:2	135
Psalms		127:1–2	15	26:3	10
6:1	121	129:1–2	106	29:13	353
16:6	360	131:1	18	30:15	34, 286
16:8	247, 248	132:1	26	38:2	131
16:11	149	133:1	172, 219	40:28	213
23:1	239	133:3	219	42:8	209
27:8	155	136:3, 23	131	43:19	156
29:2	290	138:2	75	45:15	25
30:5	169	139:14	21	54:1	309
35:13	281, 282	142:1–2	213	54:1–7	169
37:8	277	143:10	28	55:8	134
51:4	81, 339	148:13	373	58:6, 8	283
56:9	42			61:8	305
72:11	209			62:7	131
83:1	115